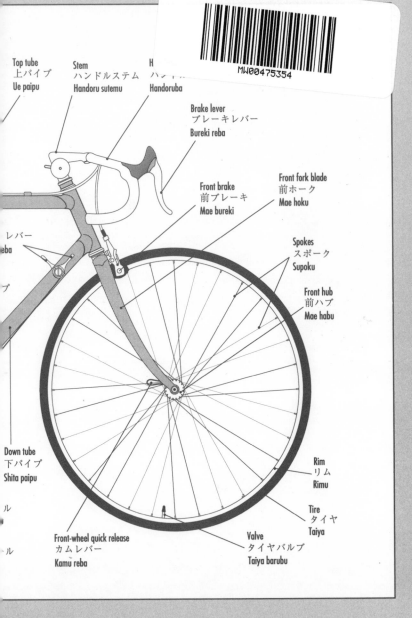

B20498

MW00475354

Top tube
上パイプ
Ue paipu

Stem
ハンドルステム
Handoru sutemu

Handoruba

Brake lever
ブレーキレバー
Bureki reba

Front brake
前ブレーキ
Mae bureki

Front fork blade
前ホーク
Mae hoku

Spokes
スポーク
Supoku

Front hub
前ハブ
Mae habu

レバー
eba

プ

Down tube
下パイプ
Shita paipu

ル

ル

Front-wheel quick release
カムレバー
Kamu reba

Valve
タイヤバルブ
Taiya barubu

Rim
リム
Rimu

Tire
タイヤ
Taiya

CYCLING
JAPAN

CYCLING JAPAN

A Personal Guide to Exploring Japan by Bicycle

Edited by Bryan Harrell

KODANSHA INTERNATIONAL
Tokyo • New York • London

Request to the reader: Every attempt has been made to ensure that the information contained in this guide is correct. However, prices go up, hotels disappear, and schedules change, to the extent that the publisher and authors cannot be held liable for any changes which occur after the time of writing. The publisher welcomes updated information for future editions.

Jacket design by Hideyuki Nakajima
Jacket illustration by Akiko Ono
Maps by Satoru Takanashi and Brian Smallshaw

Distributed in the United States by Kodansha America, Inc., 114 Fifth Avenue, New York, N.Y. 10011, and in the United Kingdom and continental Europe by Kodansha Europe Ltd., Gillingham House, 38–44 Gillingham Street, London SW1V 1HU. Published by Kodansha International Ltd., 17–14 Otowa 1-chome, Bunkyo-ku, Tokyo 112, and Kodansha America Inc.

93 94 95 96 97 10 9 8 7 6 5 4 3 2 1

ISBN 4-7700-1742-1

Library of Congress Cataloging-in-Publication Data

Cycling Japan : a personal guide to exploring Japan by bicycle /
    edited by Bryan Harrell.—1st ed.
        p. cm.
    ISBN 4-7700-1742-1
    1. Bicycle touring—Japan—Guidebooks. 2. Japan—Guidebooks.
I. Harrell, Bryan, 1954-
GV1046. J3C93 1003
796.6'4'09952—dc20   93-9116
                                                        CIP

CONTENTS

Preface 7

Acknowledgments 8

Introduction 9

1 Gearing Up 11

Bike Basics: What Bike? 12 Big Bikes and Big Frames 15 What about Tandems? 16 Which Bike Shop? 16 Alternative Sources 23 Recycling Bicycles 23 Rental Bicycles 24 Looking after your Bike 25

Getting Ready: Communication 27 Maps and Orientation 27 Packing that Pannier 30 Thought for Food 33 Looking after Yourself 35

On the Road: Rules of the Road 38 What to Watch out For 38 Getting Around with a Bike Bag 40 Riding the Trains 42 Ferry Tales 43 Shipping your Bike 46 Cycle Hitching 47 Time Out 48

2 Freewheeling 53

Tokyo Hours 55
Planning your Ride 55 Exploring the Concrete Jungle 56 Cyclin' by the Dock of the Bay 58 Paradise on Garbage 60 Tokyo Oasis 64 The Yamanote Countryside Ride 66 River Rides 83 Tokyo Lake District 98

Kanto Weekend Getaways 103
The Chichibu Trail 103 Chasing the Breeze 106 Cruising Izu 111 Fuji Five Lakes 115 Yamanashi Wine Country 122 The Chikuma-gawa River Path 127 A Slow Boat to Boso 130 Nasu Highlands Hot Springs 133

Alpine Riding 137
Japan's Shangri-la 137 The Old Post Road 140 The Oku Shiga Forest Road 145 Water, Fire, and Earth 148

Northern Japan 153
Discovering the Back Side of Japan 153   Lake and Samurai 157   Osore-zan: The Gateway to Hell 159

Hokkaido: The (Summer) Cycling Paradise 165
Hakodate: The Jewel of Hokkaido 165   Tomakomai Two Lakes Route 168   The Back Way to Hokkaido 171   The Lake District 174   Arctic Loop 177

Beyond Kyoto and Osaka 181
Bicycling Beautiful Biwa-ko 181   *Tokobashira* Country 185   Cycling the Echizen Coast 189   High on Hiei 192

Western Japan Days 201
In the Land of Lacquer 201   Coasting the Kii Peninsula 204   Cyclin' the San'in 209

Shikoku: Japan's Fourth Largest Island 217
From Tokushima 217   From Kochi 222   From Imabari 226

Kyushu 231
In the Land of the Secret Christians 231   Crossing Mt. Aso 232   In the Deep South 239

All Those Islands 243
Izu Islands 243   Rishiri Island 250   Awaji Island 251

Out of the Saddle 256

3 Nuts and Bolts 257
Bicycle Resources 258   Cycling Clubs 259   Cycle Sports Centers 260   Cycling Terminals 261   Rental Bike Stores in the Kyoto Area 266   Cycling Roads throughout Japan 268

Preface

In early 1985, after writing a short article on cycling for a small, recreation-oriented magazine I pondered the possibility of starting a cycling club which would function in the English language. I had tried Japanese cycling clubs but found their style of activity and organization not completely satisfying. Without going into much cultural and sociological detail, I felt there was a need for a more informal cycling organization, with a dynamic riding style and a laid-back attitude, much like the groups that I had ridden with during the sixties and seventies in my native Northern California. At the end of the article I cautiously added my phone number and waited.

Many readers called to say that they wanted to meet other, like-minded cyclists. I started to think it might be a good idea to send out some kind of cycling newsletter around which a bike club could form.

Some weeks later, at the crest of a downhill on the Boso-hanto Peninsula just across the bay from Tokyo, I first understood the meaning of the Japanese word *oikaze*. It was shouted by a Japanese friend just after a huge tailwind suddenly whipped up and pushed us down the long arcs of road leading to the coast. This was the final push I needed to go ahead with my idea of a newsletter. What's more, *oikaze* was also a great name.

The first issue of *Oikaze*, which has always been essentially free, appeared in late 1985 as a three-page cut-and-paste affair with crooked columns and hand-drawn maps. The issue carried a short piece on good reasons for cycling out of Tokyo, another on healthy cycling foods, and a thumbnail sketch of cycling on the Boso-hanto Peninsula. Although it was hard to get enough articles from readers for the early issues, we now receive many, all of which are eventually used. Although the articles are often heavily edited to keep the information level high, every effort is made to retain the voice of the writer as much as possible.

From the twentieth issue, *Oikaze* made its debut in the world of desktop publishing when computers were used to do the layout, giving *Oikaze* a look of significance far beyond its highly communicative grass-roots content. In the summer of 1992 we decided to make *Oikaze* a quarterly and increase the number of pages from six to eight. I intend to keep publishing *Oikaze* for as long as readers keep sending in the interesting and informative stories that have made it into one of the best reader-supported newsletters in the world.

Acknowledgments

Oikaze has been an enjoyable way to promote cycling, an activity that makes people and the world better for each other. It has also been a meaningful way for me to contribute to my community here in Tokyo, and throughout Japan.

First of all, I would like to thank Bill Womack for creating the Oikaze logo, Katherine Markulin for designing some of the early issues, and Brian Smallshaw for the countless hours he's devoted to making *Oikaze* such an impressive newsletter.

This deluxe edition of *Oikaze* does not attempt to be a comprehensive guidebook, but rather aims to encourage cyclists and would-be cyclists to get out and explore Japan by bicycle. For sharing their cycling adventures and helping to bring this book together, I owe special thanks to Adam Adamski (AA), John Ashburne (JA), Sam and Laurie Cohen (SLC), Jean-Pierre Denis (JPD), Brian Hanke (HB), Joe Hlebica (JH), Nathan and Grace Hoover (NGH), Jill Ishii (JI), Jeff Kadett (JK), Seiichi Kaneko (KS), Sue Kocher (SK), Paul Lehnert (PL), Kim Longmine (KL), Bob Lowe (BL), Giselle Mortimer (GM), Roger Northridge (RN), Phil Ono (PO), Mike Schultz (MS), Kevin Palmquist (KP), Don Todt (DT), and the many other readers who have contributed to *Oikaze*.

Finally, I must express deep appreciation to my editors at Kodansha International, Hilary Sagar and Taro Hirowatari, for their original idea to create this book and for their great patience and hard work in seeing the project to completion.

Introduction

Why Tour Japan by Bicycle?

Dense and compact, Japan offers the cyclist a diverse and unusually fascinating selection of sights and scenery within relatively short riding distances. The roads are generally good and interesting, while the topography in most places is complex enough to offer both exciting tour possibilities and short-term riding challenges. With the help of a bike bag and Japan's well-developed public transportation system, it's simple to get where the good roads and riding begin.

Best of all there are some great places to stay, among them the small, privately operated inns called *minshuku* which include both dinner and breakfast in their modest (for Japan) rates. Some feature natural hot spring baths, which are particularly exhilarating after a long day on the bike. If you're lucky, the inn may also have an outdoor hot spring bath, where the steam rises into the fresh, cool air and a blanket of stars adds a pleasingly unusual texture to the blackness of the night. There's no better way to finish a day and prepare yourself for another day of cycling.

You may also find, for the most part, deep generosity and civility among the local people, particularly away from the cities. When seeking assistance or directions, the cyclist is sometimes overwhelmed by offers of food and lodging from total strangers. Consider this a good way to enjoy Japanese culture and language, but be careful not to wear out your welcome.

What to Be Careful About

Although bicycle theft, belligerent drivers, and crime in general aren't nearly the worry they are in some other countries a sense of caution and awareness of your surroundings should never be totally abandoned. Bicycles should always be locked, and valuables kept with you or in a safe place (virtually every innkeeper is trustworthy), and the rarely encountered inconsiderate driver should not be allowed to spoil what is otherwise a great cycling day.

What will certainly be difficult to get accustomed to, however, will be the Japanese sensibilities about space within the traffic context. Most roads in Japan's towns and cities are woefully narrow and crowded. As a result, acceptable tolerances are smaller but people usually know how much space is enough. These difficulties are compounded somewhat by the fact that, in Japan, traffic moves on the left. Continual caution and street-smart awareness are the best way to prevent accidents. Although careless and stupid drivers do exist in Japan, there are far fewer deliberately malicious drivers than there are, say, in North America. In spite of what it may seem, nobody wants to have an accident—especially the Japanese, who tend to find sudden and intimate contact with strangers particularly embarassing.

The Bicycle as Part of Your Japan Lifestyle

The first bicycle I had in Japan, in 1977, was a Bickerton Portable—I was hesitant about getting something I couldn't take back to California as airline baggage.

After experiencing the limitations of small wheels and a folding frame on a particularly hair-raising downhill stretch, I decided to buy a National Demontable, a full-size portable that breaks into two pieces for easy bagging.

Later, I realized that almost any kind of bicycle can be taken apart and bagged, and so I went out and bought a no-compromise lightweight bicycle and a bike bag. Ever since, the bike has made my trips a real pleasure, not only for its great ride, but also because its light weight makes it easier to carry than the heavier folding bike which I'd previously ridden.

The point I'm making is that, rather than mess around with folding or portable bicycles, in which performance or the ride must be compromised, it's best to get the right bicycle from the start and learn to bag it if you plan to take it on public transport. Of course, what constitutes the right bike, be it for racing, touring, or off-road riding, is a matter only you can decide.

While most people can get by with only one bike, I recommend two. If you do a lot of city-riding for shopping, errands, and runs between your home and train station, you might consider a cheaper second bike (with rugged tires, and a big rack or basket) that will take everyday wear and tear and rain, while your good bike stays clean and dry indoors, ready for the next long ride on the weekend. Keeping a utility bike, even a trashmo special, is the best way to make sure the bicycle is part of your complete lifestyle in Japan.

I
Gearing Up

Bike Basics

What Bike?

Despite the current popularity of mountain bikes, <u>road bikes</u> are still the best for touring. Characterized by the conventional diamond-style frame, road bikes run the gamut from heavy-duty rack and pannier models to ultralight racers.

While most riders wouldn't think of touring on a racing bike with tubular (sew-up) tires, I have found them to be the easiest and most exciting way to go—provided that you stay on paved roads most of the time, don't pack more than a small bag or two, and travel less than a hundred kilometers per day. Although a good set of tubular tires can take the punishment of a bit of gravel, the ride is harsh and uncomfortable. Should you encounter more than a few kilometers of "road under construction," you'll wish that you'd taken a bike with balloon-type clincher tires. More than about ten kilometers of rough road and you're likely to start pining for a full-blown mountain bike.

Because of the tighter frame geometry, racing bikes are not always easy to handle when loaded down with a full set of pannier bags, front and rear. Moreover, while the ride is more lively and responsive, you're likely to feel stiff and sore yourself after spending many hours in the saddle.

If you're more interested in LSD (long, slow distance) riding, however, a touring-style road bike may be a better choice. The wider, more rugged tires and more relaxed frame angles will afford a more comfortable ride during long stretches in the saddle, while accommodating more luggage without strain. For cycle camping, this is it.

Many people mistakenly believe that a mountain bike can only be used for traveling deep in the countryside, or up in the mountains on dirt paths, or for just thrashing around on a race course. However, the image of a mountain bike as heavy, clunky, and hard to pedal has quickly faded. Available at reasonable prices and in a wide variety of designs—over a thousand models in 1993—MTBs are proving to be ideal for commuting, touring, and for use as a city bike for errands and shopping. Price is mostly a factor of weight: the lighter the bike the more it costs. MTB frames and wheels are made to last and are a bit heavier than their road counter-parts—hazards like the unseen pothole and the partly flattened soda can are not so fearsome on a MTB. Frames come in three basic designs: the traditional triangle (the most common), the sloped top-tube, and the ele-vated rear stay. The sloped top-tube tends to weigh less and there's more room betweeen the crotch and the frame to allow for rougher terrain, bumps and jockeying without hurting yourself. Elevated rear stay bikes are designed for better climbing, wider tire clearance, and avoidance of chain problems. Most riders have no need of suspension; it also weighs more and costs more. The most expensive frame material is high-tensile steel, followed by cromoly steel (the most common), aluminum, titanium, and carbon composites. With a judicious use of different tires, a mountain bike can serve a variety of purposes: use slick tires for commuting, change to strong rims and knobby tires for playing in the mountains, light wheels with lighter, knobbier tires for racing, and for touring go back to commuting slicks and add clip-on tri-bars, a rear carrier, panniers and mudguards.

Lighter than the mountain bike is the "hybrid" bike—half mountain bike and half road bike. The frame is somewhere between the two, usually more road-bikish, while the tires are sanely sized at about 35 mm width. Gearing is wide ratio, in the MTB tradition, for use just about anywhere. In fact, these bikes are a match for mountain bikes in all but the roughest ter-rain—you know, jumping tree stumps and clambering down rock faces.

Which bike you choose depends on the type of riding you want to do. Many people buy a bike that's better (and more expensive) than they real-ly need. Be careful of "overbuying"; the cheaper model in a line is invariably good enough.

Once you've chosen the bike, make sure the tires are right for the kind of riding you intend to do. For on-road riding, a rather smooth tread is best; for off-road, the tread should be rougher. Tires with big rubber knobs are useful for lots of loose dirt and mud, but on pavement can be squirrelly in the turns and uncomfortable all around. A good dealer will substitute tires on a newly-purchased bike for free, or for the minimal difference in cost.

Finally, make sure the gearing is low enough. Mountain roads can be mighty steep in Japan, and many road bikes have racing gearing, which won't get you up the hills at the end of a long day. The lowest gear should be at least 40 wheel inches, which is equivalent to a 42-tooth front chain-ring and a 28-tooth rear cog. A 100-inch gear is the standard high gear on most road bikes, usually 52 in front and 14 in back. Right between them is a 70-inch gear, which is what most riders find comfortable for use on flat ground.

Learn to use a gear chart to calculate the ratios of all the gears on your bike, and pay attention to which ones you use for which situations. With a little experience, you'll know which gear to shift to when you see a rise up ahead so that you maintain a smooth pedaling momentum. You'll also have a better idea of how to change the gearing on your bike to suit your riding style.

After you've selected the right model, with the right tires and gearing, you'll finally come to the most important consideration: fit. What model to choose is not nearly as important as how well the bike fits your body. A good fit depends not only on frame size, but also on the height and angle of the saddle and handlebars, as well as the distance between them.

Most riders select frames that are slightly too large. The best way to determine if a frame is right for you is to straddle the bicycle with both feet flat on the ground: there should be about ten to fifteen centimeters of clearance between your crotch and the frame's top tube. On a frame that's slightly too big for you there may be too much distance between the saddle and the handlebars. This could require you to stretch forward too much, causing discomfort in a myriad of areas during a long trip.

Set the height of the saddle so that when you're sitting on it your leg is fully extended with your heel on the pedal in the downmost position.

The tops of the handlebars should be set between ten and fifteen centimeters lower than the saddle. A good rule of thumb is to set the bars the same distance lower than the saddle as the distance between your crotch and the frame's top tube when standing astride the bike. The handlebars and the saddle should be far enough apart to let your torso extend fully so that even deep breathing is comfortable, yet should be not so far apart as to cause you to stretch your torso. The distance between the handlebars and the saddle can be adjusted by moving the saddle back and forth on its rails, and by changing the forward length of the handlebar extension. Generally, bikes are factory equipped with handlebar extensions of a length suitable for use with the frame size. If it is too long or short, however, the dealer should change it free of charge to achieve a proper fit. Some dealers in Japan may be reluctant to alter the bicycle in any way; should this be the case, you may have to pay the dealer to make the change. If you're using dropped handlebars, the outside tops of the bars should decline just slightly, with the brake levers mounted just high enough to be used from the top, yet still reachable from the bottom position.

Another important consideration is crank length. Most bikes come equipped with 165 or 170mm cranks, but riders under 160cm may find the shorter 160mm cranks more comfortable, while those over 185cm may find 175mm or even 180mm cranks a better ride.

Comfortable crank length is also dependent on riding style. Generally, those who spin faster in lower gears will find shorter cranks more comfortable because the circle the foot describes is smaller; those who pedal more slowly in higher gears will appreciate the extra leverage of longer cranks.

You may find that U.S. valve stems don't fit the Japanese clip-on tire pump. The best solution seems to be to buy an aluminum frame pump for Schrader valves to avoid any hassle in finding an adapter. The next time you change your tires, consider changing over to tubes with Presta valves (used for sew-ups and lightweight clinchers) because the design is superior, particularly in regard to ease of inflation.

Big Bikes and Big Frames

If you're looking for big frames your best bet is Cycland in Shinagawa (see page 15) which will order export-size models. For example, the Bridgestone 400, a decent Sunday sports bike with drop bars, 27 x 1–1/8 tires, 12-speed derailleur, and no mudguards, is available with a frame size of 635mm (25"), and that's big. Alps, the Kanda bike manufacturer and dealer (see page 20), accepts orders for touring, racing, and all-round sports frames and bikes in large sizes. The final option is to do some bike shopping when you're back in your home country. I bought my own fairly big frame in Britain, mainly because the absurd exchange rate meant the frame cost less than anything in Japan that I was certain would be as good, and I knew I'd be returning with little luggage. A juvenile desire to be different plus a fleeting concern for the British economy encouraged me to make my decision.

What About Tandems?

A bicycle built for two is the great equalizer, keeping two riders of disparate ability together. For couples, a tandem could be a lifesaver for your relationship, but the most appealing aspect about tandems is that they're fun, fun, fun, because they're fast, fast, fast! Imagine the strength of two riders pushing against the wind resistance of one, on a bike that weighs only about fifty percent more than an equivalent single bike, and you have the recipe for an exhilarating ride.

Unfortunately, tandems are not street-legal in Japan, and must be ridden off-road on bicycle trails. The only exception is the happy wilds of Nagano Prefecture, where tandems are street-legal by virtue of the fact that the law doesn't specifically say they aren't. Many resort areas in Nagano rent tandems of less than optimal quality to riders often unfamiliar with how to ride them safely.

In some areas, particularly rural places, you can get away with riding them. Off-road mountain bike tandems are just beginning to make an appearance, with many riders reporting harassment-free riding on fire roads and mountain trails. Still, the determined tandem enthusiast will need a special tandem bike rack to transport a tandem to a trail head.

Which Bike Shop?

When you first arrived in Japan, you probably thought, "Wow, I'm finally in cyclist's paradise, land of Shimano, Suntour, Miyata, and Fuji." Then, passing the long rows of screechy-braked, rusty clunkers in front of the train station, you make your first trip to the neighborhood bike store only to be greeted by a disappointing selection of bikes and accessories, nearly all with Bridgestone or National labels. And, very often your friendly local *jitenshaya-san* has never even heard of a tubular tire.

However, don't lose heart. There are a few stores around that cater to the serious cyclist. Although bike prices in Japan are about the highest in the world, some bargains are available. When choosing a bike, consider your needs carefully, find your size, set your budget, and window shop. Dealers do not, unfortunately, allow test rides so take home catalogs and have a look at the latest issue of *Cycle Sports*, a Japanese magazine with lots of adverts.

The best time to buy is from January to March when both manufacturers and dealers start offering discounts to clear stock and make room for the new models that start to appear around December. Dealers will often discount to near buying price and are sometimes willing to bargain. Factory outlets sell scratched and returned models at great discount. However, the bike is sold as is, no service is offered, and there is no guarantee.

Most Japanese customers of bike shops put themselves at the mercy of the dealer, who recommends not only the bike but how it should be set up. My experience over the past fifteen years is that the enthusiast who wants to order something different from what's in the store is, at best, a pest. Finicky Westerners (most of us) should proceed with caution, yet be insistent about what you want to order and what you're willing to pay for.

Many bike shops in Japan are reluctant to repair bikes they didn't sell. If the bicycle is foreign, a dealer may not even want to look at it or consider it for repair, even if all the components on the bike are Japanese. Most dealers assume, incorrectly, that parts will not be available for it, and that repair or adjustment will be a totally unfamiliar experience.

Finally, while the selection of cycle clothing, bags, and accessories carried by the average bike shop has improved in recent years, it still pales by comparison with that carried by similar shops in North America. As extra-large sizes are a rarity here, it's best to stock up when you're back home.

Buying from a local dealer can be very satisfying if you become a regular customer. Dealers tend to favor regulars with discounts and free repairs, are great sources of information, and often host riding clubs. If you find a helpful dealer, consider yourself lucky and treat them well with lots of business.

The following bike shops have been tried and tested and have consistently proved their worth over the years.

Asahi Shokai

   2-27-18 Kyodo, Setagaya-ku, Tokyo ☎ 03 3428-4276
   • A few minutes walk from Kyodo Station on the Odakyu Line
   • Open 10:00 A.M. to 7:00 P.M.; closed Wednesdays

Asahi Shokai is just a step above the neighborhood *jitenshaya-san* when it comes to parts and accessories. But the friendly owner has, or can get, some famous European bikes at rather reasonable prices.

Cycland

4-6-4 Ebara, Shinagawa-ku, Tokyo ☎ 03 3783-7881
* Musashi Koyama Station, Tokyu Mekama Line; off Nakahara-Kaido opposite a big NTT office
* Open 9:00 A.M. to 7:00 P.M.; closed Thursdays

Cycland's friendly establishment will do their best to pander to your every whim; they have a good reputation for friendly service.

Durango

4-6 Motoyoyogi-cho, Shibuya-ku, Tokyo ☎ 03 3481-9801
* Yoyogi Hachiman Station, Odakyu Line
* Open daily from 11:00 A.M. to 8:00 P.M.

Modeled after a West Coast-styled triathletic outfitters, Durango is stocked with a full line of both road and off-road bikes, foreign and domestic. It's probably worth the few extra thousand yen to buy from Durango, as the shop can be relied upon for generous, conscientious after-sale service. The manager is very helpful, speaking passable English if the need arises.

Durango has a wide variety of athletic shoes, jogging wear, cycling clothes, and even the odd windsurfing wetsuit. The store also takes special orders. There are some real bargains in the baskets of sweats and running shorts in front of the store. Even if you're not looking for a bike, drop by to pick up some good cheap, knockaround duds. And get this—large sizes!

Friend Shokai

Main Store

1-8-4 Minami Asagaya, Suginami-ku, Tokyo ☎ 03 3311-8930
* Four minutes walk from Minami Asagaya Station, Marunouchi Line
* Open from noon to 8:30 P.M. weekdays , 10:00 A.M. to 8:30 P.M. Saturdays, 10:00 A.M. to 7:00 P.M. Sundays and national holidays; closed Tuesdays

Nishi Kokubunji Branch

3-33-2-108 Izumi-cho, Kokubunji-shi, Tokyo ☎ 0423 23-6690
* A two-minute walk from Nishi Kokubunji Station, JR Chuo Line
* Open from noon to 8:30 P.M. weekdays, noon to 7:00 P.M. Saturdays, 10:00 A.M. to 8:30 P.M. Sundays and national holidays; closed Tuesdays

Friend Shokai opened in 1933, and is sort of a department store for the seriously cycled. Two floors offer a wide selection of parts and accessories, but don't expect many discounts. Custom orders are their specialty.

Hara's Azabu Cycle Center

> 3-2-4 Shirogane, Minato-ku, Tokyo ☎ 03 3441-5910
> • Hiroo Station, Hibiya Line
> • Open 10:00 A.M. to 7:00 P.M.; closed Wednesdays

Right behind the shopping bikes at Hara's store there is a wide selection of goods for the serious cyclist. Hara-san is an avid cyclist himself, and doesn't try to push you into buying new-fangled gadgetry you don't really need.

Mr. Charley—American Bike Shop

> 1-43-6 Higashi Ikebukuro, Toshima-ku, Tokyo ☎ 03 3983-8694
> • Open daily from 10:00 A.M. to 8:00 P.M.
> • In D-Box Building, a five-minute walk from the east exit of Ikebukuro Station

Mr. Charley offers a wide choice of imported bikes at discounted prices. At Galaxy, a bike shop affiliated with Mr. Charley, located opposite the Sunshine 60 Building in Ikebukuro, a variety of bikes are available, including tandems.

Narushima Friend

Main Store

> 2-37-7 Sendagaya, Shibuya-ku, Tokyo ☎ 03 3405-9614
> • Short walk from Sendagaya Station, JR Sobu Line
> • Open 11:30 A.M. to 6:30 P.M., until 8:00 P.M. Saturdays; closed Wednesdays

Tachikawa Branch

> 1-17-22 Nishiki-cho, Tachikawa-shi, Tokyo ☎ 0425 22-6632
> • Open 11:30 A.M. to 6:30 P.M., until 8:00 P.M. Saturdays; closed Wednes days and Thursdays
> • A few minutes walk east of Tachikawa Station, JR Chuo Line

Narushima Friend is very well stocked, especially with brakes and derailleurs. Some discounts are available, with good buys on bike packages and frames. While they know their business, they tend to be understaffed and poor at customer relations. Cyclists with few tools will appreciate that the staff is rather free about letting regular customers make use of tools at the shop.

Outside

Sanko Meguro Bldg. 1F, 2-13-29 Meguro, Meguro-ku, Tokyo
☎ 03 5704-1561
- On north side of Yamate Dori, between Komazawa Dori and Meguro Dori, about a twelve-minute walk from JR Meguro Station, or Nakameguro Station on the Tokyu Toyoko Line
- Open weekdays 11:00 A.M. to 7:00 P.M., Saturdays 11:00 A.M. to 8:00 P.M., national holidays 11:00 A.M. to 6:00 P.M.; closed Sundays and Mondays

Opened amid considerable fanfare involving the Canadian Chamber of Commerce and a canoe-full of iced Labatt's Blue, Outside is the first Canadian-owned and operated outfitter in Japan. Rallying beneath the motto *Natural Touring*, Outside specializes in kayaking and off-road riding and there is talk at Outside of organizing off-road cycling tours.

Though only the upper-echelon off-road units from the extensive Rocky Mountain catalog are stocked, anything in the line can be ordered, even custom-builts—good news for those with North American builds. Along with cycling accessories, Outside offers an eye-catching array of outdoor wear, as well as backpacks, tents, and expedition accessories—try the freeze-dried vegetarian meals, or the dehydrated non-alcoholic wine.

Sports Cycle Alps

3-17-8 Uchi Kanda, Chiyoda-ku, Tokyo ☎ 03 3256-8288
- A few minutes walk from the west exit of Kanda Station
- Open 10:00 A.M. to 6:30 P.M.; closed Thursdays and the third Wednesday each month

Alps, located near the Central Hotel, specializes in touring bikes and accessories for the touring cyclist. Quality is high, and so are the prices.

Pro Shop Nakamura

2049 Fussa, Fussa-shi, Tokyo ☎ 0425 51-0773
- A two-minute walk from Higashi Fussa Station on the Hachiko Line out of Hachioji Station
- Open 10:00 A.M to 7:00 P.M.; 10:00 A.M to 6:00 P.M. in winter; closed Thursdays

This friendly establishment specializes in MTBs and racing bikes, and stocks major imported and domestic frames and parts.

Westy Cycle Products

1-23-10 Sugamo, Toshima-ku, Tokyo ☎ 03 3943-5140
- Five minutes from JR Sugamo Station
- Open from noon to 8:00 P.M.; closed Thursdays and New Year holidays

On Sunday mornings, Oi Futo, south of Shinagawa with its wide streets, bridges, overpasses, high winds, and lack of traffic, is a hot spot for the road bike crowd. If you've been there, you may have noticed many riders sporting jerseys, or riding bikes, emblazoned with the name of Westy Cycle Products. This shop tries hard to appeal to all types of riders, who ride all types of bikes.

The most interesting way to discover the shop is to go to Oi Futo on Sunday morning and introduce yourself to any Westy riders you see. They, in turn, may introduce you to Westy's owner, Mr. Hayama, though he may not be at Oi if there is an interesting race somewhere else that Sunday. Since English isn't a strong point of the Westy group, the common language is cycling. Your efforts to communicate in Japanese will be met with enthusiasm. Back at the shop, everyone who goes is offered a free cup of coffee or tea, served by Mrs. Hayama. Not really an avid cyclist, her job is to watch over the shop's two mascots, Tora the cat and Snoopy, the Westfield terrier after whom the shop was named.

You may be surprised by the sleek decor and lack of jumble here. There's a coffee bar, video player, and huge windows, making the atmosphere quite different from ordinary bike shops in Japan. Much of the merchandise, including components, is tucked away in cupboards or in the frame shop in back. Only representative examples are attractively displayed. You can order a custom frame here, or pick a ready-made off the rack, and choose components as you like. Mr. Hayama is especially good at fitting frame dimensions to the rider, and at explaining the principles involved. The emphasis is on road and triathalon bikes, although mountain bikes and kid's bikes are also sold. Along with the interesting array of accessories, including shorts, jerseys, and shoes, the shop will also fit you with a wetsuit, considered a necessity by Japanese triathletes. Unusual items, and things in large sizes, can easily be ordered.

Westy is worth a visit even if you don't buy anything. As you sip your coffee, you can watch a video of a triathalon or a road race while you chat with Mr. Hayama and any knowledgeable customers who happen to drop by. They frequently organize group participation in various races, even some overseas, and the atmosphere provides the motivation many of us need to keep training consistently or to set higher goals.

The Yoshida Group

Yoshida Main Store

 1-6-9 Hon-cho, Shiki-shi, Saitama ☎ 0484 71-0069
 • Fifteen minutes from Shiki Station on the Tobu Tojo Line from Ikebukuro
 • Open from 9:00 A.M. to 7:00 P.M.; closed Wednesdays

The Yoshida Group has a chain of nine stores throughout Tokyo, all run by serious cyclists who are very helpful in making suggestions and lending assistance after taking your concerns into consideration. Each store is well stocked with foreign and domestic frames, accessories, and complete bike packages generally ten to twenty percent cheaper than comparable bikes in other stores. And what they don't have they can order from one of their other stores. Bicycles can also be ordered directly from their factory in Kawagoe (3301 Maeda Kugedo, Kawagoe-shi, Saitama, ☎ 0492 35-6333).

Yoshida branch stores:

Shibarakku

 2-23 Kanda Awajicho, Chiyoda-ku, Tokyo ☎ 03 3255-8530
 • Near the Nikolai Cathedral, a few minutes walk from Ochanomizu Station on the JR Sobu Line
 • Open noon to 7:00 P.M.; closed Wednesdays

Spica

 3-8 Sakuragaoka, Shibuya-ku, Tokyo ☎ 03 3462-2546
 • A few minutes walk from Shibuya Station on the Yamanote, Ginza, Inokashira, Hanzomon, Shin Tamagawa, Toyoko lines
 • Open Mondays and Fridays 12:30 P.M. to 7:00 P.M., other days noon to 7:00 P.M.; closed Wednesdays

Roue

 2-10-1 Higashi Oizumi, Nerima-ku , Tokyo ☎ 03 3978-4111
 • Opposite Toei Movie Company near Oizumi Gakuen Station on the Seibu Ikebukuro Line from Ikebukuro
 • Open 10:00 A.M. to 7:00 P.M.; closed Wednesdays

Alternative Sources

Alternative sources do exist in Japan for purchasing bikes at discounted prices. Independent dealers, many of them long-term foreign residents, buy bikes from manufacturers, and then sell them with a mark-up of ten to twenty percent, offering service in addition.

Mail order from overseas is another option, particularly for the more expensive models. Even taking shipping costs into account, mail-order is always cheaper, but warranties may not apply, and service is a problem.

Cycle Sales Newsletter

2-2-A6-303 Minami Ai, Ibaraki-shi, Osaka-fu ☎ 0726 41-6213

After finding sales channels for domestic and export-model bicycles, Michael Schultz of Osaka set up an English-language cycle sales newsletter to list his current lineup of low-priced bikes, both new and second hand. Those in the Osaka area can schedule showroom visits and end up riding away on a new purchase.

The newsletter also includes cycling tips on sizing, accessories, maps, foreign and domestic magazines, small ads, information on bike races and tours, and recommended sources in the local bike market. To receive the newsletter, contact Michael Schultz at the above address.

Recycling Bicycles

Tokyo is a city with a tremendous appetite for new, used, abused, and abandoned bicycles. Yearly production of bicycles in Japan must be in the hundreds of thousands of units, with as many more imports pouring in from Taiwan, the United States, and Europe. As a result Tokyo appears to be in the throes of an ongoing bike boom, and the casualties in the form of discarded mounts are piling up at an alarming rate. Think of it as another contribution to the entropy of the environment. Or in lay terms, more waste.

So, what can you do about it? Recycle bikes. Whenever you spot a good bike gone to waste, make a cursory assessment of its quality and condition. There are simply too many bikes on city sidewalks to make a comprehensive adoption program practical, so limit your involvement to bikes with exceptional potential.

Why so many bicycles are abandoned each year is open to debate, but one explanation is that many people buy bikes at discount from retailers who do not provide good (or any) service. Real bike shops are often reluctant to work on bikes sold by other stores, so when the bike needs attention, the owner just abandons it and buys another new bike at discount, starting the cycle of bicycle pollution over again.

The question you might be asking at this point is how to distinguish, for moral as well as legal purposes, between bike recycling and bike theft.

The answer is time. Very simply, if a good bike has remained locked and obviously unmoved in the same location for more than a few weeks, chances are it has been abandoned. Once the police notice it, the bike is likely to be tagged with an appeal to the owner to move it or lose it. At this point I usually act. Try recycling a bike sometime and see if it doesn't make you feel good inside.

Rental Bicycles

In the Tokyo Metropolitan area, rental bikes are available at certain designated cycling courses, usually in large parks:

Palace Cycling Way: Chiyoda-ku, 5.5km, 500 bikes, Sundays only

The Outer Gardens of the Meiji Shrine: Shinjuku-ku, 2.5km, 300 bikes, Sundays and national holidays only

Ueno Onshi Park Cycling Road: Taito-ku, 0.8km, 70 bikes

Tama-gawa Cycling Path: Denenchofu to Ota-ku, 12.5km, 80 bikes

Yoyogi Park Cycling Course: Shibuya-ku, 1.5km, 150 bikes, closed mondays, children 12 years and under

Setagaya Cycling Course: Setagaya-ku, 5.2km, 56 bikes, Sundays and national holidays only

Kinuta Ryokuchi Cycling Course: Setagaya-ku, 3.2km, 200 bikes

Komazawa Olympic Park Cycling Course: Setagaya-ku, 2.4km, 205 bikes

Zenpukuji-gawa Cycling Course: Suginami-ku, 2.1km, 170 bikes

Suginami Traffic Safety Park for Children: Suginami-ku, 1.3km, 170 bikes

Johoku Central Park: Itabashi-ku, 2.7km, 120 bikes

Koganei Park Cycling Course: Koganei-shi, 2.7km, 120 bikes

Showa Memorial Park Cycling Course: Tachikawa-shi, 7.0km, 860 bikes including 220 tandems

In the Kyoto area, some bike shops and hotels rent out bicycles for the day or by the hour. These bikes are ideal for seeing the main sights in the city. For more information, see pages 266-67.

Looking After Your Bike

Even in the land of the low crime rate, bicycle theft is becoming an increasing problem. Lock your bike every time you leave it, although it doesn't take much of a lock to deter Japanese bike thieves.

One attempt at theft prevention is the bicycle registration system, a one-time procedure automatically performed on new bikes by most bike dealers, whereby a small yellow sticker with a number and regional identification is stuck on the frame. (This registration, by the way, is not mandatory.) The main problem is that thieves have found that these stickers can easily be removed by heating them to loosen the adhesive, so the chances of the police recovering your stolen bike are slim.

In recent years, the police have, however, been stopping "suspicious-looking" foreigners on bikes to check, among other things, if the bikes are being ridden by their registered owners. If the bike is a hand-me-down, or a garage-sale special, the registered name may not match that of the rider, causing much consternation among the police and many hours of detention until the ownership issue is resolved. While this may never happen to you, having your bike registered in your name is a good way to prevent misunderstandings between you and your local police. Have your bike registered at your local bike shop, or ask at your local police box for details.

Bicycle parking is prohibited around train stations, but free or inexpensive parking areas are provided. If you leave your bike in a No Parking area for any length of time, it could be carted away to a municipally operated compound; a small charge is levied when you reclaim it. Also, some municipalities periodically collect bicycles which appear to be abandoned in public. Unfortunately, most are disposed of as garbage, although a small but increasing number are reconditioned by enlightened local governments and sent to needy overseas countries.

Another problem in Japan is rust. The humid climate and frequent rains cause bicycles to start rusting remarkably quickly. If you don't have covered parking, it's best to put a cover over your bike, fastening it tightly with clothespins. A better alternative, particularly for more expensive bikes, is to store it indoors. In Japan it's likely that floor space will be at a premium, but the creative use of a few hooks and straps are all it takes to mount your mount up on the ceiling. The rigging needn't be particularly strong because your bike shouldn't weigh any more than fifteen kilograms, right? Some older wooden buildings feature a sturdy moulding on the walls at head level; both wheels can be slotted into it while the top tube can be held by a strap attached to a single hook mounted in the ceiling.

Continual display in a prominent place indoors is also a good incentive for keeping it clean and polished. Even if you store your bike in a shed, you should clean it regularly, as mud and grime dull the finish over time.

You should do most maintenance on your bicycle yourself. Not only will you avoid repair bills and difficulties in dealing with bike shops, you'll also gain an understanding about your bike that will definitely come in handy should mechanical trouble occur on the road. Modern cables are of very high quality, so brakes and derailleurs rarely need adjustments due to cable stretch. The only repair you're likely to make is fixing a flat tire, or possibly straightening a wheel that has gone out of true. Apart from that, regular maintenance should include adjusting the brake cables to compensate for brake shoe wear and a little oil on brakes, chain, and derailleur to keep them moving smoothly.

On tour, a pump, a tire repair kit, and tools are a must. Just as important is a spoke wrench: If you have a mishap and a wheel bend way out of true, the bike may not be rideable and you could get stranded somewhere. Having a spoke wrench—and knowing how to use it—can allow you to true the wheel enough to get rolling again. Only on long trips will you need to carry a full tool kit, as today's hubs, headsets, and cranks are very reliable.

Getting Ready 🚲🚲🚲🚲🚲🚲🚲🚲🚲🚲🚲🚲🚲🚲

Communication

Central to any discussion of cycling in Japan is language, both spoken and written. Can you ask which is north or south? Can you distinguish one *kanji* from another? Should this stop you from touring? Of course not. However, it certainly helps if, before your trip, you spend some time and effort to study words and phrases having something to do with geography, distance, scenery, directions, accommodation, and how to make reservations or ask for a bicycle repair shop. Either way, make sure you take along enough patience, humor, and flexibility to handle potentially frustrating attempts at communication.

Maps and Orientation

Just take a look at a map of Tokyo (or any Japanese city other than Kyoto and Sapporo), and you'll quickly surmise that town planning has not been high on the list of priorities of the city authorities. I recommend you accept the insane maze that is made up by the streets of Tokyo as an exciting challenge to test your navigation and orientation skills. Besides, you can also have some fun in the bargain.

The first thing you will need in addition to your bike and cycling accessories is a good map, and preferably not one of those oversimplified folders that the tourist office puts out for foreigners. These are inadequate because they feature trains and subways primarily (we're cyclists, remember), but above all, the fact that names are printed in roman letters rather than Japanese *kanji* makes them harder to navigate by. After all, location and route signs in the real world are written in *kanji*. While a map in English may be helpful in planning your trip if you don't read Japanese, once you're on the road, a Japanese map is the best way to go.

Since there is more demand in Japan for maps in Japanese than for maps in English, there is a much better selection. Also, maps in the vernacular are updated more often for greater accuracy. Should you get lost, you don't have to be fluent in Japanese to match the characters on the roadsigns with those of your destination on your map, which will also be easier to read by any local person you stop and ask directions from.

Large bookstores are good places to buy maps. The best road maps are usually available by prefecture for about ¥750 each, so buy one for each prefecture you'll be riding through.

A common practice among mapmakers is to print the same map on both sides of the sheet; one in full color and the other in black and white only. You can use the monochrome side to draw in your route and make notes while leaving the color side clean and easy to read. Be sure to get maps done to at least 1:25,000 scale for optimum detail because you may often find yourself searching for an alternative route, particularly a small, quiet road that parallels a busy highway. Some Japanese map books tend to be somewhat bulky; make a copy of the pages that you need and leave the book at home. These map books cost from ¥1,500 to ¥2,000.

I have relied for years on the maps published by Shobunsha, and available at practically all Japanese bookstores. One of my favorite maps is *Tokyo Midokoro*, published by Tokyo Chizu Shuppan, an award-winning combination of page-by-page, ward-by-ward maps featuring tedious detail, accompanied by essays on points of interest, festivals, markets, etc. Though devised for use by walking tourists, the recommended routes can be just as rewarding for city cyclists. It's a little on the heavy side, but folds in thirds and fits nicely in a jersey pocket.

Something considerably more compact is Shobunsha's Tokyo booklet, featuring maps only, starting with regional transit and working its way through all of Tokyo's wards and neighboring cities. Note that the compass roses printed on maps in Japan are seldom consistently oriented. What this means when following a map book through Tokyo is that you may leave one ward and enter another, and on turning the corresponding pages it's not unusual to find that the orientation has shifted cataclysmically. In order to compensate, you must reorient with every turn of the page.

The Bridgestone cycling maps available at the Bicycle Culture Center (see page 258) and some major bookstores are in *kanji* and are extremely detailed, marking all the usual features in addition to cycling paths, suggested routes, and recommended bicycle shops. They make for fascinating armchair reading but their usefulness on the road is more limited. There are at present seven maps in the series, including Tokyo, Kanagawa, Saitama, Chiba, and the Kansai area.

On some maps the names of the big cities are written in roman letters as well as *kanji* and hard-to-pronounce (even for Japanese) place names are given in *hiragana* (easy-to-learn Japanese phonetic letters) to aid identification. Finally, if you're still worried about following a Japanese map, ask someone to write the names of the big cities on the map in roman letters.

An alternative is to try and find a map which has both English and *kanji*, or carry two maps, one in English and one in Japanese. Kodansha International's bilingual maps of Japan, the Tokyo area, and Kyoto and Osaka are useful, but for on the road the more detailed Japanese maps are the best choice.

Paradoxically, when on the road, the most obvious navigational aids—road signs and asking the locals—are often the least help. Road signs tend to steer you to major roads that lead toward the bigger cities, while asking for directions often means asking for similar trouble. Invariably, signs and locals steer you to the fastest way to get someplace, whereas for you the act of getting there is the real destination. Watch out for kind old ladies who tell you it'll take all day to get to your destination; more often than not you're there an hour later. Beware, too, of hand-drawn maps, or even showing the average bystander your detailed map. Many folks out there have a very non-map mentality, used to expressing distance in units of time regardless of variables such as speed, traffic, weather, and how much was drunk the night before. Road construction signs are also often unreliable; a road indicated as impassable can often be passed on a bicycle. I've found that a "Road Closed" sign is generally worth a go—the odds are definitely on your side.

Another very useful though highly underestimated tool is a good compass, and it is essential if you wish to dispense with maps altogether. I recommend a compact watchband compass like the ones scuba divers use. They are tiny, practically weightless, weatherproof, shock-resistant, and usually come with a Velcro band that can just as easily wrap around your handlebars as around your wrist.

The final option is to navigate as ancient sailors and pathfinders did, focusing on your position relative to the sky and the whole surface of the earth. Remember that, although Tokyo has been strewn haphazardly over the face of the Kanto Plain like an upset Monopoly game, the fact remains that Mt. Fuji is west, the surrounding mountains decline in altitude and increase in distance toward the north and east, the big rivers and the bay lie north and east, and the sun rises in the west and appears to journey east here as it does elsewhere, Japanese "uniqueness" notwithstanding.

One flight of fancy I find very helpful is to visualize the Yamanote Line as a vast surrealistic clock. Turning clockwise you'll find Ikebukuro's mammoth Sunshine 60 building at 12 o'clock, Tokyo Tower at 3 o'clock, air traffic in and out of Haneda at 6 o'clock, and that cluster of skyscrapers just west of Shinjuku at 9 o'clock. Though following visual orientations can be frustrating most of the year thanks to grey sweatshirt skies, pack your map and compass and get out on the streets and hone your navigation skills.

Packing that Pannier

"Bare Bones Biking" is the practice of planning an extended bike tour with no more baggage and equipment than you would require for a day ride.

This may well sound impractical, particularly in other parts of the world such as the United States, Canada, and Australia where the tours that attract cyclists cover vast unpopulated tracts of land. In Japan, however, with its excellent travelers' support services and low-cost, quality accommodation, Bare Bones Biking is the most intelligent way to go. Starting with a full-dress touring bike and all the trimmings, let's pick our way through the rig and see if we can't come out with a more streamlined outfit.

Since camping on Japanese campsites can be more a trauma than a pastime, it is assumed that cycle tourists will favor the many excellent and inexpensive alternatives, which include hostels, minshuku, and rider houses. So we can begin by dropping the tent, sleeping bag, ground pad, cookware, and anything else needed for camping. This leaves the panniers, rack, and handlebar bags, none of which I presently tour with. That's right, once you've dumped the gear that requires the bags, you can dump the bags too.

First of all, the panniers and rack can go for obvious reasons, but what about the handlebar bag? Don't we need that for clothes, toiletries, and other personal items, not to mention the essential camera?

Well, we can forget about the need for an extra change of clothes—

today's miracle fabric cycling wear can be washed and dried in less than an hour, during which time we are probably lounging around in a *yukata* (cotton summer kimono provided by many *minshuku*) anyway. I will admit that we still should carry some sort of rain gear, since there seem to be fifty-two distinct rainy seasons in Japan. A thin parka can be rolled up tight and wrapped around your *rinko bukuro* (bag for carrying your bike), which should then be lashed under your seat with its own straps.

Next stop: the Toilet Zone. Don't we need lots of toiletries? First of all, just how clean do we need to be on a bike tour? Certainly no cleaner than you can get every evening in your own bath or at the nearest *sento* or *onsen*. Bar soap, small containers of shampoo, toothpaste, and razors are almost always available, and a wash towel can be purchased en route, while your own toothbrush can be stashed in your jersey pocket.

Now, the only item that remains between us and freedom forever from that imposing handlebar bag is the camera. Forget it. Nothing spoils a good downhill more than the urge to stop and take a picture. Postcards are cheaper, usually feature better photographs, and can be gotten rid of en route at any mail box. Though cameras are devolving into ever more compact and lightweight formats, any camera still requires something to carry it in, so you will need a bag as long as you feel you need a camera. Liberate yourself from your camera and you'll find you enjoy the ride much more—although you will inevitably run into those situations that make you think "I wish I'd brought my camera."

Now we're down to the bare bones. Your bike has regained those sleek lines that made you want to own it in the first place. So what *do* we need? Regardless of how naked you want to get, you will still probably need that *rinko bukuro*, and a few tools for assembly, unless you are fortunate enough to be able to ride out of town and all the way back home again. A pump is still a requirement, but that goes on the frame nice and tight.

Finally, you will have to contend with your wallet or bag. Dump the contents and take only your passport (or alien registration card), and your credit card and/or bank cash card. A little cash in your jersey pocket and you're ready for the pleasure of superlight touring.

For those who adhere to the philosophy of Bare Bones Biking in theory but wish to deviate slightly in practice, particularly when on an extended tour, one extremely practical idea is to keep those extra essentials in a medium-sized wedge-shaped bag that straps under the saddle, requiring no extra hardware.

This bag serves nicely for holding all those extra essentials that tend to accumulate when planning a tour of up to one week and helps keep jersey pockets free of too much stuff. Stuff your spare sew-up tire (or inner tube only if you're riding clinchers) into an old sock and throw it in the bag—flats do happen. Together with your bicycle bag, roll up two hex wrenches (one for unbolting the seatpost, the other for the handlebars and pedals) and one glove (for handling the chain, etc. during the assembly and disassembly). In the bag's tiny side pocket, I slip in a small patch kit, a spoke wrench, and a Swiss Army knife for opening cans and bottles.

Along with your parka, don't forget to include a very light nylon backpack. This will come in handy when somebody gives you armfuls of fresh fruit or when you decide to buy after-dinner drinks or snacks.

If you wear cleated cycling shoes, which aren't good for walking, it's nice to be able to slip into a different pair of comfortable shoes for strolling around in the evening. Many minshuku provide Japanese geta (wooden block sandals), but after a day of pushing pedals, they're not particularly comfortable. A handy item to pack in the extra bag is a pair of those cheap black Chinese casual shoes that fold flat.

There's also room in the bag for a razor, toothbrush, and small plastic vials of shampoo and shaving cream—wrap them up into one of those long, narrow Japanese bath towels and keep them together with a rubber band. Most of these things are usually available in hotels and minshuku, but the disposable razors are at best unpleasant for anyone with more than a very thin beard and it's a rare place indeed that has anything more than a bar of soap to shave with. And, those disposable toothbrushes never seem to get the job done and often leave a bad taste in the mouth.

And finally, a map. You need one, especially in the deep countryside where signs are sometimes few and far between.

Weighing about one kilo in all, this bag doesn't interfere with cycling and fits neatly on top of the disassembled bike in its bag.

No matter how much or how little you take on a tour, it's a good idea to question your choices before you leave. Stuff has a way of piling up before you realize it, weighing you down with not just extra weight, but the responsibility of keeping track of and caring for your possessions. Remember, the idea is to get away from it all, not take it all with you.

Thought for Food

After about two hours of hard cycling, chances are you'll want something to eat to maintain your energy level. There are as many ideas on what the ideal cycling food is as there are cyclists on the road, and most people eventually find the foods that work best for them.

Apart from the "what's healthful versus what's tasty" battle everyone must come to terms with, there are a few requirements for cycling food that go beyond taste or nutrition. Food to take with you must pack well and not spill easily. It should not require refrigeration, additional preparation, or any utensils to eat it.

This might be an excellent physical description of candy, but candy isn't the most excellent thing to eat. It's better to aim for fresh fruit and complex carbohydrates such as bread or rice. Unfortunately, it's hard to find whole-grain breads or brown rice out of the big cities, so you might have to make do with the white versions.

A good choice is *onigiri*, the triangular rice balls wrapped in seaweed available in virtually every convenience store; they are inexpensive, often about the same price as a candy bar, but much more filling and nutritious. Plus, they're easily packed in your bag or stuffed in a jersey pocket, so buy a couple for the day when you find them.

Lightly sweetened *kombu* strips, known as *Nakano Kombu,* are sort of the beef jerky of seaweed and can provide many interesting moments of chewing. Look for them in the little red boxes next to the chewing gum. Tastier and without sugar is *yakinori*, or dried seaweed. Although the packages of larger sheets are more economical, the smaller individual packages are more convenient. A lookalike variation is *ajitsuke-nori,* which is heavily seasoned and salted, with most brands containing MSG.

Dried fruits and nuts pack and keep well, and are a good snack on the road. Go easy on them, though; dried fruits are high in sugars (which can stimulate thirst), while nuts are high in fats (which can be hard to digest in large quantities.) A good source of these and other Western-style natural food items is Tengu Natural Foods (Umehara 50-2, Hidaka-shi, Saitama, tel 0429 85-8751 fax 0429 85-8752). Contact them for a catalog; they will deliver anywhere in Japan.

Another temptation is the assortment of ice cream bars found in small freezers in even the smallest of stores. Few of these are any good and fewer actually qualify as real ice cream. Lots of sugar and unfamiliar fats combine with a cornucopia of artificial flavorings to give some bizarre taste sensations. What might look good on the packet will probably leave you thirsty for what might be hours on end.

Many cyclists spurn the idea of carrying a water bottle and rely on drinks to quench their thirst from the ubiquitous vending machines. Some riders report good results with the sugared mineral-added "sports drinks," although I've found that in the long run they tend to stimulate thirst rather than quench it. If it's minerals you're after, a better alternative is a little sea-weed to chew with just plain water.

The next time you find yourself face to face with the impressive array of drinks ranging from Calpis to Pocari Sweat to Toughman, spare a thought for all the natural resources that went into the building of all those machines, and the amount of electricity (much of it nuclear generated) that is used by them all. And we haven't even started to think about the containers yet. Just imagine all the natural resources that go into the manufacture of those bottles and cans, most of which are used only once. Many are unburnable, and will find their way into landfill dumps if they don't end up as litter.

The sheer waste is especially shocking when one considers what all this consumption is for—just to give people something cold to drink. Imagine what would happen if only half of all the people who buy from these machines decided to carry water bottles, much like the water bottles cyclists use on their bicycles. The more you think about it, the more possible (and perhaps practical) it seems. Belt-mounted canteens for the casually dressed. Slim and elegant stainless steel canteens that fit into briefcases for business people. Canteens that can be easily refilled from drinking fountains in stations and buildings.

But I'm tired of just water, you might well say. Most people with a little cycling experience have already thought about that. When I'm cycling, I carry a little squeeze bottle of pure lime juice and give each water bottle filling a little squirt. Just about a teaspoon or two of pure lime juice makes plain water surprisingly refreshing. Some people just cut a lemon up into quarters and put them in their water bottle. Other people get powdered versions of their favorite sports drinks and pocket the packets. Those who are into really cold refreshments put their bottle in the freezer the night before, and take it out the next morning so they can sip ice water in the time it takes the big chunk to melt inside the bottle. All it takes is a little imagination and you'll find there are many ways to adapt the water bottle habit for times when you're off the bike.

Finally, a few words of caution. Riding during the hot summer months may work up a thirst for cold beer, but try to resist the temptation until the end of the day. The first few gulps may well be invigorating, but the alcohol actually tends to warm the body, making one hotter and sweatier and ready for more beer.

Outside of Tokyo, Seven/Eleven and other convenience stores can be found almost everywhere. However, Denny's and some of the other chains ubiquitous in Tokyo are few and far between. Be ready to try some new eating places. Noodles, which come in a bewildering choice of shapes, sizes and colors, offer the perfect antidote for flagging cyclists. Not only are they rich in carbohydrates, but they're inexpensive, too. Look for _soba_, thin buckwheat noodles, _udon,_ white wheat noodles, and _ramen,_ Chinese egg noodles. In summer _zarusoba_ (cold _soba_) and _somen_ (thin white wheat vermicelli) are particularly refreshing.

Looking after Yourself

Anyone living in the twenty-three wards of Tokyo can join a public insurance fund (_Kumin no Kotsu Saigai Kyosai_) which provides compensation should you be injured or killed due to a traffic accident. Cyclists and pedestrians are also covered but damage to vehicles or other property is not. With a choice of three annual premiums of ¥500, ¥1,000 and ¥2,000, corresponding to coverage of ¥1.5 million, ¥3.5 million and ¥6.0 million respectively, it's the best insurance value in town. Apply at any ward office, or at your local Sogo or Shinyo-type bank.

However, as hazardous as biking in Tokyo is, nobody ever expects to have an accident. No matter how careful you are, it can happen to you, and the more you know about the laws, medical care, system, and customs of Japan, the less likely it is that you will have to undergo any unpleasant experiences with the medical profession during your stay in Japan.

Experience has shown that competent medical care cannot always be taken for granted in Japan. One major difference is that Tokyo's ambulance service is operated by the fire department, and its personnel receive only minimum training. One evening while riding home, my wife, through no fault of her own, became involved in an accident. Lying crumpled on the pavement, she told me she had hurt her back and couldn't move. An ambulance arrived on the scene within minutes, but to my horror it was immediately clear that we weren't dealing with highly trained medical professionals but several individuals who more closely resembled delivery truck drivers. It might have been comic had it not been so potentially dangerous—after carefully assessing the situation (they looked at her), they started to lift her onto a stretcher, but it was only after I protested loudly that it wasn't clear how bad the injury was and that she should be lifted onto the stretcher more carefully that they tried to lift her without moving her back.

Never assume that emergency medical care is readily available. Many hospitals refuse emergency cases, or say that they don't have any space to handle arrivals late at night. When we confronted the problem of where to go that night, we were told that one large and relatively highly regarded hospital close to our apartment had no free beds. Only after some searching did the ambulancemen find a small hospital that was willing to take us.

Don't assume that general care of the patient will be undertaken by the nurses. On arrival at the hospital we were told that relatives or friends were expected to carry out general nursing duties such as washing and changing. Our problems were compounded when we found that the only free bed was in a women's ward where men were not allowed to enter. The search for a suitable hospital began again.

Do your best to check out the nearest hospital that offers decent medical care. Realize that some small private hospitals are of a shockingly low standard and seem to exist primarily to make money. The next hospital we visited did come up with a private room—but one with peeling paint and a plainly inadequate number of roach motels.

Having an idea which hospitals are best before you have an accident is definitely an asset. Our experience illustrates what can happen by going to the nearest hospital that will take you. Unfortunately, late at night you may not have much of a choice. If your Japanese is less than perfect you should try to find hospitals with English-speaking doctors.

Prevention is obviously better than a cure, and if you are one of the few surviving cyclists that still doesn't wear a helmet, consider what a watermelon that has rolled off the back of a pickup truck would look like on the road. The last thing my wife remembers before the excruciating pain in her back was the sharp crack of her plastic helmet hitting the road. Head injuries are the leading cause of bicycle-related deaths, so you need all the help you can get. Today's lightweight helmets are not all that uncomfortable and they also provide some protection against the sun, more if a visor is added. Brightly flashing belts or bike-mounted red lights to signal one's presence are a must for riding through the frequent dark tunnels on coast and mountain roads in Japan. If you wear contact lenses, consider taking along some form of eye protection as passing trucks throw up plenty of dust and dirt.

Before starting out on any ride you should get in the habit of checking tire pressure (by hand is okay) and that both front and rear brakes are working properly. Those with quick release hubs should also make sure that the levers are in their proper closed position. It has been noted that bicycles are occasionally tampered with when parked and that quick release levers are an easy target for pranksters. You won't get too far with a loose rear wheel, but a loose front wheel could go undetected until the first bump, causing the front wheel to come off, leading to certain injury.

If you ride in Tokyo regularly—and even if you don't—it may be wise to consider extra health insurance. In our case the expenses were not so high, but they could quickly become a problem if you are confined to a hospital for any length of time. If no nursing care is available and you cannot provide your own, hiring a private nurse is expensive. Emergency ambulance services are free (and considering their quality they should be), but if you require one to move from one hospital to another it will cost.

In the meantime, ride carefully.

On the Road 🚲 🚲 🚲 🚲 🚲 🚲 🚲 🚲 🚲 🚲 🚲 🚲 🚲 🚲 🚲

Rules of the Road

"What are the rules for bicycles, anyway?" Even after a number of years in Japan, you'll still find yourself asking that question. The reality is that, regardless of the official rules, police are inconsistent in their enforcement of them, and that casual cyclists, in city and countryside alike, seem to be able to do pretty much as they please. Bicycles roll on roads, sidewalks, footpaths, and sometimes even station concourses.

While this may seem like a recipe for a chaotic riding situation, the reality is that the lack of clearly observed and enforced rules for bicycle traffic can work in your favor—as long as you exercise caution. Naturally a lack of clear-cut guidelines exposes the cyclist to all kinds of traffic hazards.

If traffic is heavy on the road (where you should normally ride) and you have trouble making progress through lines of tightly packed vehicles, you can always move over to a sidewalk. Often there are openings in the barriers between the road and the sidewalk; if not, you can dismount and heft your bike over and proceed. Although the going is much slower because people and other bicycles seem to pop out suddenly in the most unlikely of places, it's faster than staying stuck in the traffic. Keep an eye on the road, though, because you can return to it when the traffic opens up.

Finally, the best advice on safe cycling in traffic is to practice defensive riding tactics. Remain aware of traffic coming at you from both sides and behind—as much as possible go "with the flow." Almost all motorists are courteous, and it's easier on the nerves to give up right-of-way than to insist on it with drivers who abruptly cut you off. After all, you shouldn't be in that kind of hurry, it's only tiring in the long run. Besides, there are plenty of stretches on the open road where you'll be able to ride as fast as you please.

What to Watch Out For

Although the rulebooks prefer cyclists to use the sidewalks, a number of bad habits chronic among local sidewalk users emphasize the ironic fact that you are actually far safer riding your bike out in the traffic. Tokyo is one of the few Japanese cities I am familiar with that can boast an extensive infrastructure of sidewalks. Unfortunately, my experiences on these sidewalks, both as a cyclist and a pedestrian, have taught me that they are hair-raisingly hazardous.

Some examples of the alarming behavior of sidewalk cyclists I have observed and encountered in Tokyo include:

The tendency of others "sharing" the sidewalk's bike lane with you to ride on the wrong side of it.

The stupefying practice local housewives have of overloading poor quality, unmaintained "shopping" bikes with heavy cargoes of groceries and children (sometimes as many as three) and plowing along like the vanguard of an armored battalion.

The breakneck antics of kids who think nothing of standing precariously on special long "spikes" threaded onto the rear axle of their friends' bikes. (These dangerous accessories continue to be sold despite the fact that doubling up on a bicycle is illegal.)

The malicious "rear attack" in which a speeding cyclist closes in from behind and narrowly misses you without the courtesy of ringing the bell—which, in spite of regulations which require it, the bike often does not have.

At the same time, a number of bad habits among pedestrians which can impede a cyclist's progress (or worse) include:

Without the least caution, bolting onto the sidewalk from storefronts, restaurants, doorways, and alleys. Or out of taxis, buses, and private cars. This includes the potentially lethal practice of "door-jamming," flinging a car door open into a sidewalk or curb so that the approaching cyclist must either swerve dangerously to avoid it, or eat it whole.

Pedestrians who suddenly stop and turn around without purpose, or who sidestep back and forth with the apparent intention of confounding the approaching cyclist. (Or, perhaps their behavior is merely an outward manifestation of the stresses inherent in city life.)

The only way to avoid all of the above is to ride well out in the lanes with motorized traffic. Despite the illusion of danger out there, a competent, alert cyclist who obeys the rules of the road is actually far less likely to encounter problems there than on the sidewalk. For one thing, traffic is always going just one way. Motorists also tend to be more cautious and, at least in Tokyo, far more aware of cyclists sharing the road with them. (Think about this: people who flunked driver's training must use the sidewalks.)

One of the most civilized ideas in Japan is the parallel pedestrian and bicycle tunnel dug alongside some tunnels (perhaps a fifth of them). Keep an eye open for these side tunnels as they may not be visible until you're almost inside the main tunnel. For the rest of the tunnels you must go through, we suggest that you wait for traffic to clear in both directions and ride in the center of your lane rather than near the left line. Since the lighting is often poor, you may not be able to see bad pavement or sand along the side of the road. If you're trying to get out of the tunnel as fast as possible before cars come, beware of overriding your headlight. As noted before, be sure to take along a good flashing bike- or belt-mounted light for use in tunnels.

Getting Around with a Bike Bag

If you live far from good cycling countryside, getting there by bike can sometimes take all day. By putting your bike and yourself on a bus or train, you can avoid all the traffic hassle. All you need is a bicycle bag (*rinko bukuro*), available at any well-stocked bicycle shop. Getting a bicycle bag and learning how to use it gives you the freedom to explore the entire country by taking advantage of Japan's comprehensive rail system. I've also taken numerous domestic airline flights, and have found that Japanese baggage handlers take especially good care.

People often assume it's a nuisance to take apart their bicycle and stuff all the pieces into a bag. But it's definitely not if you take a few minutes to learn how to do it. All you have to do is take the front and back wheels off, strap them to the frame in three places, then put the whole bundle in the bicycle bag. Then put your tools, grease rag, and other small parts in the small carry bag supplied with the bicycle bag and drop it in with the bicycle. Zip the bag, hook up the strap, and you're on your way.

You might want to reposition things that stick out to make the bike fit more easily and make the bag easier to carry. I always remove the pedals and saddle and pull out the handlebars while leaving all cables connected. Mudguards and racks can create problems, so they'll also have to be removed. If it's only a short trip, consider leaving them at home and using a small front bag, or a rear bag that straps to your saddle.

Removing the back wheel looks far more complicated than it really is. Make sure you've shifted to the highest gear, loosen the wheel, pull the derailleur body back a little (it's spring loaded), and slip the wheel right out. Putting it back on is just as easy: move the wheel in, hook the upper side of the chain on the smallest cog, pull the derailleur body back, slide the wheel in and tighten the wheel nuts. If you feel uncertain about the whole process, spend a few minutes staring at the whole setup to get an idea how it's put together. And round up some cheap cotton gloves to keep grease off your hands. After a few times doing it, you won't need them anymore.

When you unpack and assemble your bike, roll the bicycle bag up and put it in the carry bag (with your tools, work gloves or rag, etc.) and strap that to your saddle or wherever is convenient. Check the brakes and gears by making a short test ride. Now you're ready to roll.

Choosing a Bike Bag

When considering the purchase of a commercially manufactured bike bag, a general rule is that the heavier your bike, the heavier the bag you'll need to get for it. Ostrich, one of Japan's leading manufacturers of bike bags, offers a wide range of bags for both road and mountain bikes, with prices ranging from ¥7,000 to over ¥13,000. This may seem expensive, but a properly designed bike bag will last for years if treated with care and is worth every yen when you consider the advantages of using Japan's superb transportation network.

Bags by Ostrich are available at most bike shops; the bike section of Tokyu Hands in Shibuya can be relied on for having regular stock. A good idea is to order one at your local bike shop, checking with the dealer to make sure it will fit your bike.

Some bags only require that you remove the front wheel, and these are tempting to a lot of first-timers. However, these bags tend to be larger and bulkier, and are harder to carry than the bags designed to hold a bike with both wheels removed. Most bags don't require removal of the handlebars and other parts, but it's safer to remove the pedals—even though they are covered by the bag, catching a passer-by or yourself in the side while you're hefting the bag can really hurt.

Choose a bag made out of good quality nylon fabric—not only is it stronger for its weight than canvas-type fabrics (which can become unmanageably heavy when wet), it's also thinner, allowing the bike bag to be packed into its carrying bag a lot more easily.

Once you've bought the bag, practice putting your bike into it; not just once but a few times in order to find how to fit everything in with a minimum of stretching and pulling. Also, check out what kind of extra room the bag has for other gear like helmets, handlebar bags, and cycling shoes.

Those who skip this important orientation will run the risk of being stuck at some train station, furiously trying to pack the bag in time to catch the last train home. After a long and tiring ride is not the time to start trying to figure out what goes where in your bike bag.

An alternative to buying a commercial bag is to improvise your own. All you need is a lightweight nylon sheet, 1.5 by 2.5m, six clothes pins, and a bungee cord.

First, take off the front wheel and place it against the frame just in front of the rear wheel, which you don't have to remove. Then tie the front wheel to the bike with the cord, which you can also loop around the handlebars to keep them tied sideways in line with the frame. Next, drape the nylon sheet over the top tube, and fasten each side together with the clothespins. Leave the saddle and handlebar exposed for carrying purposes.

This all takes about three minutes, and pedals and racks stay on. Should a carry strap be necessary, you can use a baggage strap with plastic end clips. Just loop it around the seatpost and handlebar and hook it together.

The cost? Only ¥950. The nylon sheet also doubles as a groundcloth, a raincape, or a tent. It's washable, weighs less than 100 grams, and compresses into a cylinder about 9 x 9cm.

Riding the Trains

Bikes may be taken on any train or subway providing that it is properly bagged—or at least covered to look like it is. When using the bag in stations and on public transport, do your best to stay out of everyone's way. You might find the bag heavy or awkward to carry at first, so it might be better to let people go ahead of you and then continue at your own pace. Once on the platform you can make things easier by entering at the very front or back of the train and resting your bagged bike on the wall out of the way. Try to avoid rush hour because it's hard enough just handling yourself in the crowd, much less the large, lumpy bag that's your bike. I learned this lesson the hard way when trying to get off at Ueno Station around 8:30 one weekday morning. In the onrush of people, I couldn't even lift my bicycle until the train had gone all the way down to Kanda. One solution is to leave earlier—most trains are fairly empty until 7:15 A.M. or so, and if that's too early, plan for a more leisurely 10:00 A.M. start.

However, the rather curious, bulky nature of the bag can help to break the ice, particularly out in the countryside—for a friend, a long bus journey passed quickly when the other passengers, after a false start with a tuba and a hang-glider, became convinced that there was a collapsible helicopter in her bag....

Finally, you should know that a special ticket is required to carry a bagged bike on the train. It's called a *temawarihin kippu*, and costs only ¥260 whatever the length of the journey and regardless of the lines you subsequently change to. The ticket can be purchased from the fare adjustment window by the ticket gate and is actually a small tag with wires to attach it to your bag.

However, experience has shown that subway people or railway officials rarely ask for it when you enter or exit a ticket barrier and they often don't even know how to sell it to you. Some people have used the same *temawarihin kippu* for a whole season, as station personnel never remove it at the exit and are rarely known to check the actual date. Nonetheless, the ticket is far from expensive, and you should purchase one in the event it is demanded. Besides, it makes a simple little souvenir of your journey.

Ferry Tales

For those who don't like to bag their bikes and who don't have cars to carry them on, Japan's ferries present an appealing solution to the problem of finding a quick way out of Tokyo into some great country/off road cycling, particularly if the dock is nearby. For example, the car ferry that plies Tokyo Bay between the cities of Kawasaki (Kanagawa Prefecture) and Kisarazu (Chiba Prefecture) offers one of the best adventure values to be had by Tokyo urbanites. Following a seventy-minute bay cruise you'll wind up on the Chiba side of the bay, where there is unlimited bayside cruising and back country riding available in almost any direction.

Depending upon where you live in Tokyo, the ride through town to the ferry need not be an unpleasant one, and my recommendation is that you take your most direct route to the Tama-gawa River Bikeway, and then head downstream. Eventually, you'll want to cross the river to the south, or Kawasaki side, as it is only a short ride from the south side of the estuary, adjacent to Haneda Airport, to the ferry terminal.

For centrally located Tokyoites, the most direct route to the Tama-gawa is along the Toyoko Line which connects Shibuya and Yokohama. After passing through stately Denenchofu, take a short jog to the left and cross the river using the Maruko-bashi Bridge, turn left again, and follow the bikeway until you cross the Keihin Kyuko Line. From there, road signs (if you read Japanese) or your friendly neighborhood police box (if you speak the language) will direct you to the ferry. The ride from the bridge to the ferry should take about forty-five minutes.

The round-trip fare is ¥2,530 including bicycle, which you simply wheel on board and park on the car deck. Crewmen will usually secure the bike for you, as the ride can be choppy, and when the ferry reaches midchannel, it must yield right of way to other vessels in what is the world's busiest inland shipping lane, sometimes causing the ferry to swerve dramatically. Another transportation sideshow is to be had on departure from and arrival back at Kawasaki, when the ferry passes under the final approach for Haneda Airport.

When the ferry arrives at Kisarazu, it turns into a channel domineered by an industrial seascape that looks like a monstrous motion picture painted by Edward Hopper. The opposite, bayside shore, however, is pleasantly picturesque, and there you'll see a long quay from which anglers tug at bay denizens, a well-groomed, lawn-covered island yacht club connected to the mainland by a towering footbridge, and broad stretches of tidelands where seasonal clam digging is reputed to be first rate.

Kisarazu, in fact, lies adjacent to the last remaining remnants of unspoiled tidelands on Tokyo Bay, though if developers get their way, this will not be so for long. A preposterous plan to span the bay with a combination tunnel and causeway by the turn of the century is bound to eradicate what little precious tideland remains. Get out there and explore it by bike while you can.

Top the day off with a fresh seafood meal at any of Kisarazu's fine Japanese restaurants, get back to the ferry by its final 8:00 P.M. departure, and enjoy a satisfying twilight cruise back to Tokyo. Bus service is also available between the ferry terminal and Kawasaki Station, for bike baggers who prefer not to ride after dark.

Other popular weekend destinations accessible by boat include the Izu Islands (see page 243). These islands are particularly convenient for riders living in central Tokyo, as the docks are a short ride from Hamamatsucho Station on the Yamanote Line.

Long-distance ferries are also available, providing a means of entry into some of the more inaccessible areas. Although the Tokyo Long-Distance Ferry Terminal is further out beyond Tsukiji, there's nothing like riding your bike to the ferry terminal, rolling up the gangplank, and cruising off to some faraway place for a cycling getaway. Long-distance ferries take a long time—usually from thirteen to over thirty hours, depending on the route. It may seem like a lot of empty time, but it does give the industrious person a chance to catch up on letters or reading. Even for those who end up napping and bumming around, hours and hours of doing nothing may be just what's needed.

A whole fleet of long-distance ferries plies the waters from one end of Japan to the other. The ferries have large open group compartments, smaller compartments (at higher fares), and lounges of various types. Many have both communal bath and sauna in the lower decks. The Japan Long-Distance Ferry Association prints a brochure in English describing all the major lines, ports, and schedules along with numbers to call. The guide is available from the Tourist Information Center in Yurakucho or by writing to Nihon Chokyori Ferry Kyokai, Iino Bldg. 9F, 2-1-1, Uchisaiwaicho, Chiyoda-ku, Tokyo.

One example of a good start for a cycle tour is the Blue Highway Line that operates cruises between Tokyo, the Kii-hanto Peninsula in Wakayama Prefecture, and Kochi (on Shikoku), both great places to start or finish a tour. The boat leaves the Tokyo Ferry Terminal at 6:20 P.M. every other day, pulling into Nachi-Katsuura in Wakayama Prefecture at 7:40 the next morning. You can bail out there and ride the area's scenic coastal roads, or stay on until Kochi at 3:40 P.M., giving you enough time to find where you're staying and take a short ride around the city. The return ship leaves Kochi at 5:50 P.M., puts in at Nachi-Katsuura at 1:00 A.M., and arrives in Tokyo at 2:40 the next afternoon. One-way fares to Nachi-Katsuura are ¥8,800, and to Kochi ¥13,500; bicycles are a bit extra. This is not exactly inexpensive, but is good value for those coming from Tokyo because it's a quick way out of the city with an overnight thrown in. The ships are new and clean, and have public-bath–style bathing facilities for both men and women. Phone 03 3578-1127 for more information.

The wonderful Shin Nihonkai Ferry leaves Niigata at 10:30 A.M., arriving in Otaru a little after four the next morning, a great time during summer. Going the other way, the departure from Otaru is at 10:00 P.M. with arrival in Niigata the next day at 5:40 P.M. The lowest fare is just ¥5,150 and the ship has its own free public bath. Departures most days; contact Shin Nihonkai Ferry at 03 3555-3211 for more details.

These are just two examples of what's in store for you when you discover the world of long-distance ferries. Other ships sail from Tokyo to Tomakomai (Nihon Enkai Ferry 03 3573-1911) and Kushiro (Kinkai Yusen Ferry 03 3447-6561) in Hokkaido, and to Tokushima in Shikoku and Kokura (Ocean Tokyu Ferry 03 3567-0971) in Kyushu. Kansai residents are just as lucky, with overnight ships leaving from Minami-ko Port south of Osaka for cities in Kyushu and Shikoku.

Shipping your Bike

After a long-distance cycling trip, a convenient method of avoiding having to juggle your souvenirs and your bagged bicycle on packed trains is to ship your bike back to your home via the door-to-door parcel delivery service called *takkyubin*. However, not all *takkyubin* agents (usually convenience stores and mom-and-pop stores) welcome items as large as a bicycle.

One *takkyubin* company called Footwork (03 3763-0210) has no objection to bicycles and ships them at a very reasonable rate to boot. For example, the cost of shipping a bagged bicycle from Kyoto to Tokyo is only about ¥5,000. If the bike is sent as is, the price goes up to more than ¥10,000. If you want to ship your bicycle in Japan, start by looking around your neighborhood for Footwork's orange dachshund trademark. Many different kinds of general stores offer pickup services for other well-known delivery companies, such as Pelican-bin (you can't miss the pelican mark, 03 3253-1111), Sagawa Kyubin (03 3699-3333) and Yamato Takkyubin (with the black cat mark, 03 3541-3411). Call them up for more information if you find yourself in the middle of nowhere and unable to locate their office.

Cycle Hitching

Many people assume hitchhiking is impractical or inconceivable in Japan as the Japanese don't hitchhike (in their homeland at least), so drivers can't be expected to know the custom. Even rarer alongside Japanese roadsides than the walking hitchhiker is a cyclist leaning on his bike with his thumb jabbing in the direction he wants to go. Cycling purists, of course, won't even consider the merits.

Five years ago, my girlfriend and I decided to cycle around the five lakes near Mt. Fuji (see page 115). On the morning of the trip, we stuffed my bike into its bag and began to struggle to push her brand-new bike into the old bag. After wrestling more than an hour, we decided to give up the fight, reassemble the bikes, pedal out of Tokyo, and start hitchhiking. My first thought was that drivers who'd pick up two people with two bicycles would be few and far between. Cycling in the mountains of northern Aomori during bad weather the summer before, I'd been picked up one day by a microbus and the next day by a huge truck. But in neither case did I flag down the vehicle; the people in the microbus offered me a ride, and the truck driver was asked on my behalf by a shopkeeper.

We left home jauntily with the idea that if we couldn't get a ride we'd chain our bikes to a pole and catch a bus or train to the lake. Just beyond Hachioji, we stood hot, dusty, and tired by the roadside holding our bikes, sticking out our thumbs, and looking imploringly into the faces of surprised drivers.

We waited about thirty minutes before the first vehicle stopped, a truck whose kind driver helped us lift our bikes onto his flatbed and tie them down before driving us to Sagami-ko Lake. Refreshed by the lift, we pedaled on again.

By the time we arrived at our *minshuku* near Kawaguchi-ko Lake, we'd cycled about sixty kilometers and ridden in trucks and vans for the remaining hundred-plus kilometers. Best of all, we hadn't spent a single yen, had avoided the bother of assembling and disassembling and toting our bikes, and weren't even the least bit tired. By cycle-hitching we were able to cover long, uninteresting stretches by truck, saving our energy for cycling through and stopping to enjoy the beauty spots.

This was the first of many pleasant experiences of cycle-hitching. Out in the countryside, the chances of being picked up are much greater, as vans, microbuses, and trucks make up a larger portion of the traffic than in big cities. The puzzled drivers who stop usually act out of curiosity and the chance for a novel encounter—just sit back and enjoy the fun.

Time Out

For the cycle tourist, finding appropriate lodging is a bit of an art in Japan. For pure comfort, in absolute terms, nothing beats a first-rate hotel or *ryokan* (higher-priced Japanese inn). Most cycle tourists, however, will find such hotels in Japan not only far too expensive, but also rather formal as guests are expected to maintain a certain level of dress and decorum.

At the other end of the scale are youth hostels and *kokuminshukusha* and *kokumin kyukamura* (government-sponsored accommodation) and the like. For more information on youth hostels, visit the Tourist Information Office in Tokyo and get hold of their *Public Youth Hostels Guidebook* and their *Youth Hostel Map of Japan,* or write to the Japan National Tourist Organization, 2-10-1 Yurakucho, Chiyoda-ku, Tokyo. Rates are much lower in these type of places but so are the levels of comfort and privacy. Guests are expected to be in at early hours and are sometimes asked to pitch in with cleaning chores. While young people on very small budgets may find this acceptable, older people with a little more to spend may feel out of place. *Kokuminshukusha* and the like are convenient and often located in beautiful sites—perched on headlands or guarding uninhabited islands. However, their appeal is somewhat limited by the utilitarian look and feel about them and the fact that reservations are usually necessary.

For these reasons, my favorite places to stay are *minshuku*, the smaller family-operated Japanese inns that can be found practically everywhere. Here, the atmosphere is very "down home," and service is light enough not to be oppressive as it can be in the more expensive *ryokan* or good hotels.

Although they can be best compared to bed and breakfast establishments, the overnight rate (usually from around ¥5,000 per person) includes dinner as well. Invariably the food is Japanese and while not on a par with that served at the average *ryokan*, it is nevertheless good and usually in sufficient quantity.

Note that breakfasts are also Japanese, which I find to be quite tasty, nicely filling, but not too heavy. However, some Westerners, even after several years residence in Japan, find the usual mix of fish, seaweed, rice, raw egg, and pickled plum too much to face in the morning. Sometimes, if given advance notice before check-in, the more friendly and accommodating *minshuku* will prepare some sort of alternative breakfast, often thick slabs of toasted white bread, a cold fried egg, and thin instant coffee.

In larger cities, unfortunately, *minshuku* are not easily found, particularly around large stations. The urban alternative, then, is the business hotel. Favored by ordinary lower-level Japanese businessmen, these establishments are usually clean, efficient, and utterly lacking in any distinctive character whatsoever—if you've stayed at one, you've stayed at them all. While some may find that judgment harsh, everyone who has ever stayed at a business hotel will agree that the rooms are as small as they are boring, the bathrooms somewhere between cramped and impossible depending on one's size, and that, if one is alone, the loneliness can be stupefying.

Still, for the uninitiated, staying at a business hotel is a new and uniquely Japanese experience. Besides, if bad luck or bad weather suddenly finds you in a large city at nightfall, there is often no alternative apart from a hotel with room rates often three times higher than the ¥6,000 or ¥7,000 for a business hotel. And, like *minshuku*, business hotels usually provide guests with *yukata* robes to wear after the bath, a special plus for those who travel light and wash their quick-drying cycling gear every evening.

Available nationwide and usually in places of great scenic beauty, often alongside cycle paths, cycling terminals offer low-price accommodation for the cycle-tourist. Currently, there are fifty-three cycling terminals, many of which offer additional facilities such as hot springs, and even glider rides. Bicycles are also available for hire and terminals are equipped with cycle workshops which can be invaluable if you're cycling in the vicinity.

Although some of the designers of the earlier terminals took the minimalist concept to heart, many of the more recent buildings have been designed with more imagination and fun in mind. At prices competitive with *kokuminshukusha* and youth hostels, cycling terminals shouldn't be overlooked when considering lodgings for the night. Reservations are recommended, particularly during the holiday seasons. For a full list of cycling terminals, see page 261.

A phenomenon seemingly found only in Hokkaido, rider houses offer extremely inexpensive and fun lodging for riders, whether they be of the motor- or pedal-bike variety. Rider houses are listed in the Hokkaido chapter (see page 165), but every summer in Hokkaido new houses seem to pop up, so the best way to find them is to look out for makeshift signs along the road.

The first time we stayed in a rider house, my wife and I were heading north along the Sea of Okhotsk. As we approached the town of Esashi we kept noticing signs to "Esashi You Rider House." At noon, we pulled up to a normal–looking house right in town. Inside we found many motorcyclists lounging around in a huge tatami room. The manager asked us to register—by drawing a self-portrait in the log book. Accommodation cost us only ¥260—the price we paid to visit the *sento* (public bath) next door. The beer was for sale at liquor-store prices, and we spent a great afternoon hanging out with all the motorcyclists. Later that evening the local fishermen delivered free crabs by the dozen; we all ate heartily and the refrigerator was still full to brimming. Talk went on until midnight and then everyone settled down on their *futon* to sleep. By 6:00 A.M. the heat had woken most people and the two of us left early for Wakkanai.

Some weeks later after a late start leaving Sapporo, we only managed to make forty kilometers or so before it was 6:00 P.M. and rain seemed imminent. Luckily the rider houses we'd been seeing became more frequent and soon, after some tricky navigating, we rode up to an A-frame building on a pleasant-looking potato farm. The very drunk owner seemed very pleased to see us and beckoned to us to join him around the fire where ten or so motorcyclists were having trout stew. Normally the place charged ¥300, but, scoring high in the novelty stakes we were invited to stay for free and urged to get some stew before it disappeared. We spent an enjoyable evening trying to make sense of what the alcohol-impaired man was saying and enjoying his trout stew. From what we could work out it seemed that he ran the farm for a profit and the Rider House as some kind of tax write-off. In addition, he wasn't totally against young motorcyclists showing up with bottles of *shochu,* either. We also enjoyed our second *goemon-buro* there, a bath that basically works like a large kettle over a roaring fire except that you have to keep adding cold water if you don't want to end up as soup of the day. We were given the honor of sleeping in the "Capsule House," which turned out to be a cylindrical trailer with a hemispherical plexiglass window and a purple shag carpet. The next morning there was trout *sashimi* for breakfast and fresh goat's milk. As a parting gesture the owner offered us all the potatoes we could dig.

If you're in Hokkaido and you're money's a bit thin on the ground, or if you simply want a chance to meet interesting people, try dropping into a rider house.

Camping is one of the cheapest ways to see Japan and enjoy some of its more scenic areas. For a list of official campgrounds, get hold of the *Camping in Japan* leaflet from the Tourist Information Center.

However, when out on the road, nothing beats spotting a perfect place to make a campfire and give the wheels a rest for a while. For a long time, I was hesitant about camping just anywhere in Japan, no doubt out of fear of the police or an irate farmer shouting abuse at my insolence. Out of dislike for official Japanese campsites and fear of camping in the socalled wild, I felt I was doomed to seeing my tent only in the closet. However, talk of successful camping in Japan gave me newfound confidence. Rapidly reaching the status of an urban myth, the story goes that friends of friends camped with little fuss or bother right in the middle of Hiroshima Park. They pitched their tent and, rumor has it, spent a quiet, pleasant night in very historical surroundings. You might say it was luck that the local police didn't appear. But perhaps not. During a recent cycling trip to Mt. Akagi in Gunma, friends and I tested what I've come to call the Hiroshima Theory for three nights with great success.

We discovered that in the countryside, people are oblivious to cyclists taking a break, be it by the road, or a river. The trick is to make it look like a short break. Then, when night falls, pitch your tent and suddenly you have an authentic camp. When sunrise comes, get going and nobody will be any the wiser. A benefit of being by water is that a campfire is possible—we found evidence of campfires in all three places we stayed. Riverbanks and lakeshores are ideal because they provide water and seclusion along with a fair amount of green. Public parks are a hip alternative, though you can forget about the campfire.

Camping is in theory forbidden in public parks; the important thing is to try and make sure that you're not on private property and to leave things as they were when you arrived. If you are quiet about camping, and considerate of the environment, the Hiroshima Theory can be most successful. And, best of all, it's free.

And finally, what do you do when it's getting dark and you find the nearest *minshuku* is fifty kilometers over the other side of the mountains and you haven't got either a bike bag or a tent? Short of bedding down in a nest of leaves, one option is to ask at a temple. Although this is not a failsafe solution, many priests have been known to offer floor space to needy cyclists. While delicious vegetarian meals sometimes accompany the floor mat, making a habit of staying in temples is not recommended—sleeping in extremely close proximity to a row of benevolently smiling Buddhas can be an unnerving experience. In more urban areas, finding a temple may not be so easy. Be prepared for some unusual invitations—we once ended up spending the night in an open-ended shed at a bicycle parking lot after having trouble finding somewhere more conventional to stay. Our bathroom was the lavatories at the train station, and our wardrobe a couple of coin lockers. The attendants let us sleep on a couple of old mats on the ground from closing time at 11:00 P.M. until opening at 6:00 A.M. the following morning. The cost of our accommodations? ¥200 for the bikes, nothing for us.

For tourist information, call the Tokyo Tourist Information Center 03 3502-1461 (toll-free 0120 222800) or the Kyoto Tourist Information Center 075 371-5649 (toll-free 0120 444800). If you have problems with language and need an interpreter immediately, or have a question or problem while traveling, try telephoning a hotline set up specially for foreigners in Japan. Call toll-free 0088 222800 in the east of Japan and 0088 224800 in the west for answers to your questions.

2
Freewheeling

Note to the reader: The maps in this book are not drawn to scale. Recommended routes are shown by a solid line.

A Cyclists' Wordbook

doro, dori, tori, michi	road
jitenshaya-san	bicycle shop
-ken	prefecture
-ku	ward
-cho, -machi	town
mura	village
koen	park
kawa	river
hashi	bridge
umi	sea
wan	bay
hama	beach
misaki	cape
hanto	peninsula
-ko, numa	lake
yama	mountain
minshuku	family-run inn
ryokan	inn
onsen	hot springs
ofuro	bath
rotenburo	open-air bath
sento	public bath

Tokyo Hours 🚲 🚲 🚲 🚲 🚲 🚲 🚲 🚲 🚲 🚲 🚲 🚲 🚲 🚲

Planning Your Ride

The oft-touted notion that Japan has four distinct seasons is one of the three most mistaken ideas about this country. The real truth is, in terms of weather, that Japan has somewhere between 14 and 365 distinct seasons each year, and some sort of rain is involved in most of them.

Over the years as I've tried to attune myself to Japan's unique and mysterious seasonal makeup, I've come to understand that there's a very simple and fundamental relationship between good weather and planning a cycling trip: If you plan a cycling trip, either far in advance or on the spur of the moment the night before, you can be sure that it will rain on the day of departure and if there are one or more days on which you have no plans to cycle, you can be sure that the weather will be perfect throughout.

Seriously, though, the best way to ensure enough cycling in good weather throughout the year is to plan to go cycling every weekend and every other chance you get. The odds are that at least some of those times it won't be raining and you'll actually go someplace. When rain does dampen your plans, however, you'll be left with some free time you didn't count on—perfect for cleaning and oiling your bike and patching a few old tires.

The idea is planned spontaneity—if you plan to go somewhere every chance you get, and thus are always ready, you can decide on the departure morning whether to actually go or not. This does, however, present problems of a minor nature, such as the inability to reserve domestic flights, seating on trains, or suitable lodging. Nonetheless, for day rides and weekend trips of limited distance, the notion of planned spontaneity will assure you the maximum amount of good weather cycling.

Generally, the weather is best from early October (when the typhoons stop coming) through the end of the year. The temperature ranges from warm to a bit cool, humidity is low, the sky is high and expansive, and there is usually a little wind. Best of all, the chance of rain is at its lowest. From January through mid-March conditions are similar, but it's much colder. From April through mid-June the weather warms up as spring swings into full gear, but there is also a greater chance of rain. From early June through July is the so-called "rainy season," although the constant drizzle throughout these weeks is easily eclipsed by occasional torrential downpours during the typhoon season from the end of August through mid-October. The month of August is very hot and humid, and only really bearable in the north in some parts of Tohoku and throughout Hokkaido.

☃ Hours, Days, and Weeks

One thing you should determine is where you want to go. Your route and destination, of course, depend on how much time you have.

Those living in the country or in small cities close to good cycling have the luxury of planning routes and times as they please. For most of us, however, planning requires a little more foresight. If you only have a day, or part of one, the plan is made in hours. This might mean a good route near-by, or someplace just out of town. If you have a weekend or more, you'll be planning in terms of days, so take the opportunity to head further out and start, for example, someplace about two or three hours away by train.

If you have a week or more, regardless of where you live, you have the luxury of touring the greater part of any area in Japan—Hokkaido, Tohoku, the Japan Alps, Kansai, Shikoku, or Kyushu. You also have the luxury of enough time to take a long-distance ferry for one or more legs of your trip. By using trains or airplanes, you'll be able to see a lot of the country while avoiding areas of heavy traffic and/or little interest.

Finally, if you have a month or more and, importantly, sufficient funds, it's possible to tour the entire country and gain an insight into Japan and its people that just isn't possible any other way. If you fall into this category, consider yourself lucky and go for the Japan cycling experience which will stay with you for a lifetime.

☃ Exploring the Concrete Jungle

If I were to restrict my cycling activities to out-of-the-city tours alone, I would be on my bike only once or twice a season, and that is simply not often enough to stay in shape or even maintain interest in the sport. The obvious alternative for us city-bound, wanna-be tourists is to day-ride in Tokyo. Most riders I know are either terrified of, or politically opposed to, riding in traffic. I recommend you give it at least a try because you may not know what a thrill you're missing. Drafting a speeding bus down Shibuya's busy Dogenzaka and then threading the taxi cab needle at the Hachiko-mae intersection is one of the world's great cycling adventures.

However, riding in traffic is not what most of us would prefer to do, so let's take a look at the alternatives. Excellent rides within the Yamanote Line in the center of Tokyo are available to all of us, as are beautiful rides in the adjoining countryside with trees, streams, hills, and friendly people. Rides like this can be made by anybody every weekend—just get out and explore the paths and roads.

An easy solution to the problems of traffic, air pollution, and ghastly summer heat and humidity, is to go riding in the wee hours of the morning.

The most important preparation for the red-eye special is making the commitment to do it. On Friday night, decide to either cut the partying short, or go for an all-nighter. Get friends to join in the fun, to prevent the alarm clock from *accidentally* getting turned off or *somehow* not getting set. Start as early as it is light enough to ride safely, when the air really feels much fresher, and whizz down boulevards ignoring (after looking, of course) the red lights at normally the busiest of intersections.

Take a look at Tsukiji Central Fish Market, already buzzing with business at 5:30 A.M. Hundreds of frozen carcasses of tuna, auctioneers speaking some extraterrestrial language, mountains of styrofoam boxes, and the traffic jams of push-carts and miniature forklifts all contribute to the surreality of the whole experience. Get a map of the market from a policeman and enter the labyrinth of squirming eels, mounds of seaweed, and more fish than you could ever shake a chopstick at.

To remind you that the earth is covered with soil, not concrete and asphalt, try the trails through bushes and trees at Kitanomaru-koen, northwest of the Imperial Palace. By around 7:00 A.M. the place starts to get crowded—going early seems to be the key to enjoying the bigger parks.

For mountain bike fun, get pictures of yourself riding down staircases of prominent Tokyo landmarks. With the exception of some shrines, temples, and government buildings, you're limited only by your imagination. When you get home, enjoy a huge breakfast and plan your next great Wee Hour Ride.

Cyclin' by the Dock of the Bay   🚲

Route: Round the Imperial Palace via Yasukuni-jinja Shrine finishing with a ride past one of the world's biggest fish markets to a shogun's garden overlooking Tokyo Bay
Start: Kudanshita Station (Tozai, Hanzomon, Toei Shinjuku lines)
Goal: Shiba-Koen Station (Toei Mita Line)

Believe it or not, Tokyo is a port city. Granted, it may not seem so to those who've lived and played in other port cities in the world. This is probably because Tokyo's residential neighborhoods, for the most part, lack water views. Only in recent years has the city taken to constructing high-rise apartment complexes on bay fill land parcels. Otherwise, the bay is kept largely from our view by a wall of warehouses, elevated turnpikes, and office buildings miles in length. Sadly, Tokyo is not proud of her bay.

But, when the tide begins to tug at the blood in your heart, and the breezes wafting over town carry the faint fragrance of the wetlands, how does the cyclist get down to the water for the essential maritime hit.

Try Hama Rikyu Detached Palace Garden, the adjacent hubbub of the Tsukiji Waterfront, and the tangential concrete stretches of Takeshiba, Hinode, and Shibaura Piers. I recommend this part of Minato-ku for its accessibility to riders living in central or northwest Tokyo. Hama Rikyu Garden is, in fact, the nearest bay shore to ground zero—the Imperial Palace—presumably since the grounds were set aside long ago for the Imperial family's seaside strolls.

Cyclists in search of relatively pleasant city riding should try a triangular route that takes in the Imperial Palace circuit (closed to automotive traffic on Sundays and holidays), adjacent Hibiya-koen Park (Japan's first Western-style park), Hama Rikyu, and Shiba-koen Park. Start at either Iidabashi or Kudanshita stations and head up toward Yasukuni-jinja, the controversial state Shinto shrine enshrining Japan's war dead, including a couple of A-class war criminals. Have a zip around Kitanomaru-koen, a pleasant park with a couple of museums. After a lap (several if you're in training) of the Imperial Palace, it's a straight shot down Hibiya Dori and then left onto Harumi Dori. Just before the concrete expanses of Nishi Hongan-ji Temple, turn left for Tsukiji Central Fish Market, the world's largest dry aquarium; note that the place closes down in the early afternoon so be sure to get there in time for breakfast or lunch.

Cyclin' by the Dock of the Bay

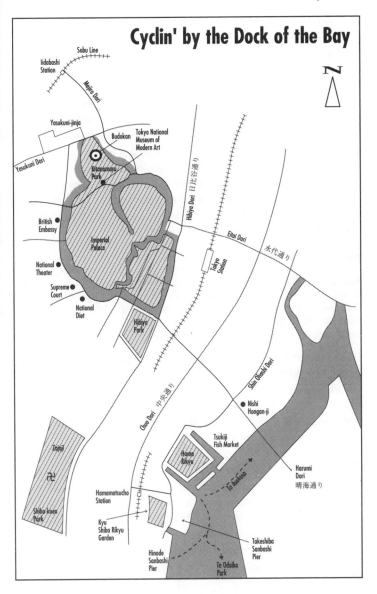

Sobu Line

Iidabashi Station

Mejiro Dori

Yasukuni-jinja

Tokyo National Museum of Modern Art

Budokan

Yasukuni Dori

Kitanomaru Park

British Embassy

Imperial Palace

Hibiya Dori 日比谷通り

National Theater

Eitai Dori

永代通り

Tokyo Station

Supreme Court

National Diet

Hibiya Park

Shin Ohashi Dori

Nishi Hongan-ji

Zojoji

卍

Chuo Dori 中央通り

Tsukiji Fish Market

Hama Rikyu

Harumi Dori 晴海通り

To Tsukishima

Hamamatsucho Station

Shiba-koen Park

Kyu Shiba Rikyu Garden

Hinode Sanbashi Pier

To Odaiba Park

Takeshiba Sanbashi Pier

N

Continuing along Shin Ohashi Dori, you'll find Hama Rikyu on your left, an ideal location for a stroll and picnic overlooking the yacht basin, but no bikes are allowed. Bring a lock and pasture your mount on the USDA-choice gravel outside the gate. In February, an unusual sight for Tokyo is the field of bright yellow rape blossoms here. Entrance is ¥200; closed Mondays.

From Hama Rikyu, it's a short hop over to Shiba-koen and Zojo-ji Temple. Alternatively, take the waterbus (*suijo basu*)from Hama Rikyu to Odaiba-koen Park and check out the waterfront area. The waterbus departs from Asakusa every one and a half hours, calling at Hama Rikyu, Hinode Pier, and Odaiba-koen.The cost is ¥400 for you, ¥200 for your bicycle.

As with all city riding, earlier is better, and Sundays or national holidays usually have the least auto traffic, although note that Tsukiji Fish Market is closed on Sundays and national holidays. Buses also run less frequently, and trucks tend to be at rest, meaning less diesel exhaust.   ✐ JH

Paradise on Garbage

Route: Along the waterfront from the man-made beaches of Odaiba-koen Park to Kasai Rinkai-koen Park via the garbage islands of Yumenoshima and Wakasu
Start: Hinode Pier (Hamamatsucho Station, Yamanote Line)
Goal: Kasai Rinkai-koen Park (Kasai Rinkai Koen Station, Keiyo Line; Nishi Kasai Station, Tozai Line; or waterbus back to Hinode Pier)

Tokyo's waterfront is a respite from the crowds, cramped spaces, and concrete jungles of the megalopolis. The wide roads, parks, and sea breezes will delight any cyclist. Much of Tokyo's waterfront has been created by filling in the sea with Tokyo's garbage. For a long time large tracts of this land remained unused until a few years ago, when construction of a bay bridge and new urban center was started.

Four areas are worth exploring by bicycle: Odaiba, Yumenoshima, Wakasa, and Kasai Rinkai-koen Park. The suggested route described here covers about twenty-five kilometers. It is possible to cycle through all these places in one day, but if you want to take it more leisurely and visit the various attractions along the route, set out early or divide the route into two.

The most efficient way to start your cycling tour of Odaiba or Kasai Rinkai-koen is to start at either end of the eastern waterfront. In the summer of 1993 cyclists (as well as pedestrians) coming from south or west

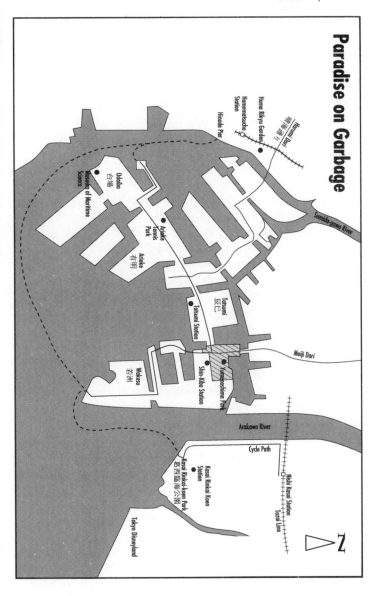

Paradise on Garbage

Hama Rikyu Gardens 浜離宮庭園
Hamamatsucho Station
Hinode Pier
Hinode Dori
Sumida-gawa River
Odaiba 台場
Museum of Maritime Science
Ariake 有明
Ariake Tennis Park
Tatsumi 辰巳
Tatsumi Station
Meiji Dori
Wakasu 若洲
Shin-Kiba Station
Yumenoshima Park
Arakawa River
Cycle Path
Kasai Rinkai Koen Station
Kasai Rinkai-koen Park 葛西臨海公園
Nishi Kasai Station
Tozai Line
Tokyo Disneyland
N

Tokyo may well be able to cross to Odaiba-koen from the Shibaura end by using the Rainbow Bridge (via elevator). Until then, the best way to cross to the park is to use the waterbus (*suijo basu*) from Hinode Pier near Hamamatsucho Station on the Yamanote Line. The fare is ¥400 for adults and ¥200 for your bicycle, which need not be bagged. The first boat leaves at 10:00 A.M. and takes about twenty minutes. From Monday to Saturday, boats to Odaiba run once every hour and a half until 4:00 P.M. and on Sundays and National Holidays every forty-five minutes. On the return trip, the last boat leaves Odaiba at 4:55 P.M. for Hinode Pier.

If you plan to start at Kasai Rinkai-koen, take the Keiyo Line which originates at Tokyo Station, and get off at Kasai Rinkai Koen Station. You could also take the Tozai Line to Nishi Kasai Station and cycle to the park.

For starting points between Odaiba and Kasai Rinkai-koen, Tatsumi and Shin-Kiba stations on the Yurakucho Line and and Shin-Kiba Station on the Keiyo Line are closest to the waterfront.

Odaiba (which also masquerades as Daiba and the No. 13 land parcel) is characterized by two square islands, the bay bridge, a ship-shaped museum, and a host of windsurfers. The closest thing Tokyo has to an ocean beach, the Odaiba area used to be a very quiet place with a wide open grassy area until all the construction started. Fortunately, Odaiba's seaside park will be preserved and cyclists will still be able to enjoy riding along the water's edge. From one of the square islands connected by a short isthmus, there is a good view of the bay bridge.

From the island, ride along the water's edge all the way to the Maritime Museum (*Fune no Kagaku-kan*). This appropriately shaped museum has a 70m-high observation deck affording a bird's eye view of the Odaiba area and beyond, giving one a good idea of the scale of the construction work going on. Museum admission is ¥500. From the Maritime Museum you can ride further south straight down to a little waterfront park at the end of the road. The park faces another island: Tokyo's current garbage dump. Although the mild stench gives the game away immediately, people continue to picnic and fish at the park. From Odaiba ride east past the Ariake Tennis Park and Coliseum until you reach Shin-Kiba Station. Then turn left and ride north to Yumenoshima (Dream Island) Park. The park and sports ground are not very large and you can zip through them quickly on a bicycle. However, the Tropical Plant Dome (*Nettai Shokubutsu-kan*) and the museum housing the *Daigo Fukuryu Maru* fishing boat, which was exposed to radioactive fallout from the 1954 hydrogen bomb test at Bikini Atoll, make for an interesting visit. You can also swim in the public indoor pool adjacent to the gymnasium; the restaurant there is a good place to have lunch.

Across the highway (Meiji Dori), the Yumenoshima Undo-jo features a pleasant cycling path along the waterfront. If it's cherry blossom season, be sure to ride through the adjacent Tatsumi no Mori Park. From Shin-Kiba Station, go south on Meiji Dori all the way down until you reach the water. Then turn left and ride along the littered shore, from where you'll soon see the Wakasu-bashi Bridge.

After crossing Wakasu-bashi, you'll be on Wakasu, another island built on garbage, which is now a golf course, park, and campground. There is an excellent cycling path (slightly over four kilometers long) encircling the park and golf course. The ocean view is even quite picturesque: just across the water you can see Kasai Rinkai-koen and the row of bay hotels flanking Tokyo Disneyland. Rental bicycles are available for ¥200 for two hours. Camping is possible for ¥200 per night; apply at the service center office. At the northwest corner of the cycling route is a small pier for the water bus, which leaves for Kasai Rinkai-koen at forty minutes past the hour every hour between 10:40 A.M. and 4:40 P.M. (From December to March there are fewer runs so check the timetable at the pier when you get to Wakasu.) The trip costs ¥200 and takes ten minutes. For ¥100 your bicycle goes on as is. Boats to Hinode Pier leave at ten minutes past the hour every hour between 11:10 A.M. and 5:10 P.M.; the cost is ¥620.

Kasai Rinkai-koen has recently become one of Tokyo's major attractions. Besides the green grass and the Sea Life Aquarium, there are cycling paths in and around the park; mountain bikers can enjoy various hills and bumps off this path. However, bicycles are not allowed to cross the bridge leading to a sandbar offshore.

After Kasai Rinkai-koen you can either take the boat back to Hinode Pier or get on the train at Kasai Rinkai Koen Station. The last boat for Hinode Pier (with a stopover at Wakasu) leaves at 5:00 P.M. The boat takes forty-five minutes and the fare is ¥800 and ¥400 for your bicycle.

There are at least two cycling paths from the park leading to Nishi Kasai Station, about two kilometers away. One shoots out from the west end of the park and follows right along the water's edge along the Ara-kawa River all the way up to the Tozai Line bridge. Then just turn right and follow the elevated subway tracks to the station.

The other cycling path, well marked on maps around the park, starts from the park's northwestern side. After going under the train tracks and express-way, follow the path to the station through a green belt and park.   ✍ PO

Tokyo Oasis   🚲

Route: A circuit round several pockets of green at one of Tokyo's busiest wharves, dropping in at a bird park and Tokyo's Sunday cycling mecca
Start: Showajima Station (Tokyo Monorail)
Goal: Shinagawa Station (Yamanote, Keihin Kyuko, Keihin Tohoku lines)

There's always something new and interesting happening down at Tokyo's waterfront, and the area near Haneda Airport is no exception. From Showajima Station on the Tokyo Monorail, head west toward Kyowa-bashi Bridge and cross to Keihinjima. This island is bordered by two narrow parks: Tsubasa-koen, popular with young couples and video buffs shooting landings and takeoffs at the neighboring Haneda Airport, and Green Park, frequented by people fishing, typically the hardcore Tokyo Bay fishermen who dot the bay and canals between here and Harumi. I have also fished the canals with friends, but have not been to keen to eat anything we've caught. My friends, however, are still alive to tell the tale.

From Keihinjima, ride over the tall bridge (Keihin Ohashi) to the area that includes Tokai, Oi-futo, and Yashio. Stay on the left side of the bridge—coming up will be Kan-nana Dori and the beginning of a nice little trail leading to Oi-futo Chuo Kaihin-koen Park. From here you will be between sports fields and an expressway, surrounded by trees and unseen by ball players and motorists alike. This section of the trail is flat, with one street crossing. At the next intersection, which is not busy, the road goes under a bridge, and the best part of the trail unfolds from here. The loca-tion is behind a huge apartment complex and adjacent to the expressway. This part is a little hilly, with wooden stairs and a small stream. You'll have to make some choices on direction here, but there's no need to dismount.

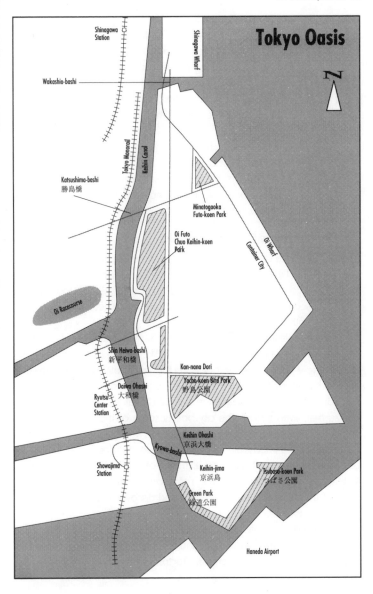

Tokyo Oasis

N

Shinagawa Station

Shinagawa Wharf

Wakashio-bashi

Tokyo Monorail

Keihin Canal

Katsushima-bashi
勝島橋

Minatogaoka
Futo-koen Park

Oi Futo
Chuo Keihin-koen
Park

Oi Wharf

Container City

Oi Racecourse

Shin Heiwa-bashi
新平和橋

Kan-nana Dori

Yacho-koen Bird Park
野鳥公園

Daiwa Ohashi
大和橋

Ryutsu
Center
Station

Keihin Ohashi
京浜大橋

Kyowa-bashi

Showajima
Station

Keihin-jima
京浜島

Tsubasa-koen Park
つばさ公園

Green Park
緑道公園

Haneda Airport

I like to ride over this part several times before going on. Emerging on the ridge-top, you will be facing the Keihin Canal. On one side will be more parkland, and opposite stands the Tokyo Monorail. Turning left will take you back to Kan-nana Dori along paved pathways through a series of parks. Illustrated maps on signboards abound. Find your own place to picnic. If you haven't brought a picnic basket, you can go to the large Daiei supermarket in the apartment complex, which also has several restaurants and even a bike shop.

Other parks in the area, such as Yacho-koen, a bird park where volunteers are on hand to answer your questions, and Minatogaoka Futo-koen, a mecca for cyclists on Sundays, are worth a visit after enjoying this continuous stretch of riding. Take a look at your map and check out all the green spots because you never know when you'll find something worthwhile.   ✍ BL

🚲 The Yamanote Countryside Ride

The JR Yamanote Line is not known as the most exciting leisure or sightseeing spot in Tokyo. For most people, this big train loop is rarely a goal, but rather a convenient circle around Tokyo's center. Visitors look at their maps and see the Yamanote Line as a handy way to get from Shibuya or Shinjuku to other places, like Ueno Park.

Many people like being in Japan and enjoy the advantages of its capital city, but few foreigners actually love Tokyo like people adore Venice, London, or New York. A cycling tour along the Yamanote should change this approach entirely, leading to the discovery that Tokyo is quite a nice village and sometimes even a pleasant provincial capital. Moreover, cyclists will realize that, even though the city boasts some of the most up-to-date architectural fantasies in the world, Edo life has not disappeared completely. Somehow it's impossible to have any understanding of this Tokyo by using the subway: you'll never get all the pieces of the big puzzle together. Instead, try riding a bike along the Yamanote—you'll get to know something of the general shape of the city, and discover many sides that you never knew existed.

Traditional urban life has often been enclosed within protective walls. Before becoming a green vacuum and *terra incognita* on Tokyo maps, the Imperial Palace was a truly defensive fortress with a moat supplied by the big river network of the Kanto Plain. Northwest of the palace, the valley linking Akasaka, Iidabashi, and Ochanomizu provides natural water protection with its long canal connected to the Sumida-gawa and Kanda-gawa rivers. The Sumida-gawa itself, together with the narrow Shibuya-gawa, completes this circle on the eastern and southern sides of the palace: to get into the shogun's retreat one had to permeate the natural obstacles before getting within reach of the man-made waters.

Parts of these rivers have since been filled or obscured by motorways, but the system is still effective. Rediscovering these waterways is interesting, even though you may find it deplorable that such a valuable part of history has been deeply mutilated by shortsighted traffic bureaucrats. But, despite these changes, you can still see many people out for a stroll along their banks and even fishing boats in some places. Landscape gardening has already begun to give the rivers back to nature lovers in quite a lot of areas, and more aesthetic surgery is planned in the future.

Defining the limits of the seemingly endless urban sprawl, the Yamanote provides the city of Tokyo with a frontier. As befitting a citadel's ramparts, the Yamanote is a powerful wall dividing the inner from the outer world and those on bikes in particular. For example, from Yatsuyamabashi, south of Shinagawa, to Mita, the only way to cross the tracks is the drawbridge connecting the west and east entrances of Shinagawa Station. Two kilometers or so without a single gate from the sea to the city, in such a busy area! Similar examples occur all along the Yamanote, especially near the big lookout towers of Ikebukuro and Shibuya.

In old citadels, forlorn and forgotten areas creating a no man's land are often found between a city and its walls. The Yamanote is no exception—small pieces of wasteland, usually beginning with an empty street, an apparently deserted foodstall in the foreground, and a train on a bridge as a background, are ubiquitous. The chances of enjoying such desolate places have been increased by the downturn in the Japanese economy. During the booming years of land speculation, the compulsive search for free land within the city caused small pieces of land to be turned into golden triangles full of pencil-shaped buildings. Recently, many projects have been frozen with the result that the golden triangles are turning into Bermuda triangles, some with brand-new but completely empty offices. Others await better times—for instance, the centrally located land between Shimbashi, Hamamatsucho, and the Tokaido Line is a meadow but without the cows. Here you can cherish the dream that just a few more years will be enough to change it into a true forest, a natural park in the heart of Tokyo.

Geographically linked to these deserts are some of the liveliest little places in the whole city, giving one a whiff of the old *Edokko* spirit. Riding along the Yamanote is like making an inventory of the dead ends, tunnels, and small corners where *izakaya*, sake shops, and other small meeting places prosper. These strategic points might be called the heart of Tokyo life, revealing the pulse of the city. Yurakucho, Komagome, Gotanda, Shimbashi, and Kanda provide good opportunities to see this life, particularly in the early evening: a great way to end a ride.

Totaling forty-five kilometers in length, the Yamanote Countryside Ride has been designed to link the busier centers, avoiding crowded pedestrian crossings and traffic-heavy avenues. Whether you decide to do the whole route or just half of the trail with stops along the way, you're sure to discover flowers and trees, temples and cemeteries—a more real and a more human city. A vanishing Tokyo? Maybe. But all the more reason for you to get on your bike and look for the last shreds of evidence.

The Northern Loop

Route: Freely following the general shape of the northern Yamanote Line through Nippori, Ikebukuro, and Mejiro, the route runs parallel to the tracks, sometimes veering away to an old temple, or a quiet garden
Start and Goal: Tokyo Station, or any station along the northern Yamanote Line

How you view Tokyo depends very much on your attitude: city riders can still see Tokyo as a magic box, full of anecdotes and adventure. An early start is advisable because of the early sunset and because cycling in such a big city is slower than, say, cycling between tulip fields in Holland. Frequently the route is lively and colorful: from Kanda Station to Yushima, for example, Tokyoisms as well as alien items abound. Tokyoisms? Have a look at the small soba restaurants around the station, or the red brick Dowa Hospital with its old chimney, contrasting with the nearby Kenwood building. Coexisting alongside traditional restaurants and tea houses is a small building with a concrete grid pattern designed by Unemura Meisho. Alien

The Northern Loop

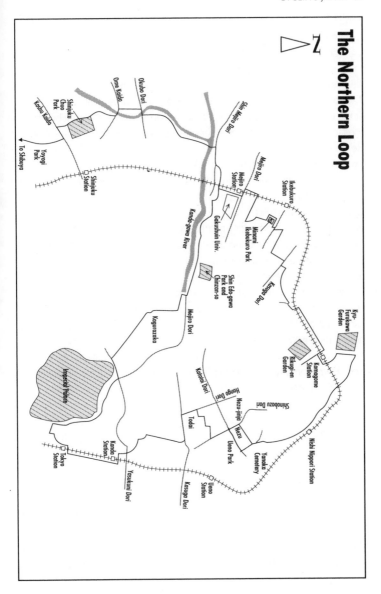

N

To Shibuya
Yoyogi Park
Koshu Kaido
Shinjuku Chuo Park
Okubo Dori
Ome Kaido
Shinjuku Station
Shin Mejiro Dori
Kanda-gawa River
Mejiro Dori
Mejiro Station
Gakushuin Univ.
Ikebukuro Station
Minami Ikebukuro Park
Shin Edo-gawa Park and Chinzan-so
Kagurazaka
Kasuga Dori
Kyu-Furukawa Garden
Rikugi-en Garden
Komagome Station
Mejiro Dori
Imperial Palace
Kototoi Dori
Nezu-jinja
Nezu
Shinobazu Dori
Hongo Dori
Yanaka Cemetery
Nishi Nippori Station
Todai
Ueno Park
Yasukuni Dori
Kanda Station
Tokyo Station
Kasuga Dori
Ueno Station

items? The Russian Orthodox Nicolaï Cathedral and Yushima Seido, the Confucian shrine, form exotic parts of the kaleidoscope.

The route is also intellectual, visiting Tokyo University, where you may meet some of the next-generation leaders while looking around Sanshiro-ike Pond for the spirit of Soseki and other famous figures of the Meiji and Taisho eras. Look closely and the route provides a convenient history lesson: at the otherwise banal Chuo Church in Hongo 3-chome, the dark board on the facade reads "Central Tabernacle—Established 1890, Destroyed 1923, Re-erected 1929." Stop for a while at Yasukuni-jinja and ponder a moment on its nature—peace monument or kamikaze memorial?

Redolent with atmosphere of a bygone era, the route passes through temple gardens and cemeteries. At Kishibojin-do, even if you miss the lantern procession held in mid-October, a beautiful gingko tree, the wooden temple, and its Indian deity protecting children will hold your fascination.

More often than one would expect in such a city, the Northern Loop offers plentiful greenery. Try Tokiwabashi, an old fortress gate now home to tramps and pigeons or leave the bike to graze while you stroll around Rikugi-en, one of the best feudal gardens in the city. There's also Kyu-Furukawa Garden, an intriguing juxtaposition of Japanese and Western gardening traditions, and don't forget the intimate Shin Edogawa-koen, near Kanda-gawa. In spring the Northern Loop is a riot of color, with the plum trees of Yushima-jinja Shrine and the city out-of-parks cherry trees from Komagome to Sugamo, in Minami Otsuka, and along the Kanda-gawa River. You'll also cycle under gingkos, plane-trees, weeping willows, and plum trees, and beside banks of azaleas. Tokyo is green, but it's up to you to notice it, and to catch the seasonal variations of nature.

The Northern Loop is also a *shitamachi* ride, dedicated to the lower city, which, paradoxically, is sometimes uphill, as in Yanaka. Unlike most parts of Tokyo, Yanaka escaped the big 1923 earthquake and World War II. Not a particularly fashionable place, but worth visiting to taste the rarified atmosphere of one of the most fragile ecosystems in Tokyo. Yanaka is basically a large cemetery, but somebody must have mixed up the pieces of the puzzle on purpose, scattering a couple of temples here, a few doll shops there, and a gaggle of gravestones over there, all with the muffled rhythm of the Yamanote in the background. Unexpectedly, the cemetery has quite a lively atmosphere, with colorful flowers, young couples on benches, and the feeling of wandering in a carefree environment—enough to make you want to come back to look for graves, names, and *genius loci*.

Unfortunately, this heady perfume is mostly a speciality of Yanaka and of a few other select places. But, along our ride many little pieces of the puzzle, busy streets as well as small neighborhoods, retain much of the Edo atmosphere. Near Yanaka you'll find Nezu-jinja, a shrine with clouds of pigeons, hills of azaleas, and a neglected garden, as well as a tunnel of *torii* zig-zagging up a small hill. The shrine is also the stage for the Sanza no Mai, a unique Shinto dance performed around September 20. Around the shrine are wooden houses and a wooden church which would look more at home in a remote part of northern Europe. And don't miss what I call the *ukiyo-e* garden, the small park above Nishi-Nippori, which inspired many famous prints, some of which are shown on a board in the park.

And, finally, if you have time, three magic places: the charming neighborhood of Komagome, the fairy-tale shops at Mejiro, and the old geisha quarter hidden away in the narrow backstreets of Kagurazaka.

⇨ From Tokyo Station to Nishi Nippori

From Tokyo Station's main square, ride by the covered tracks, cross the Yamanote on Eitai Dori and turn left to follow the tracks again. After 200m you'll see the Italian Commercial Bank building with Tokiwabashi-koen Park just beyond it. Follow the Yamanote to Kanda Station (500m), but instead of turning left near the first entrance, veer under the bridge at the second one, onto Chuo Dori. Turn left again at the next crossing, and then right onto a street lined with plane-trees (the New Central Hotel is a useful landmark). After 200m, the street becomes narrower, leading to a corner of Yasukuni Dori; detour to the traffic lights to get onto it. Dowa Hospital is on this little street, the little Unemura Meisho building 20m further on the right.

The street slopes straight up to the Nicolaï Cathedral (250m). Passing Ochanomizu Station turn right onto Hongo Dori. Yushima-seido is just after the bridge; park your bike and walk down the steps to visit it. Behind this Confucian temple is a road that passes the entrance to Kanda Myojin. If you don't have time, ride 600m to the well-signposted Yushima-jinja Shrine.

In front of this shrine, turn left, and then left again to reach Kasuga

Dori—on the left side you'll find an antique shop, a traditional pharmacist, and a second-hand bookshop. After the Chuo Church turn right onto Hongo Dori, which passes the Akamon (Red Gate) of Tokyo University on the right. Go through the gate to the garden and turn left to some interesting Western-style buildings. From Sanshiro-ike Pond go around the left side of Todai Hospital to reach Shinobazu-ike Pond, about 50m from the Todai exit. Take Shinobazu Dori on your left for a kilometer. About 100m after the Kototoi Dori intersection, turn left for Nezu-jinja Shrine; the narrow streets with wooden houses are in the immediate vicinity.

Go back to the Kototoi Dori intersection and turn left. About 500 m further uphill you'll come to a major intersection. Don't turn right to Ueno Library, but left to Yanaka. Then turn right after the street to Yanaka Cemetery, passing between Yanaka 5-chome and Yanaka 7-chome—the abundant signboards in the neighborhood will help you navigate through this labyrinth. On the way you'll pass Joko-ji, Fujimizaka, Suwa-jinja, and the *ukiyo-e* garden before plunging down to Nishi Nippori Station.

However, Yanaka is a great place to get lost—ask in a local shop for a map of the neighborhood.

▷ From Nishi Nippori Station to Ikebukuro (Sunshine City)

After a ride beside the tracks to Tabata Station, the street veers away from the Yamanote, but then crosses it more than a kilometer later at Fujimi-bashi Bridge as the train turns westward.

A great place for a rest is the Kyu-Furukawa Garden, just 800m across the bridge; the entrance is opposite the Takinogawa Kita Ward Office. This street leads to Komagome Station, but it's better to take a smaller one on the left to Komagome Station's east exit and the nearby shopping area. Go through a narrow tunnel to cross the line.

To visit Rikugi Garden, ride past Komagome Station to Hongo Dori—the garden is on the right.

Follow the Yamanote to Sugamo Station, sometimes called the Hara-juku for the elderly, cross the wide Hakusan Dori, and go on to the second bridge after the station. The second street after the bridge takes you downhill. After less than 200m you'll see a cemetery wall on your left. Enjoy the downhill, but don't forget the cemetery, as it's highly important to take a little street here on the right. Go straight for no more than 5m, and then turn left at the pine tree. You're actually in a valley now, although it's difficult to tell. Go up again in the same direction and you'll stumble across one of Tokyo's frequent urban enigmas: this street, which at first seems to be more a path than a road, suddenly changes into a cherry-tree-lined avenue leading to the Toden Arakawa tram line.

Go straight along the tram line for about 100m, then turn right onto Kasuga Dori, crossing the tracks. Take the first road on the left and follow it round to Sunshine City.

⇨ From Ikebukuro (Sunshine City) to Mejiro

From the bottom of the tower, cross the expressway and turn left to Green Odori (250m). You should find Minami Ikebukuro Central Park on the other side of this avenue, in a little street between Dai Ichi Insurance and the Shizuoka Bank.

From the Seitai-ji corner, the street leads to another cemetery, following its left wall and becoming quite narrow. Don't be too surprised when it ends in three small steps. The street gradually becomes a paved alley, then a proper street again leading to the Kishibojin-do precincts. With the temple behind you on the left go across diagonally Meiji Dori crossing to a pedestrian road between a Honda showroom and a food shop. The road snakes down to the Seibu Line (200m), and, after a tunnel under the tracks, a countryside-style level crossing on the Yamanote, and another tunnel on your left under the Seibu Line, you'll find yourself along the Yamanote again, Mejiro Station being 200m farther up the tracks.

⇨ From Mejiro to Tokyo Station

From Mejiro Station, follow the Yamanote on the left side for another 200m. (If you prefer to do the complete Yamanote Loop, turn right through the tunnel—see p. 74). To complete the Northern Loop, turn left at Gakushuin University; 300m further, you'll see the big cube of Takeda Chemicals. Turn right and then take the first left onto a parallel street leading to Meiji Dori. Cross this avenue and the Toden Arakawa tram line. The next street on the right (50m) leads to the Kanda-gawa. For nearly two kilometers the riverside path winds by Shin Edogawa Garden and the tiny tree-shrine of Sui-jinja, ending at the Edogawabashi–Mejiro Dori intersection. (If time is short, simply take Mejiro Dori all the way to Otemachi and the Imperial Palace, 4.3 kilometers further.)

For a more scenic route, cross the busy intersection, go past the Fuji bank, and turn left 200m later onto a pleasant, bustling, semi-pedestrian shopping street known as Jizo Dori. At the next traffic lights, turn right onto a busy street lined with printing factories, which leads uphill to Kagurazaka. Turn right at Akagi-jinja Shrine and then left at the traffic lights to go sailing straight down to Iidabashi. Cross the JR Chuo Line and go straight on— you can't miss the pedestrian alley on your right, leading to Yasukuni-jinja. In front of you will be the Budokan and Kitanomaru-koen Park. Turn left, following the Imperial Palace moat to the Palace Hotel. Turn left onto the first avenue after this hotel for Tokyo Station.

➪ From Mejiro to Shibuya

From Mejiro Station, follow the tracks southward, cycling down between the Yamanote and Gakushuin University for 200m. Then take the tunnel on the right. (Otomeyama-koen is on your right 100m. farther ahead). About 300m after the tunnel, you'll notice a Shinto shrine. Turn left here and cross Shin Mejiro Dori (50m). This avenue leads, on the right, to the nearby Shimo-Ochiai Station. Turning left just before the station, you'll pass both a little concrete-sided river and the Seibu Shinjuku Line. The little street on your right will give you access to a second river, the Kanda-gawa. Follow the riverside path on the right. Part of the route doesn't appear on maps, but you can go on for about 1.6 kilometers, to Okubo Dori. While cycling along the peaceful riverbank, think about the bizarre legend of the servants who were killed and dumped in the Kanda-gawa nightly after carrying their master to visit the Kumano-jinja Shrine. Change to the right bank, although the street isn't exactly on the riverside. Change to the other side of the river again after 600m, taking Ome Kaido on your left. (You could keep on in the same direction and cross the river later, but this area, although nicer, is really a labyrinth.)

Heading toward Shinjuku, turn right after 200m onto a wide street leading directly to Kumano-jinja (600m) and Shinjuku Chuo-koen Park. an area currently being revamped. Behind the high trees, beyond the quiet little pond with a tiny Shinto shrine, loom the twin towers of Tange's Tokyo Metropolitan Government building, destroying the usual perceptions of Shinjuku as a city of concrete and glass. About 600m after the shrine, turn left onto Koshu Kaido in the direction of Shinjuku Station. After about 200m and before Bunka Women's College, you'll see a small street on the right which goes through Yoyogi 3-chome. On the left corner you can't miss the humongous gingko, which also serves as a sort of shrine. The shape of the pencil building on the right corner adds, deliberately or not, the perfect symmetrical finishing touch to the scene.

After less than 800m, cross the Odakyu Line and go on underneath an expressway. Turn right as if you wanted to visit Meiji Jingu Shrine; cycle alongside the Yoyogi-koen Park on what first seems to be an expressway but fortunately becomes the green Inokashira Dori (after one kilometer you'll see a small park on the other side; on the rear street is a new building, a concrete cubic grid). After about a kilometer, you'll cross an avenue leading to the National Yoyogi Gymnasium and Harajuku (on your left). But head in the opposite direction, to a small pedestrian path about 20m from the crossing. This trail actually follows Inokashira Dori quite closely, but is far quieter. Later it becomes narrower, merging into a road leading to Seibu Department Store and the Yamanote Line. Immediately after Seibu, go under the tracks and turn right, going past cozy *izakaya*. You should now be in front of Shibuya Station.

(To join the Southern Loop, turn left, cross Meiji Dori in the direction of Tokyu Bunka Kaikan, then follow the instructions below.)

The Southern Loop

Route: Snaking along the Meguro-gawa River and passing some of the last remnants of seaside Tokyo, the route visits some of the architectural wonders of Tokyo
Start and Goal: Tokyo Station, or any station along the southern Yamanote Line

A little girl walks beside the Meguro-gawa River carrying an enormous white rabbit. It's not a dream, nor a reminiscence of any Wonderland; just another facet of Tokyo life. Further on, a group of workers gaze at a beetle, and are reminded of the caged insects of their childhood. Rabbits, insects, chicken, fish, cats, donkeys, and, of course, crows. Even if you're not lucky enough to see a rabbit, you're sure to find cats and crows, mostly in cemeteries. It's more difficult to meet a donkey. But Hie-jinja Shrine, near the

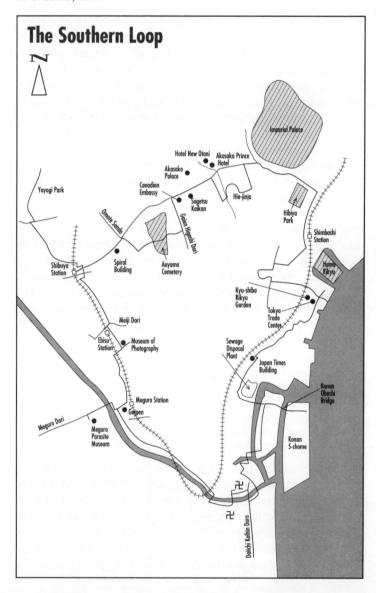

The Southern Loop

N

Imperial Palace

Hotel New Otani

Akasaka Prince Hotel

Akasaka Palace

Canadian Embassy

Yoyogi Park

Sogetsu Kaikan

Hie-jinja

Omote Sando

Golen Higashi Dori

Hibiya Park

Shimbashi Station

Shibuya Station

Spiral Building

Aoyama Cemetery

Hama Rikyu

Kyu-shiba Rikyu Garden

Tokyo Trade Center

Meiji Dori

Ebisu Station

Museum of Photography

Sewage Disposal Plant

Japan Times Building

Konan Ohashi Bridge

Meguro Station

Gajoen

Meguro Dori

Meguro Parasite Museum

Konan 5-chome

Daiichi Keihin Doro

Diet, has an interesting stone donkey guarding the inner steps of the sanctuary and serving as a messenger for the gods. At the same shrine, half a dozen chickens wander around a pocket bamboo forest. For fish, go to Shinagawa harbor and have a look at the fishing boats, or go along the sea canals between Shibaura and Hamamatsucho at lunch time and you'll meet many an amateur fisherman. But more exotic are the strange little things you can find at the Kiseichukan Museum in Meguro, where four thousand parasites are enshrined.

A different kind of animal gives the rider a strange feeling of wandering between dream, nightmare, and reality. Let's call them by their real name: Architects. These creatures invaded Tokyo in the boom years, making quite interesting dens. The first one on our route (Higashi 3-chome, south of Shibuya) is the East Gallery, a banal glass-and-metal cube beautifully wrapped in a concrete sheet torn like a sheet of paper—a futuristic vision of Tokyo after an earthquake, or perhaps a prosaic symbol of the Japanese fondness for wrapping. Anyhow, it's worth a stop for its art gallery and open terrace, a concept still exotic in Tokyo. Further south, an interesting example of International-Japanese architecture is expected to be provided by Sapporo Breweries. The original plan to dismantle an eighteenth century French chateau and rebuild it at Ebisu was stymied by French officials, so the brewery has decided to make do with a copy. Those looking for a convincing link between Japanese tradition and modern urbanism should take a look at Meguro Gajoen, a huge and luxurious wedding factory which also harbors a museum, laquerware items, and even an old building surrounded by a small river inside the modern one. On weekends, the bevies of gold kimono–clad women add a lively touch to this fairy-tale palace.

Getting back to the real world, have a (brief) look at the hideous white cubes of Osaki New City, the last big urban item before Tokyo Bay. Many interesting skyscrapers are located in this area, including the Japan Times headquarters, and Seavans in Shibaura, a new complex with a huge glass roof and a musical fountain serenading jaded Tokyoites with New Age music. For a panoramic view of the cycling route, park your bike and take the (expensive) lifts at the World Trade Center Building. If the weather is fine, Yokohama, Hakone, and Mt. Fuji are visible. In the next century this cycling ride may well include a visit to the Millenium Tower, but for the moment this 840m-high project is nothing more than a Norman Foster-styled utopia, a dream in an economic bubble.

If you happen to be in quest of fashionable shapes, the Akasaka-Aoyama part of the route will prove more attractive. Behind you when you leave Hie-jinja is a building with a huge model boat on its roof, advertising Nagasaki Holland Village, evidence of the marriage between modern Tokyo and the Disneyland aesthetic (another fine example is Yumi Katsura Bridal House, a big cardboard castle on Gaien Higashi Dori). Akasaka is more like a permanent open-air exhibition of the stars of Japanese architecture—here you'll find not only Tange's Sogetsu Kaikan, but also his giant accordion (Akasaka Prince Hotel), and Moriyama's Canadian Embassy, a huge glass building partially hiding the old residence.

Echoing the concrete and granite volumes of the Supreme Court (Okada) is the Collezione Building near the Nezu Museum, practically the only important Tadao Ando building in the Tokyo area. The two Oxy buildings (one on Gaien Higashi Dori, the other with a Castelbajac shop before Nezu-jinja) offer a minor but virtuoso version of the intelligent combination of concrete and light. You may want to make two other stops in the immediate vicinity of Collezione: the first at Yokku Mokku deluxe coffee and cake shop, and the second at Spiral Building (Maki), a vain box for a spiraling slope leading almost nowhere. It would be fun to try it on a bike . . .

After this architectural feast you'll be in need of a break. Try Nezu Museum, either its collection or its beautiful park filled with maple trees. Tea ceremony in one of the tea houses is the ultimate antidote for the ragged nerves of Tokyo cyclists.

History buffs are well catered for on the Southern Loop—at Nogi-jinja Shrine try and catch an echo of the cannon shots which rang out from the palace on a quiet evening in September, 1912, marking the departure of the coffin containing the Meiji Emperor on his last journey to Kyoto. General Nogi, hero of Port Arthur, was to commit suicide immediately after. Many years earlier, the Emperor made a last stop at Ebara-jinja Shrine, also on our route, on his journey from Kyoto to Tokyo for the Imperial Restoration. This shrine, however, is more famous for its fishermen's rituals in June than for its Imperial connection. Elsewhere we are reminded of former days, even if they were not particularly tragic or epic. Hie-jinja, for instance, was the most popular in the city during the Tokugawa period. On Children's Day (November 15), you can catch a quiet glimpse of the old atmosphere, but in the crowds at the famous ox-drawn carriage festival (Shinko Gyoretsu, June 15 in even-numbered years) you'd do better to leave the bike at home. Zojo-ji, at Shiba-koen, is also associated with the Tokugawas, as it served as their family temple. Today, its 1974 version is hardly worth a stop, but have a look at Sanmon, the big red gate (1605) and the rows of small *jizo* armed with brightly colored paper windmills in a rather quixotic manner. Compare them with the small army of lilliputian statues (also *jizo*) in the Daien-ji garden at Meguro, evoking the terracotta soldiers of Xi'an, with their two cohorts marching along a gravel drive.

Enjoy the Southern Loop according to your own mood—some areas are very lively, like Meguro, Gotanda, and the street from Meguro-gawa River to Shinagawa, which seems to retain something of the time when it was the last stretch of the Tokaido Highway from Kyoto. Others are full of activity, like Shimbashi, with its shoeblacks, newspaper vendors, begging monks, and old people holding up ads for massage parlors. Other places, on the contrary, are very select, like Hitotsugi Dori, the nighttime enclave of the Japanese elite, within gunshot of Akasaka Palace, the residence of the Emperor.

A handful of truly quiet spots also exists: Seiko-in in Minami Shinagawa is ideal for a picnic, with a pleasant garden and tea house. Stop for lunch at Shinagawa, either at the harbor, overlooking the floating restaurants and fishing boats, or on one of the artificial islands of the bay (Konan 4-chome or 5-chome), with dramatic views of the new suspension bridge. Until Takeshiba Pier, you'll actually see nothing but quays, wharves, and other vanishing souvenirs of the seaside city.

⇨ From Shibuya to Meguro

Cross the expressway south of the main square at the east side of Shibuya Station. From Meiji Dori, turn right onto the little street which goes under the Toyoko Line and meets the Yamanote Line. Proceed left along the tracks. After a kilometer you'll pass the East Gallery on your left.

To reach Ebisu Station, turn right onto the next avenue after Fit-to-Art. Cross this wide street after about 50m and go up the steep slope parallel to the Yamanote Line which leads to the station. (Turn left before the bridge to visit the Tokyo Museum of Photography, located 100m up the road on the left.) Cross the bridge over the tracks and follow the train line again. On the other side, you'll see the huge Sapporo Brewery construction site. After 250m the route curves to the right around a driving school. At the fork, turn left or keep on the same, much quieter street; they join again before Meguro. Cross Meguro Dori 500m later and, after crossing a second wide street in front of Meguro Station, bear right down to the Meguro-gawa River and Meguro Gajoen. Daien-ji Temple is located halfway down the slope.

➫ From Meguro to Shinagawa

To visit the Parasite Museum, cross the river and turn right, following the river for 200m to Meguro Dori. Turn left; the museum is 100m on the left after the Yamate Dori crossing.

From Gajoen, don't cross the Meguro-gawa, but follow it for 1.2 kilometers toward Gotanda. Although it may sound unbelievable in such a built-up area, the first part of the path is a dirt track, but this, of course, could change any time. Further on, the path changes into a quiet riverside street lined with cherry trees and weeping willows. Just after you've crossed the second of two major avenues leading to Gotanda Station, you'll find a small area strung along the river and down a couple of narrow little streets full of soba restaurants, *izakaya*, and coffee shops.

Continue along the river. It's pure concrete for a few hundred meters, but then you'll find cherry trees and wild flowers again. For more than a kilometer from Gotanda there isn't a single traffic light until Yamate Dori; note the new glass and metal Sony Building. Keep on Yamate Dori for about 200m, then cross the river at the first bridge after the Yamanote Line and before the Keihin Tohoku Line. Just after this Japanese-style bridge, take the dirt path on the left, and ride along Meguro-gawa for another 300m. You'll soon arrive at what is actually a T-junction, as the riverside path ends at a barrier. The road on the right leads to Seiko-in and the one on the left heads across the river to an avenue 100m away. Turn right on the avenue for the Tokai-ji Temple entrance.

If you're not in the mood for a temple, cross the river, turn right, and continue along the river. The track seems to end at a concrete factory, but cross Daiichi Keihin Doro and you'll find the path continues south of the river. About 200m after passing under the Keihin Kyuko Line, cross the river to visit Ebara-jinja. Unfortunately, the riverside path ends soon after, making it impossible to reach the bay, so turn left at the next bridge after Ebara-jinja and say good-bye to the river. This shop-lined street leads to Shinagawa Station, but turn right after about 500m for Shinagawa harbor.

⇨ From Shinagawa to Hibiya

Ride around the southern side of the harbor. Turn left onto Kaigan Dori and cross Tennozu-bashi Bridge, then take the first bridge on the right to get onto Shin Konan island (Konan 4-chome). Follow the canal heading north until the second bridge, Shin Konan-bashi.

To check out warehouse city at Konan 5-chome, an area tightly packed with concrete factories, customs houses, and storehouses, turn right at the first bridge, go under the expressway and the monorail, and then cross the Konan Ohashi. Join the main route again at Shin Konan-bashi.

Cross the canal again at Shin Konan-bashi. Immediately after the rectangular waters of Shibaura Sewage Disposal Plant, turn right up the concrete slope to Shibaura Chuo-koen Park. Leave the garden by its north exit (it may close early, especially in winter) and turn right to go north, crossing Shibaura-bashi Bridge over a canal. Just after the Japan Times building, cross the bridge and continue along the canal and under the monorail. Some 300m farther, the road curves to the left, heading for the monorail. Instead, turn right along the canal, passing the Seavans and Toshiba buildings. Cross the canal under the expressway and turn left. The first street on the right leads to Takeshiba Pier.

Turn left at the Tokyo Trade Center; the road goes past the Kyu-Shibarikyu Garden, under the Tokaido Line, past the World Trade Center, up to a very big *torii*, finally leading to Zojo-ji, with Tokyo Tower in the background. (From the *torii*, you can turn left and go to the Shibuya-gawa River, 400m away, to discover its unexpected harbor under the expressway.) Cross Hibiya Dori and turn left up the quiet street between Zojo-ji and Tokyo Prince Hotel to enjoy the leafy grounds of the hotel and Shiba-koen Park. Turning right before Tokyo Tower brings you back down to Hibiya Dori again. Turn left on Hibiya Dori for a 200m ride to the Onarimon Station crossing. Turn right here; this street leads to Daiichi Keihin Doro but it's better to choose a smaller street on the left to get to Shimbashi.

From Shimbashi Station, follow the Yamanote tracks on the left side. You can even cycle *under* the tracks for about 500m along the International Shopping Arcade—the entrance is just after the Daiichi Annex Hotel on the left. At Yurakucho you'll come to a tunnel full of *yakitori* street restaurants; turn left here and follow the Yamanote tracks for about 30m and then left again to a square with a cinema and coffee shop and Hibiya Park.

(If you plan to join the northern route at Tokyo Station, go along the Imperial Palace outer garden on Hibya Dori for 800m and turn right.)

▷ From Hibiya to Shibuya

Follow the moat to the left around the palace. In front of the big cubes of the Supreme Court, turn left and then left again at the Pentax Building. heading for the rear of the Diet (Kokkai Gijido). At the Kokkai Ura traffic lights, turn right and cycle down to Hie-jinja and up and down again to the main road and Akasaka.

Cross the street, go straight on, and take the fourth road on the right, Hitotsugi Dori, to join Aoyama Dori with the Akasaka Prince and New Otani hotels further down on the right. Turn left along Aoyama Dori; you can't miss the Sogetsu Kaikan and the Canadian Embassy on the left. Turn left at Akasaka Post Office onto Gaien Higashi Dori. General Nogi's house is 500m along on the left side, just before Nogizaka Station's east exit and Yumi Katsura Bridal House. About 150m later you'll see the Oxy Building on the right; turn right on the little street in front of this concrete quarter of a cylinder. The street crosses a small avenue and seems to end in a labyrinth, but if you turn left, you'll see an avenue at the bottom of Aoyama Cemetery. Take the large slope winding up through the cemetery. Leaving the cemetery, you'll notice the cylindrical Oxy Oribe Building 200m down on your left; the road leads to the Nezu Museum.

From the museum entrance, go back to the crossing and turn left. This street passes by several fashion shops, the Collezione Building just after the crossing, and Yokku Mokku confectionery. At the Omote Sando–Aoyama Dori intersection, turn left onto Aoyama Dori; the Spiral Building is 200m down on the left. Go straight for a kilometer to Shibuya Station.   ✍ JPD

ᗧᖇ River Rides

With Tokyo's heavy traffic and narrow sidewalks, cycling can become more of a mental exercise than a physical one. To get away from all those cars, traffic lights, and pedestrians, a river ride is just the thing.

East Tokyo has three major rivers: the Sumida-gawa, Ara-kawa, and Edo-gawa. Although the Sumida-gawa is the most romantically depicted, famous for its cherry blossoms and firework displays, which have been featured in numerous *ukiyo-e*, the river has heavy boat traffic and the cycling path is relatively short. The Ara-kawa and Edo-gawa river rides are much longer with continuous riverside paths. The scenery is not especially spectacular, but the ride is flat and the headwind makes for good exercise.

The Sumida-gawa River Bikeway ᗧᖇ

Route: A meander along the Sumida-gawa River from Hamacho-koen Park to Sumida-koen Park and the temples of Asakusa
Start: Morishita Station (Toei Shinjuku Line)
Goal: Minowa Station (Hibiya Line)

The Sumida-gawa Bikeway is an inner-city concrete trip starting in the lower reaches of the Sumida-gawa at Hamacho-koen Park, near the razed Meiji-za. Begin at the back of the park next to the river; there is a walkway from the park to Ryogoku-bashi Bridge.

Cross the bridge and ride to the first light. Don't be afraid of the *inoshishi* (wild boar) hanging from a shop window on your right as you approach the light. Turn left and ride for about 500m and you'll go under some train tracks.

On your right is Ryogoku Station and the Kokugikan Sumo Stadium, which also houses the Sumo Museum; watch out for stray sumo wrestlers as this is an area with a large concentration of sumo stables. Take a sharp left under the tracks and you'll find a long walkway under the expressway all the way to Umaya-bashi Bridge.

Cross this bridge and turn right at the police box on the opposite side. Ride straight along a narrow street that parallels the river until you come to the entrance of Sumida-koen, a large park. This bridge is Azuma-bashi, and the one you already passed is Komagata-bashi.

The Sumida-gawa River Bikeway

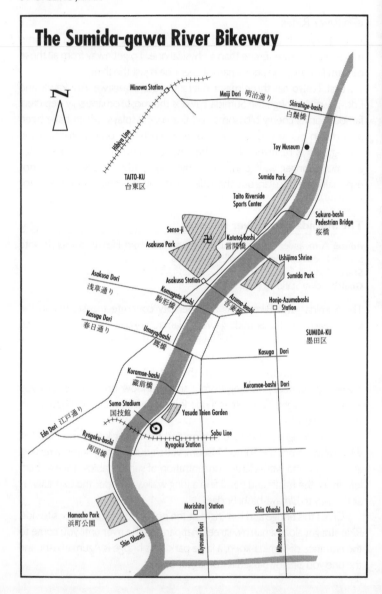

Crossing over the Kototoi-bashi Bridge and turning right at the entrance to Sumida-koen you'll find the Ushijima-jinja Shrine, where the main object of reverence is a bull complete with red bib. Going back over Kototoi-bashi again you'll see a police box and the dock for the waterbus to Hama Rikyu and Hinode Pier. Ride until you come to the Riverside Sports Center; behind it is Sakura-bashi, a pedestrian bridge. Recently a walkway has been built at the river's edge, which is far more pleasant than peering over the high concrete walls for a glimpse of the river.

In the future, you might be able to walk all the way to Tokyo Bay, but for now you can sit at stone tables on either side of Sakura-bashi and watch the river flow. After my Sunday rides I usually rest on the Sumida-ku side and watch the sun set on Asakusa.

Continuing on, cross Sakura-bashi, turn left on the walkway, and ride until you come to Shirahige-bashi Bridge. Not much to see here as you'll be under the expressway most of the time, but it's a good jumping off point if you want to get to the Ara-kawa, the next river over.

Meiji Dori runs over Shirahige-bashi. Until this point, you'll have spent very little time on streets, but from here you'd better strap on your helmet for the next few kilometers down to Minowa Station on the Hibiya Line.

All in all, the Sumida River Bikeway can serve as a main riding route, with many interesting things to see or do on both sides of the river—not only temples and tombs, and a toy museum, but also lots of traditional street life, parks, and gardens. ✍ BL

The Ara-kawa River Path 🚲

Route: Trailing the Ara-kawa River with side-trips to Horikiri Iris Garden and the Budokan martial arts stadium
Start: Minami-Sunamachi Station (Tozai Line)
Goal: Ayase Station (Chiyoda, Joban lines), or for a longer trip, Toda Koen Station (Saikyo Line)

The Ara-kawa River enters Tokyo from Saitama Prefecture and flows through Itabashi, Kita, Adachi, Sumida, Katsushika, Edogawa, and Koto wards. (Ironically it doesn't flow through Arakawa-ku.) If you are in any of these wards, the river is easily accessible by bicycle. From the river mouth to Saitama Prefecture, the river is about twenty-eight kilometers long.

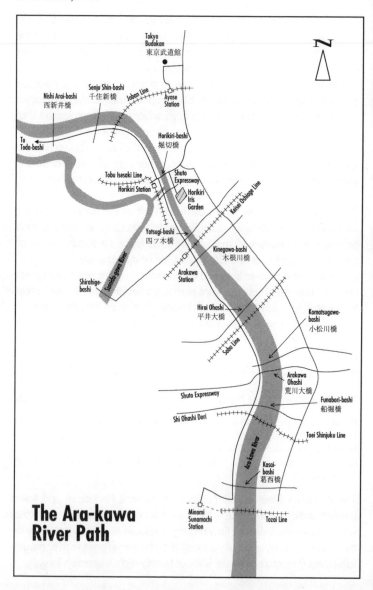

The Ara-kawa River Path

A good starting point would be in Koto-ku where the Tozai Line crosses the river near its mouth. Minami-Sunamachi Station is the closest here. Head north from the station past Minami-Sunamachi 3-chome Park. Turn right at the first major intersection and go straight until you reach the river path. The path south of the Tozai Line finishes in a dead end, but heading north are two parallel cycling/pedestrian paths on the west side. One is at ground level near the river, and the other is elevated with a better view, but you may have to duck under a low bridge or two in Edogawa-ku.

The paved elevated path continues all the way to Arakawa Station on the Keisei Oshiage Line in Sumida-ku. From there a road open to vehicular traffic takes over up to Horikiri Station on the Tobu Isesaki Line. The path on the ground is also temporarily interrupted by a canal near Horikiri Station.

If it's June, cross the Shin Horikiri-bashi Bridge into Katsushika-ku and ride south to the Horikiri Iris Garden (Horikiri Shobu-en) with its rows of colorful irises. About two kilometers north of the garden is Ayase, where you can find the distinctive-looking Budo-kan. On weekends there is usually a martial arts tournament, which you can see for free. If you find your energy waning, you can head to Ayase Station and take the easy way back.

North of Horikiri Station, the elevated path becomes bumpy; for a smooth ride, switch to the path by the river. Lined with baseball and soccer fields and parks, this riverside path will take you all the way to Saitama Prefecture. To keep track of where you are, simply go up to the elevated path once in a while to check out the names of the bridges. A suitable finishing point is Toda Koen Station on the Saikyo Line—from the west side cross the Toda-bashi Bridge and go straight on busy Route 17. Turning left at a Royal Host restaurant after the first major intersection brings you to the station.   ✍ PO

The Edo-gawa River Trail

Route: A riverside path from the lower reaches of the Kyu Edo-gawa River and the Edo-gawa River taking you to Shibamata, the home of the movie *Otoko wa Tsuraiyo*, ending at the vast Mizumoto-koen Park
Start: Kasai Rinkai Koen Station (Keiyo Line)
Goal: Kanamachi Station (Joban line)

The path along the west side of the Edo-gawa river was built especially for cyclists. It has a red (now mostly faded) grip surface. Cycling guide maps on

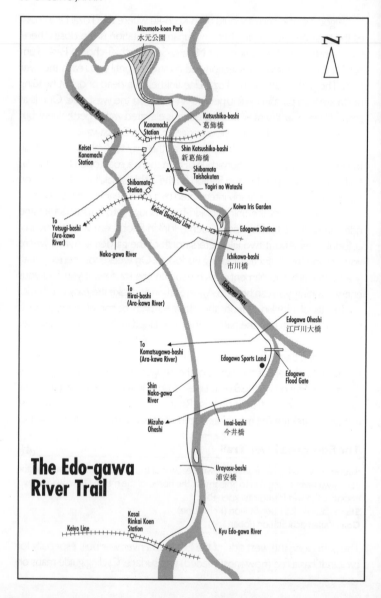

N

Mizumoto-koen Park
水元公園

Naka-gawa River

Katsushika-bashi
葛飾橋

Kanamachi
Station

Keisei
Kanamachi
Station

Shin Katsushika-bashi
新葛飾橋

Shibamata
Taishakuten

Shibamata
Station

Yagiri no Watashi

Koiwa Iris Garden

To
Yotsugi-bashi
(Ara-kawa
River)

Keisei Dentetsu Line

Edogawa Station

Naka-gawa River

Ichikawa-bashi
市川橋

To
Hirai-bashi
(Ara-kawa River)

Edogawa River

Edogawa Ohashi
江戸川大橋

To
Komatsugawa-bashi
(Ara-kawa River)

Edogawa Sports Land

Edogawa
Flood Gate

Shin
Naka-gawa
River

Mizuho
Ohashi

Imai-bashi
今井橋

The Edo-gawa
River Trail

Urayasu-bashi
浦安橋

Kasai
Rinkai Koen
Station

Keiyo Line

Kyu Edo-gawa River

metal panels have even been set up along the cycling path.

Kasai Rinkai-koen Park on the waterfront is located at one end of the cycling path. If you start from Kasai Rinkai Koen Station, ride east along the right side of the train tracks of the Keiyo Line, which runs adjacent to the park. The path will soon turn left and head along the Kyu Edo-gawa River which leads to the Edo-gawa River. Except for one or two detours around canal mouths, the red cycling path continues nonstop along the river. Go under Urayasu-bashi Bridge and eventually you will reach a fork in the river; go straight and you will be riding along the Shin Naka-gawa River. The cycling path, however, crosses the Shin Naka-gawa by the Mizuho Ohashi Bridge. Cross the bridge, then immediately turn right to ride on the river-bank cycling path next to a small children's playground. The path goes on to Edogawa Sports Land which has an indoor pool in summer and skating rink in winter. Just beyond the sports center, the Kyu Edo-gawa meets the Edo-gawa River. Where the riverbank path ends, a road lined with cherry trees begins, ending at the Edo-gawa Suimon (floodgate). Those with a taste for such things can take a detour and ride across the floodgate to take a look at the lower reaches of the Edo-gawa.

From the floodgate, the red cycling path starts again on the riverbank and continues nonstop for at least ten kilometers. Here the scenery starts to turn green with many soccer and baseball fields.

Along the Edo-gawa River there are at least three places worth a stop. The riverside Koiwa Shobu-en (Iris Garden) near Edogawa Station on the Keisei Line is hard to miss when it's in full bloom in June. Then there's Shibamata, home of Tora-san and the backdrop for the long-running *Otoko wa Tsuraiyo* movie series. North of Shibamata is the Mizumoto-koen Park with cherry trees, irises, green grass, a man-made beach, and a bird sanctuary. Lots of water, too, as is implied by its name.

After passing the Iris Garden, keep an eye out for a dinky pier and a small wooden boat full of people. This is the Yagiri no Watashi, made famous by the Tora-san movie series and now the only river-crossing boat in Tokyo, even though during the Edo period there were similar boats operating at fourteen locations on Tokyo's rivers. The fare is ¥200 for the two-minute ride. When you see the pier, get off the cycling path and look for the Shibamata Taishakuten Temple, a short walk from the river. Besides serving as a frequent backdrop to the Tora-san movies, the temple is famous in its own right for its magnificent woodcarvings on the exterior walls. The carvings are now enclosed in a glass box for protection; entrance is ¥300. Since there will be many tourists, you might as well park your bicycle and walk. The shopping mall, Taishakuten Sando, leading to the temple has many *dango* (skewered rice dumplings) and *sembei* stores offering a bewildering variety of types and flavors. One *dango* shop named Kameya Honpo is modeled after Tora-san's *dango* shop; go in and try some *kusa dango* with bean jam, washed down with green tea—great for reviving flagging spirits.

From Shibamata, get back on the cycling path and ride further north. After passing under two bridges, look out for a pleasant, cherry-tree-lined road on the left, which is easy to spot since it has red sidewalks (cycling paths). This road leads up to and then traces Mizumoto-koen Park's western fringe. You can enter the huge park at any point and ride around. The designated cycling path ends at the park's western tip. From the southern edge of the park it's a straight road south to Kanamachi Station on the Joban Line. You can also continue riding on the narrow road along the Naka-gawa River or backtrack and continue further north along the Edogawa River into Misato, Saitama Prefecture. You could even cut across Adachi-ku to reach the Ara-kawa River. The choice is yours.   ✍ PO

Looping the Green Loop   🚲

Route: Loop around the pockets of green of Omiya Hachiman Shrine, Zenpukuji-gawa-koen, Zenpukuji-koen, and Inokashira-koen parks
Start: Ogikubo Station, Nishi-Ogikubo Station, Kichijoji Station (Chuo Line) or Eifukucho Station, Takaido Station, Kugayama Station (Inokashira Line)
Goal: Stations along the Inokashira Line between Inokashira-koen and Eifukucho Station

For riders suffering from asphalt gray and sweatshirt-sky burnout, I heartily recommend a loop through the southern and western quarters of Suginami-ku, Tokyo's greenest ward.

Suginami-ku borders Setagaya-ku (the largest ward) on the south, Nakano-ku on the east and north, and Nerima-ku on the west. The southwest corner fronts Musashino City, in the quaint neighborhood of Kichijoji, and part of the route I recommend will take you through Kichijoji's popular

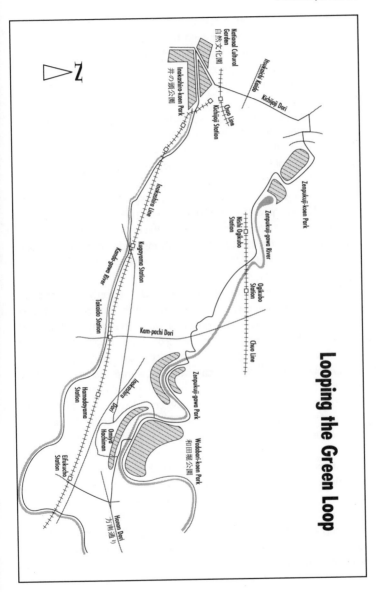

Looping the Green Loop

Inokashira-koen park. Other parks you'll visit on this ride are Zenpukuji-gawa-koen, Zenpukuji-koen (due north of Inokashira-koen Park), Wadabori-koen, and the holy forest of Omiya Hachiman, near Eifukucho Station. The latter four parks lie adjacent to one another along the meandering Zenpukuji-gawa River, and together form Tokyo's most pleasant continuous green bikeway.

Points of interest along the loop include a natural waterfowl habitat in Zenpukuji-koen, the picturesque meander of the Zenpukuji-gawa near Wadabori-koen, the expansive grounds of Omiya Hachiman, where a fabulous collection of *mikoshi* (portable shrine) are housed, and the Inokashira Zoo, whose menagerie has earned itself the nickname "Les Miserables."

As the name implies, the Zenpukuji-gawa is (or once was) a river, the modern Tokyo equivalent for which is a cement-finished canal. Tokyo is crisscrossed by a maze of canals which are the enslaved remnants of Edo-era streams and rivers. Most of these canals are bordered by bike trails, and I would recommend any of them for riding, though some are less ugly (and odorous) than others.

The Zenpukuji-gawa bikeway, though, is actually pretty, and a real surprise the first time you ride it. The high point of this ride is the greenbelt that lies between Ogikubo 3-chome and Omiya Hachiman, just north of Eifuku-cho. There is ample greenery along the trail throughout, with a sort of green-belt park flanking the trail and making a great picnic or rest stop. The Zenpukuji-gawa and the Kanda-gawa River, with its source in Inokashira-ike, form the northern and southern boundaries of this loop. Riders may join the loop at any number of easy access points along both rivers, enclosed by bikeways for much of their length. Major stations adjacent to the loop include Nishi Ogikubo, Ogikubo, and Kichijoji on the JR Chuo Line, and Kichijoji, Kugayama, and Eifukucho stations, on the Inokashira Line. If you live in Setagaya or Shibuya wards, the Zenpukuji bikeway is directly accessible by following Inokashira Dori out toward Kichijoji. Just turn north (right) at Eifukucho Station on the Inokashira Line, then turn left and go up the shopping street, cross Honan Dori (to the 7–11), then cut left onto the small side street. You'll soon see the bright orange *torii* entrance to Omiya Hachiman. Turn right at the entrance and take the little winding road to the river.

Omiya Hachiman, a shrine lying immediately next to the river, is by itself a worthwhile destination for sightseers. Its grounds create a particularly pretty meander overhung with boughs, and have been partially restored to their natural state so that there is even a clean gravel shingle along the north bank. Stairs are provided from the bike trail down to the river, and in summer I'm sure you could even bathe there, though the signs say entering the water is dangerous. Despite the warning, the water at this point is temptingly clean, and the many fish and ducks that gather along this stretch seem quite content. Just upstream from this point I saw two massive carp, one bright orange and the other a diaphanous veggie-white.

For a special surprise, turn upstream (left) on the bike trail, ride a few seconds, and then look across the stream to the south bank. There you'll see something unique in Tokyo; a real homestead. Somebody has a couple of dwellings stuck back on the river bank at the foot of a small cliff beneath the shrine. The place would look more at home in a Ken Kesey novel. A large, dirt-patched lawn with a couple of old cars, a pile of scrap wood; the only thing missing is a spray-paint-on-plywood sign advertising "Nite Crawlers—25 cents."

For most of the way the bike path meanders its way along the Zenpukuji-gawa until it narrows to the point of discomfort and then disappears altogether. Make use of some creative wheelwork to find your way to the source of the river in Zenpukuji-ike Pond in Zenpukuji-koen at the western corner of Suginami-ku. At the west end, Zenpukuji and Inokashira parks are connected by a largely straight route that runs, north to south, through Zenpukuji 2-chome, Tachinomachi 2-chome, Kichijoji Kitamachi 2- and 1-chome, and Kichijoji Honmachi 2-chome. From the western exit of Zenpukuji-koen, go west and take the second turning on the right and then turn left to reach Kichijoji Dori. From there it's straight on until Inokashira-koen.

From Inokashira-koen you can ride downstream along the Kanda-gawa Bike Path. Cross the tracks at Mitakadai Station and take the first left for about a block and a half. If you intend to return to Omiya Hachiman and Eifukucho Station, stay on the bike path until Kugayama Station. Going under the Inokashira Line at the station, the road crosses Inokashira Dori at an oblique angle in the neighborhood of Hamadayama 4- and 3-chome. Stay on it until you reach Takachiho Shoka University and, behind it, Omiya

Hachiman. Alternatively, you can ride the Kanda-gawa Bikeway all the way until the point where Inokashira Dori crosses the Kanda-gawa River.

Riders with more time and energy may enlarge the loop fifty percent by taking the bikeway that continues downstream along the Zenpukuji-gawa from Wadabori-koen into Nakano-ku. Just inside Nakano, in the neighborhood of Minamidai 3-chome, the Zenpukuji-gawa and the Kanda-gawa merge. Here you can double back and follow the Kanda-gawa Bikeway all the way out to Inokashira again. Give yourself plenty of time for this, though, as the Kanda-gawa Bikeway is not nearly as easy to follow as the Zenpukuji. You could also continue on the Zenpukuji-gawa Bike Route as far as Nakano Dori, and that's just a hop away from the big buildings on the west side of Shinjuku Station. This route, facing into the warm morning sun, would be a very pleasant commute for cyclists who work in or near Shinjuku and live in Suginami, Nakano, or Nerima wards. ✍ JH

The Tama-gawa River Bikeway 🚲

Route: A chance to observe the Japanese at play while enjoying a stiff workout in the headwinds of the Tama-gawa River
Long Route Start: Yaguchino-Watashi Station (Mekama Line)
Medium Route Start: Noborito Station (Nambu Line)
Goal: Tachikawa Station (Chuo Line), Akishima Station (Ome Line)

The Tama-gawa River Bikeway must be one of Tokyo's best unexplored cycling treasures. Here's how to find it, and enjoy some great cycling in town, without fear of two-ton metal monsters and their halitosis.

Those in Tokyo can pick it up where Route 1 crosses the Tama-gawa. The nearest station to this area is Yaguchino-Watashi Station on the Mekama Line from Kamata Station. Head straight south from the station until you hit the river. The cycling path beside the river leads up to the first bridge, the Tama-gawa Ohashi Bridge where Route 1 crosses the river. Cross the river here, as the best place to start is on the Kawasaki City side. From here, you can travel some fifteen to twenty kilometers upstream on a well-paved path, save for a few meters here and there. The scenery varies from typical city to fairly interesting, and birdwatchers will delight in the many birds to be seen.

You do have to stay alert for joggers, dogs and their walkers, kids, and (on weekends) droves of little leaguers. But it beats dodging the metal

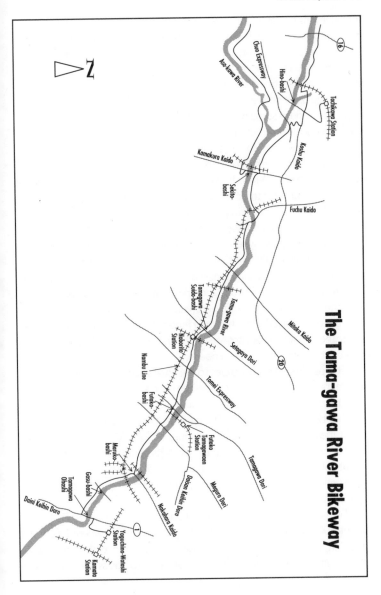

The Tama-gawa River Bikeway

monsters any day of the week. On a recent trip, my cycling was pleasurably interrupted by formation kite fliers, a Japanese drum and shamisen jam session, and an elderly man in a World War Two flying helmet breezing along on a unicycle. Try an early morning start, say at five or six, to reduce trail distractions by several orders of magnitude.

At one point between the path and the river, you'll find some interesting rapids through some rock ledges, overseen by a small shrine. Eventually, the path dumps you out onto a fairly busy road. Don't despair, however, just cross the river for more path, heading both upstream and downstream.

A particularly nice section of path about fifteen kilometers long with no stops (yes, no stops!) runs from a kilometer or two northwest of where Setagaya Dori meets the river. If you're joining the route from Noborito Station, head toward the river and follow the paved road that parallels the river. If you're riding on a weekend, you'll normally come to two spots a hundred meters apart where there are chains with a sign across the road. Go around both on the right using the paved footpath that goes around a children's play area. A few hundred meters after the second chain, the road makes a sharp right turn and immediately runs into a road parallel with the river. Ignore the turn and head straight onto a gravel path; the path becomes paved a few hundred meters later. The farther you go, the fewer the human distractions are on the trail, and eventually you'll be able to see Mt. Fuji if the sky is clear enough.

This paved section continues to my usual short-ride turnaround point where the Chuo Expressway crosses the river, a bit before Tachikawa City.

Those wanting to keep going can take the path that continues for another two kilometers or so. The pavement ends just after the path goes under the Chuo Expressway. To continue, just turn right and take the small road away from the river. After the road starts uphill, take the first left turn, about 150m away from the bike path. Follow this narrow, virtually car-less road until you have to turn right, and you'll wind up on Route 20, the busy Koshu Kaido.

Turn left onto Route 20, but don't panic; salvation from traffic is only about 500m away. Go through the major intersection where Route 20 goes left and later crosses the river. Don't cross the river, but instead go straight and turn left about 300m later, right after you cross a large drainage canal. (Bike baggers who want to leave the path at this point can turn right at the intersection and go to Tachikawa Station.)

There may still be some construction that requires a short 50m detour over gravel, where you'll face a set of stairs to the top of the dike along the river. Take the stairs, go left on the path at the top, then make a big 180-degree loop, and you'll soon find yourself on a low, scenic part of the path with playing fields on your right and the river on your left. Early one Saturday morning, while riding in this part we saw a large male green pheasant. Black kites, the feathered variety, can be seen most anywhere.

Keep to your right as long as you can, and in a few kilometers you'll go up to the top of the levee where the bike path turns into a real road, but with very few cars. Stay on it, crossing a major road if you miss the little turn to the right that goes under it. Eventually the path ends, but a right and then a quick left onto a road closed to cars will take you to Route 16, just north of the Hachioji exit of the Chuo Expressway. Cross Route 16, and go left on the sidewalk for about 30m. The bike path continues to your right for another couple of km. Just north of this point is Akishima Station on the Ome Line. This point is as far as I've been able to explore, but maybe poking around on other back roads will turn up another section.

⇨ The Asa-kawa Connection

If you get tired of the Tama-gawa, an alternative is to head out along the adjoining Asa-kawa River. From Sekito-bashi Bridge (you'll easily recognize it by a large building nearby that sports a giant bowling pin—presumably there's a bowling alley inside), where the Kamakura Kaido crosses the Tama-gawa River, head west (to your right) by first going down to the left to go under the bridge on the path. (The path also goes east, but ends after about two kilometers.) After a few kilometers west, the path ends. Go a little further, cross right over a small bridge, turn left off the bridge, then right onto the first small road into the neighborhood on your right. That small road takes you back to the Asa-kawa, which can be followed west, on either path or parallel road, for another four or five kilometers.

⇨ Tama-gawa Extensions

From the end of the Tama-gawa Bike Path it's just another twenty kilometers or so to countryside I consider heaven for cyclists.

The road to enlightenment begins on Route 16, which takes you north past Yokota Air Base. At the second stoplight after you cross Ome Kaido, turn left. Just a little after crossing the train tracks, angle right onto a country road and follow it for about five kilometers until it runs into another road. From here, you can make a long or short loop through the hills in the southern part of Saitama Prefecture, returning to this spot and taking the same road back.

Another favorite ride starts by taking Route 20 south, from the McDonald's at the end of the Tama-gawa Bike Path. This road takes you west through Hachioji. After coming down a hill into Hachioji and crossing a bridge, immediately turn right onto the road to Takao. From there, follow the signs for Jimba Kogen. After passing through Jimba Kogen, and passing the expressway and train tracks, go right on Route 20, then take a left at the bridge which goes over one end of Sagami-ko Lake.

After crossing the bridge, ride to the top of the hill, turn left and keep going until you hit a T-junction. From there, you turn right and continue until Route 413. Go left, and follow the road to Tsukui-ko Lake. Follow the signs for Sagamihara and Machida; if you go over the top of a dam, you're on the right road, just a few kilometers from Route 16.

Turn left at Route 16 and ride about half a kilometer. After going down an incline, turn right at the light under the highway and go straight toward Machida on the Machida Kaido. Well before you reach Machida, turn left onto the road that eventually becomes Setagaya Dori, and follow it back to the Tama-gawa River. From there, you'll know where to go.   ✍ JK

Tokyo Lake District

Route: A cycling path featuring fresh vegetables and the choice of one or two pristine lakes
Start and Goal: Harajuku Station (Yamanote Line) or Kichijoji Station (Chuo Line)

For those living on the western side of Tokyo, getting to Tama-ko and Sayama-ko lakes is easy and straightforward. The route is mostly flat, and the distance makes it a good day trip if you start early enough. Tama-ko is on the northern border of Tokyo, while Sayama-ko is just to the north in Saitama Prefecture . While you never really leave the greater metropolitan area until you get there, you're pretty much away from vehicular traffic

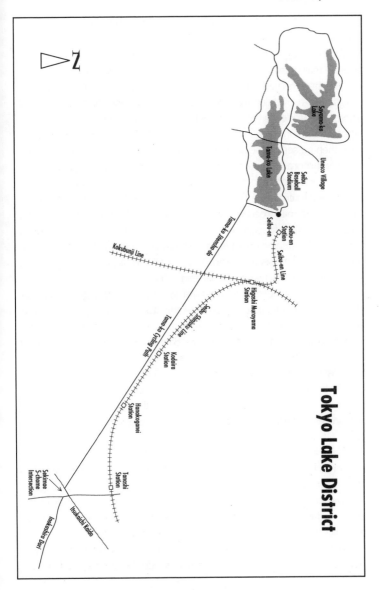

Tokyo Lake District

once you get out onto the Tama-ko Cycling Road about halfway out from Tokyo.

From Yoyogi-koen Park, which is as good a landmark as any in Tokyo, take the main road through the park, heading away from Harajuku Station. Go straight—this road becomes Inokashira Dori and runs pretty much in a straight line to Kichijoji (roughly in parallel to the Inokashira Line out of Shibuya), meandering west and slightly north through Uehara in Shibuya-ku, Kitazawa and Ohara in Setagaya-ku, and from Eifuku to Shoan in Suginami-ku. It then passes by the south side of Kichijoji Station, running straight for about four more kilometers before turning into the Tama-ko Cycling Road.

After you cross Kan-nana Dori, Inokashira Dori snakes right, then left and around to cross the Koshu Kaido. This is the only tricky part, but if you stick with the main road you won't get lost. On the other side of Koshu Kaido, it curves left again and then remains straight all the way through Mitaka and Musashino until it ends, running into Itsukaichi Kaido at the Seki-mae 5-chome intersection. From Yoyogi Park to this point is about fifteen kilometers; about halfway to the far end of the lake.

The traffic on Inokashira Dori is usually fairly heavy, though not unbearable. What is unbearable, though, are the stoplights that seem to come about every 50m on the Suginami-ku stretch. For this reason, you may want to bail out onto the Kanda-gawa Bikeway, which crosses Inokashira Dori just into Suginami-ku. This bikeway will take you to Inokashira-koen Park, just south of Kichijoji Station.

On the Kanda-gawa Bikeway, you'll have to deal with dogs and joggers and those closely spaced bars that keep cars off at the crossings. But it is a refreshing change from the red lights, taxis, and smoking trucks of Inokashira Dori.

Right after you cross Koshu Kaido (and under the #4 Expressway), Inokashira Dori turns left and goes down a hill. On the left is the headquarters of Sansui Audio. At the bottom of the hill is where the Kanda-gawa Bikeway crosses Inokashira Dori. The bikeway runs on both sides of the cemented-in river, and although there always seems to be construction going on, you can usually continue on one side or the other.

Until you get to Takaido Station, that is. Here, the path stops, and you have to cross Kam-pachi Dori. On the other side, the bikeway continues.

Until just before Mitakadai Station, that is. Here, the bikeway stops and you have to go left onto a side street, then right for about a block and a half until you get to a shopping street. Turn right, cross the tracks, and you'll find the entrance to the bikeway on your left. From here, the bikeway goes all the way into Inokashira-koen, a lovely park complete with tree-lined paths and a pond. Here you can check your gear, get your bearings, and even have a picnic lunch before you go back out to Inokashira Dori and head west. If you want to continue riding, exit the north side of the park to Inokashira Dori, go left, and ride about four kilometers to the huge Itsukaichi Kaido intersection—on one corner there's a Red Lobster restaurant with a small parking lot especially for bicycles—a nice touch. Cross Itsukaichi Kaido and continue in the same direction and you'll find the start of the Tama-ko Cycling Road, with a sign in both Japanese and English.

When it's not crowded, the trail is a good ride, free of auto traffic except at its many crossings. Should you be out on the weekend in good weather, however, you may find the constant rush of bicycles, dogs, and joggers coming from every direction every bit as stressful as Inokashira Dori. In approximately three kilometers, the bicycle path will become elevated on one side and you will go past a series of reservoirs. There is also a parallel bicycle path on the other side of the road for those people who prefer to ride at ground level. After the reservoirs, you will cross a major intersection and the bike path will cease to run parallel to the roadway.

After crossing the intersection, you will need to look for signs marking the continuation of the bike path, which begins to wander through suburbs and farmland. Along this section you can find farmers selling vegetables from stands along the bike path. At some places, you will see farmers harvesting vegetables that will be sold moments later. We saw cabbage, broccoli, spinach, carrots, and green onions at several stands. For the best selection, arrive early in the day, or on Sunday. If the attractions of a fresh salad become too great, you can always leave the bike path at Hanakoganei Station on the Seibu Shinjuku Line, where you can bag your bike (and your fresh vegetables) and jump on a train.

Continuing in a straight line, slightly uphill, the Tama-ko Cycling Road reaches the edge of Tama-ko Lake after about ten kilometers. While the cycling road continues to the left along the south side of the lake, go to the right and head uphill to the north shore. After you pass Seibu Yuen, a massive amusement park, on your right, you'll find yourself riding along with the lake to your left, and the Seibu-en Golf Course on your right.

A few kilometers later you'll pass by the Seibu Lions Baseball Stadium, and by the time you've started to wonder just how much of this area is under the control of the Seibu empire, you'll find yourself at the foot of the land bridge that bisects Tama-ko Lake. Turn right away from the water, then take the first left—about a half kilometer along you'll have Tama-ko Lake on your left and Sayama-ko Lake on your right. Turn right onto a narrow road and continue north, with the west side of Sayama-ko to your left and to your right Unesco Village, a unique park featuring models of houses from each country represented in the United Nations.

Just past Unesco village, bear left off the road onto a trail that takes you over the dam. On the other side the trail connects back up with a road that follows the north shore of the lake. While the scenery isn't exactly splendid along the shore of either lake, it's reasonably pleasant if the water level is high enough.

After you leave the north side of the lake, the road heads away from the shore and goes up a short grade, then curves around to follow loosely the perimeter of the lake, with a few ups and downs before passing the south end of Sayama-ko and returning to the foot of the land bridge that bisects Tama-ko.

From here, go right and head southward across to the other side of Tama-ko. On the other side, take the first left and breeze down this nicely wooded winding road which eventually joins up with the cycling road. If traffic is light, stay on the main road and enjoy this smooth run until the road finishes at the next major intersection. From here, go right and follow the Tama-ko Cycling Road, retracing the route back to Tokyo.   ✍ BH

Kanto Weekend Getaways 🚲🚲🚲🚲🚲🚲🚲🚲🚲

The Chichibu Trail 🚲

Route: Hills and river provide a constant backdrop for a circular route around the Chichibu area
Start: Chichibu Station (Seibu Ikebukuro-Chichibu Line from Ikebukuro)
Goal: Chichibu or Mitsumineguchi stations (Seibu Chichibu Line)

Only eighty minutes by train from Tokyo, the Chichibu region is still relatively rural and underpopulated. The area forms a basin surrounded by low hills, which are at best in May and November. Chichibu is popular with hikers, but it is also rich in culture and history. Many come to see its shrines and temples, some to walk the pilgrimage of its thirty-four Kannon temples.

Traditions are still strong in the area and it is said that you can find a festival on any given day of the year. Full details can be found in Sumiko Enbutsu's English guide, *Chichibu: Japan's Hidden Treasure,* on sale in shops near Seibu Chichibu Station and in the nearby Mokutei coffee shop.

Running through the region is the Ara-kawa River and a main road, Route 140. There are numerous minor roads radiating into the hills, which often pass through beautiful valleys, but these generally involve very steep climbs and don't always lead anywhere; good training for a triathlon, but not recommended for day trips. Certain areas—notably Nagatoro—are major tourist centers for the Kanto region and attract heavy traffic on Sundays. On weekdays, meanwhile, cyclists face the hazard of truck convoys shifting massive quantities of gravel from the many pits in the area.

However, most of the minor roads are little-used and make for quite easy cycling. If you follow a circular course without straying too far from the river basin, you can gain a good impression of the area, with the hills and the river as a constant backdrop but without any really back-breaking climbs. The following course, totalling about seventy kilometers in all, can be easily shortened by those with less time or energy.

The best way into Chichibu is by the Seibu Red Arrow Special Express (*tokkyu*), which takes you from Seibu Ikebukuro Station to Seibu Chichibu Station in eighty minutes. All seats are reserved and you must book in advance if traveling on a Saturday or Sunday.

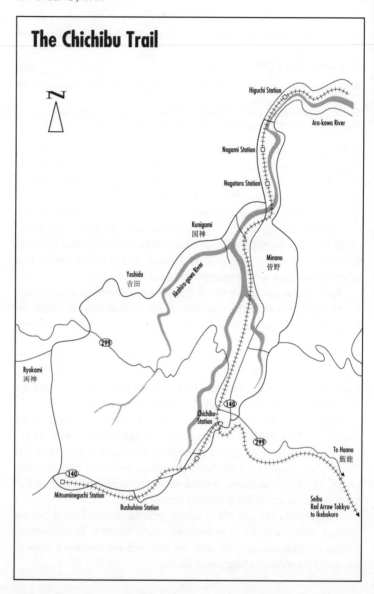

The Chichibu Trail

Coming out of Seibu Chichibu Station, go straight ahead a hundred meters to Route 140 and turn left. Turn right on the fourth street on the right, which takes you past the excellent coffee shop, Chako, and onto Route 299, the main road to Hanno. After 200m on 299, turn left at the Cosmo gas station. Go straight on for four kilometers, then turn right at Takashina primary school. Go through one set of lights, then turn left after a few hundred meters. The road is signposted to Minano. Passing temple No. 1 (known to all as *Ichiban*), continue over Sonezaka-toge Pass (the steepest climb on this route) and down into Misawa valley.

This road eventually comes out on Route 140, but about 700m before you get to it, turn right for Nagatoro. This is not signposted, but there is a sake shop just after the turn. After about two kilometers you come to a tunnel; don't go through it but around it for good views of the Nagatoro Gorge. Continue for another two kilometers past Hozen-ji Temple on the right, then turn left for Nogami Station, crossing the Ara-kawa River. Just after the bridge, turn left to follow the gorge back down the other side, past the Seibu Nagatoro Hotel and on to Naga-toro Station.

Nagatoro makes a good lunch stop. Choseikan Hotel has a coffee lounge overlooking the gorge. Within one kilometer of the station there are several museums, and the impressive Hodo-san Jinja, one of the Three Chichibu Shrines. You can also boat down the rapids or take a cable car to the top of Mt. Hodo.

Continue alongside the Ara-kawa back toward Chichibu, on the opposite side of the tracks from Route 140. This takes you past the Prefectural Natural History Museum on the right. Follow this road until, passing under the railway, it comes out on 140 before Oyabanashi. Cross over 140, past a massive pachinko parlor on the left, and follow this road 1.5 kilometers until it comes out on Route 54 at Kunigami. Turn right and continue on 54 for Yoshida-machi. Take care after 1.5 kilometers, where there is a fork in the road. Take the right fork, going uphill to stay on 54, which follows the Akabira-gawa River and then the Yoshida-gawa River on to Kami-Yoshida.

There are several roads leading off to the left which take you back to Chichibu by a shorter loop via Route 299. To complete the longer loop, however, continue through Yoshida-machi, turn left at Kami-Yoshida

Chuzaisho, and head for Ryokami-mura, still on Route 54. This takes you through Ryokami and down to Route 140 at Mitsumine-guchi. The fastest way back to Chichibu is straight down 140, but much of the main road can be avoided by turning right (away from Chichibu) and then immediately left over the bridge to Mitsumineguchi Station. On this side of the river you can go as far as Bushu-Hino, where you have to come out on 140 again, but after less than a kilometer, a right fork takes you past Kagemori Station and back to the main road just before Seibu Chichibu Station.

A final stop could be the Mokutei coffee shop, on the right just before Goho Supermarket about a hundred meters before the turnoff to the station. Mokutei often has small exhibitions of local crafts. There is also plenty to see in the town of Chichibu. Recommended are the Chichibu Matsuri Kaikan, which houses the floats for the famous Chichibu Night Festival (December 3), and the nearby Kato Art Museum, which has a small collection of paintings by Andrew Wyeth. ✍ RN

❶ Field Information
Rental bikes are available in Nagatoro
Chichibu Ryokan Association ☎ 0494 24-7538
Seibu Tourist Information ☎ 0494 24-8181
Nagatoro Tourist Information ☎ 0494 66-0307
Minano Tourist Information ☎ 0494 62-1230

⌂ Lodging log
Yoshida: Azami-so ☎ 0494 77-0096; Kaoru-so ☎ 0494 78-0311

Chasing the Breeze

Route: A refreshing eighty-kilometer coastal route round the Miura-hanto Peninsula
Start: Mabori Kaigan Station (Keihin Kyuko Line)
Goal: Katase Enoshima Station (Odakyu Line)

The perfect elixir for landlocked cyclists struck with an unending desire to see the sea can be found at Miura-hanto Peninsula just an hour and a half away from the center of Tokyo. Relaxing and refreshing, the route is an ideal two-day ride with an overnight stay recommended on Jogashima Island on the far west tip. Overall, the terrain is flat to gently rolling, making the route possible in one day, even for first-time cyclists.

From Shinagawa Station take a *kaisoku-tokkyu* express train on the

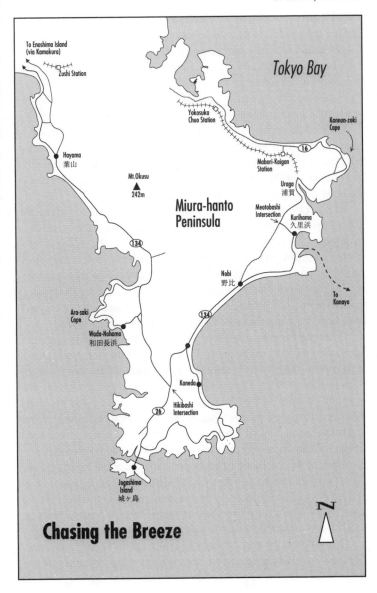

To Enoshima Island
(via Kamakura)

Zushi Station

Tokyo Bay

Yokosuka
Chuo Station

Kannon-zaki
Cape

Hayama
葉山

Mt.Okusu
▲
242m

Mabori-Kaigan
Station

16

Miura-hanto
Peninsula

Uraga
浦賀

Meotobashi
Intersection

Kurihama
久里浜

134

Nobi
野比

Ara-saki
Cape

To
Kanaya

Wada-Nahama
和田長浜

134

Kaneda

26

Hikibashi
Intersection

Jogashima
Island
城ヶ島

N

Chasing the Breeze

Keihin Kyuko Line bound for Misakiguchi Station. At Yokosuka Chuo Station, change to a local train bound for Uraga and get off at Mabori-Kaigan Station. From the station head through the residential area toward the ocean. Turn right onto Route 16; go up a long, gentle hill and then breeze down a steep slope to Kannon-zaki, the Cape of the Goddess of Mercy, where there is a quiet park. Watch out for stray fish hooks on the road as this area is popular with anglers throughout the year.

On the way to the cape, you'll pass the Kannon-zaki Keikyu Hotel, a pleasant place for a break. In the hotel cafe, sip an iced coffee while gazing out of the huge window overlooking the ocean and (in clear weather) the mountains of the Boso-hanto Peninsula on the opposite side of the bay. In the hotel lobby, don't miss the unusual, giant music-box.

At Kannon-zaki, there is a hiking path, a small natural history museum, and a 56m-high lighthouse which offers stunning views of the ocean for a small fee.

From the park, go back to the road and through the Kannon-zaki tunnel. After the Kannon-zaki Ohashi Bridge, turn left at the T-junction and then right at the fork at Kamoi, heading toward Uraga, a former shipbuilding town. In front of Uraga Station, turn left at the T-junction; on your left you'll see a huge, desolate shipyard, a great location for a music video.

Cross the Hirasaku-gawa River by the Meoto-bashi Bridge and turn left toward the port of Kurihama. Turning right at the port, you'll pass a small park on the right commemorating the arrival of Perry and the black ships to request trading agreements, one of the pressures causing the eventual collapse of the Tokugawa shogunate. Stop by at the small museum in the park to check out all these historical happenings at the end of the last century. At the far end of Kurihama is a ferry terminal from where you can catch a ferry to Kanaya on the Boso-hanto Peninsula.

After the three red-and-white-striped chimneys of the thermal power plant, the road starts to turn gently uphill. Go through Sendagasaki Tunnel at the top and then simply enjoy the breathtaking descent to the stunning coast below. This stretch from here to Nobi-Kaigan, a peaceful, relaxing beach, is one of the most beautiful parts of the route.

On the right at the start of Nobi-Kaigan is one of my favorite restaurants, Compass Point, which has a great balcony overlooking the ocean where you can enjoy a light lunch of their special pasta or scones. Their herb tea is specially recommended for cyclists feeling the effects of sedentary life.

After Nobi-Kaigan turn left at the T-junction onto Route 134 and head for the Miura-kaigan coast, one of the most famous (and crowded) areas of the peninsula. Try going in the off-season when the students are at school and the beach is quiet. Take the middle fork at the end of Miura-kaigan and ride through cabbage fields to Jogashima Island. Cross the Hikibashi intersection onto Route 26 and after the sign turn left to cross Jogashima Ohashi Bridge over to Jogashima.

If you have time, though, I would recommend that you take the left fork at the end of Miura-kaigan. The road is a bit hilly at times, although the coastal views are better. At Kaneda Port, a market (*asaichi*) is held every Sunday morning around 5:30, where you can get fresh fruit and vegetables at prices you never dreamt possible. After Kaneda the road goes inland; pass the Mitsubishi gas station and turn left. Left again at the next junction will take you to Tsurugi-zaki, the very southeast tip of the peninsula where anglers jostle for space and the chance to land the big one. The view of the rugged shore is impressive, so take a breather and watch the battle between the anglers and the sea bream. From Tsuruga-zaki it's easy to get back on the main road that takes you back to Jogashima Ohashi.

On the east side of Jogashima Island there is a picturesque park at the cape with a hiking course that takes about an hour and a half to walk around. In winter it's possible to watch cormorants from the observation tower. Try dinner at any of the excellent restaurants on the island which all serve some kind of fish including *maguro suteki* (broiled tuna) and *maguro-don* (raw tuna served on rice). To work up an appetite, have a look at Misaki Fish Market, one of the largest tuna markets in Japan.

The following day, go back onto Route 26 and then turn right onto Route 134 at Hikibashi intersection, heading up the west coast toward Hayama. Go past Misakiguchi Station and turn left, following the signs to Wada Nahama Kaisui-yokujo Iriguchi, the entrance to Wada-Nahama Beach, one of the quieter beaches on the Miura-hanto, with good white sand and warm water. If your steed is a mountain bike, ride along the shore to Ara-saki, a cape with impressive beaches and unusual rock formations.

Say good-bye to Wada-Nahama beach and go back onto Route 134. After a while, you'll be enjoying ocean views again. Watch out for a small sign on your left advertising Plage Sud. A small, comfortable cafe, Plage Sud is actually located in the middle of the cliff. The menu is not so memorable, but what is really fantastic is the stunning view of Sagami-wan Bay from the huge window.

Continuing on Route 134, cross the Shimoyama-gawa River, from where you can see the Emperor's walled-in villa on your left. Turn left toward Kamakura, and Hayama, a well-established coastal resort town; beaches from here along the coastline are known as Shonan. For Japanese youngsters, Shonan is a small-scale version of the coastline of Southern California or the Gold Coast. Those interested in marine sports should check out some of the rental shops in the area. There are great ocean views and a lot of fancy restaurants, shops, and hotels along Route 134, and, if you're lucky, you can see Mt. Fuji on a fine day.

No more time or energy? Just turn right at Zushi Kaigan and take the JR Yokosuka Line from Zushi Station back to Tokyo. On the other hand, if you intend to explore Kamakura, the home of Japan's first military government (1183–1333), Zushi offers far cheaper restaurants and accommodation. Hirako Cycle, a pro bike shop near Zushi Station, is one of the best bike shops on the peninsula.

At the Namerikawa intersection, turn right for the center of Kamakura. But if you want the scent of sea breezes and the sound of the waves, go straight toward Shichirigahama, a relatively quiet beach popular with surfers. When you see the train tracks of the Enoden Line running alongside Route 134, you'll know you're at Shichirigahama.

The final destination is Enoshima Island. Cross Enoshima Ohashi Bridge and dismount to have a look round the island. There is an observation tower with a great view of Mt. Fuji and Oshima Island on a clear day. Enoshima-jinja, a shrine famous for its nude statue of the Goddess Benten, can be reached by steps or (if the peninsula route has really finished you off) by escalator. There's not a lot to see on Enoshima Island, but a handful of craft shops and some old *chamise* (tea houses) are fun to stop by.

To get back to Tokyo, take the Odaku Line *tokkyu* express (cheaper than the Romance Car) from Katase Enoshima Station, located just across the river from the end of the Enoshima Ohashi Bridge. ✍ KL

❶ Field Information
Miura Minshuku Information (for reservations on Jogashima and Miura-kaigan area) ☎ 0468 88-5152
Perry Memorial Museum ☎ 0468 34-7531
Compass Point ☎ 0468 49-6264
Plage Sud ☎ 0468 57-4441, 4676
Hirako Cycle ☎ 0468 73-5000

⚓ Lodging Log
Kannon-zaki Keikyu Hotel ☎ 0468 41-2200
Jogashima Youth Hostel ☎ 0468 81-3893

Cruising Izu

Route: Picturesque views of Mt. Fuji across Suruga-wan Bay and exhilarating scenery along a coastal route from Numazu in northern Izu to Toi and then an inland road through the hills to the hot springs of Shuzenji, giving a hint of charms to follow further south
Start: Numazu Station (shinkansen to Mishima, change to Tokaido Honsen Line)
Goal: Shuzenji Station (Izu Hakone Line to Mishima)

The Izu-hanto Peninsula is close to Tokyo yet still full of undeveloped places. Avoid weekends and summer vacation, of course, and the east coast altogether if you dislike cars and crowds. The Izu experience is best enjoyed in three or more days, but from Tokyo or the Nagoya area it is possible to savor the flavor of Izu in just two days, just long enough to give you ideas for a longer trip. Take the shinkansen to Mishima. The Hikari #291 (quicker than the Kodama train) leaving Tokyo at 8:24 A.M. arrives in Mishima at 9:08 A.M. Riding from Mishima to Numazu on the coast is no great shakes; instead, change trains at Mishima and get off at Numazu. From Numazu south on Route 414 isn't very scenic, but when you go through the big Tabi Tunnel about eight kilometers down and turn left onto the coast highway, it becomes so distractingly beautiful that you'll soon forget what came before.

There is a bit of up and down on the road toward Heda and Toi, but the interesting views of Mt. Fuji across Suruga-wan Bay more than compensate for any hardship. Cherry blossoms were scattering across the road

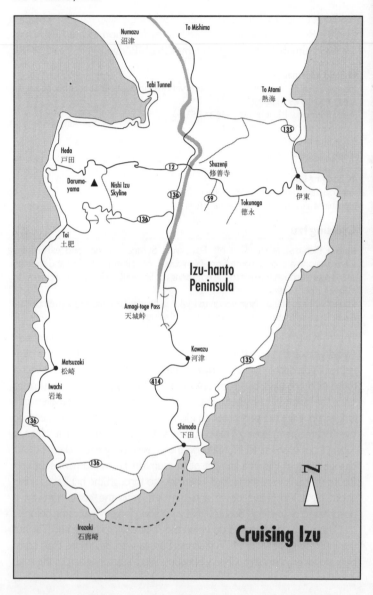

Numazu
沼津

To Mishima

Tabi Tunnel

To Atami
熱海

135

Heda
戸田

Shuzenji
修善寺

12

Daruma-
yama

Nishi Izu
Skyline

136

59

Tokunaga
徳永

Ito
伊東

136

Toi
土肥

Izu-hanto
Peninsula

Amagi-toge Pass
天城峠

Kawazu
河津

135

Matsuzaki
松崎

414

Iwachi
岩地

136

Shimoda
下田

136

Irozaki
石廊崎

Cruising Izu

N

in the breeze when we went last April, but it's nice all year round, apart from when it's raining. For a weekend trip, Toi Onsen, with its plentiful *min-shuku*, about sixty kilometers from Numazu, is the ideal stopping place for a long, hot soak in an open-air bath and a few beers.

The next day we took Route 136 inland to Shuzenji. The road goes along a river, then starts climbing. At one point you can go right onto a new road with tunnels (to avoid some uphill), or go left and take the less-traveled old road with a very gradual grade. Go left—the little extra climbing is well worth it. When you get to the entrance of the Skyline road (bicycles not permitted), you're at the top, and it's pretty much downhill or flat to Shuzenji. We found a great soba shop for lunch—it's a new Japanese-style place on your right past a couple of touristy looking places, and well worth looking for.

At Shuzenji, take a local train up to Mishima, or the Odoriko Express for Tokyo or Shinjuku. Though we didn't have time, the ride to Mishima would have been pretty nice. An alternative is to visit the Japan Cycle Sports Center, a sports complex with a variety of cycling courses (see page 260).   ✍ BH

↪ Three Days in Izu

With a long weekend to hand, Izu can provide some great scenic experiences. One day last August, some friends and I set off from Ito on the east coast (Odoriko Express from Tokyo Station, or 25 minutes on the JR Ito Line from Atami on JR Tokaido Shinkansen Line) on an epic trip around the Izu-hanto. Heading across land on Route 12, we went through Shuzenji and started the long hard climb (at least thirty minutes) up to Heda-toge Pass and the testy Daruma-yama. Before the descent into Heda, the big event of the day was the discovery of a spring right on the roadside which was rigged so that icy water flowed through green bamboo, with little bamboo cups set on a platform directly below. Several motorists were enjoying the water, but I doubt they could possibly enjoy it as much as we did after the long, steady climbing in the August heat.

Heda, a small fishing port on the western side, is really a quaint town, and special to me as my father-in-law's birthplace. We stopped at a relative's house for a few liters of *mugicha*. From Heda the route winds its way south, hugging the cliffs directly above the ocean. We weren't the only cyclists on the road—on one hill we met a fellow on a heavily laden bike who told us he was on his way round Japan and to prove it , he presented us with a pair of souvenir *geta* from Hokkaido inscribed with "Abashiri Prison."

In Toi, more relatives and more *mugicha*. And, another stop impossible to pass up: my all-time favorite coffee shop, Lennon, with its funky interior and good selection of food. You'll find Lennon in the building next to a gas station right before the main road south crosses a river.

After the caffeine, it was on again, though by now we'd been riding most of the day and we were a little fatigued. Our goal was the town of Iwachi, in the south of Izu, next to Matsuzaki. Somehow or other, we made it with enough daylight left for me to greet the poor penguin someone keeps as a pet in Iwachi. After a dip in the nice, cool ocean, we were quite lucky to find an inn, the friendly Yama-san, despite the summer crowds.

The clean white sand beach and reefs at Iwachi are exquisite, so much so that the three of us considered abandoning our plans and spending the rest of our short vacation right there. We rented a rowboat and swam quite a bit, although our pleasure was subdued somewhat by all the garbage we collected that had been left behind by other visitors. (I've come to feel that blatant garbage-gathering is the best way to jolt people's complacency about litter; a positive way for foreigners to "stand out.")

Other attractions worth visiting in the area, if you have time, are the Chohachi Art Museum in Matsuzaki, containing works by Irie Chohachi and others, and the Hakatsuzaki monkey sanctuary south of Matsuzaki, which is interesting and not too far off the main road.

Somewhat reluctantly, we started out post-noon to ride down to the southernmost tip, Isozaki, where we cheated and boarded a boat for Shimoda, saving about fourteen kilometers. From Shimoda, we headed north to Kawazu and made it to the Amagi Harris Court Youth Hostel by 6:00 P.M.

Another late start the next morning, only to stop several kilometers down the road in Nanadaru, at Amagi-so, my favorite *onsen*, along a river with a great waterfall. We were the only bathers, but there were a few observers that day, curious to see crazy cyclists jumping straight into the icy river rather than soaking in the hot water.

I hadn't climbed Amagi since high school, and it brought back memories, giving me lots to occupy my mind on the long climb up to the pass. On downhills or on the level stretches, it was easy enough to look at the scenery, or sing old songs. On uphills, it was sometimes an effort just to breathe . . . After the pass, we stopped for some soba at Joren no Taki, a tourist spot with a lovely waterfall. For dessert there was a very long downhill. Taking one of the older, less traveled roads back toward Shuzenji proved to be a wise decision: although some of the older roads are steeper than the more recent routes, our last day provided us with some of the most breathtaking scenery of the whole tour. ✍JI

❶ Field Info
Numazu Tourist Information ☎ 0559 34-2868
Toi Onsen Minshuku Association ☎ 0558 98-1152
Lennon Coffee Shop ☎ 0558 98-1790
Heda Tourist Information Center ☎ 0558 94-3115
Matsuzaki and Iwachi Tourist Information ☎ 0558 42-0745
Shimoda Minshuku Association ☎ 0558 22-8424
Kawazu Tourist Information ☎ 0558 32-0290

⌂ Lodging Log
Iwachi: Yama-san ☎ 0558 45-0036
Kawazui Amagi Amagi Harris Court Youth Hostel ☎ 0558 35-7253
Nanadaru: Amagi-so ☎ 0558 35-7711
Shuzenji: Japan Cycle Sports Center ☎ 0558 79-0001 (see p. 260); Kajika -so ☎ 0558 72-0357; Tsuyuki ☎ 0558 72-2100

Fuji Five Lakes

Route: Some fine cycling around several lakes in the foothills of Mt. Fuji, topped off with stunning downhills to Kofu and Yamanashi wine country.
Start: Fuji Yoshida or Kawaguchi-ko stations (Fujikyu Line from Otsuki Station on JR Chuo Line)
Goal: Kofu Station (JR Chuo Line)

Visiting cycle tourists often talk about wanting to "ride up Mt. Fuji." The reality, however, is that the road only goes halfway up, the trail is steep and treacherous even for mountain bikes, and the view from the top is often obscured by clouds, while the trail vicinity is often obscured by litter. The closer one gets to Mt. Fuji, the less beautiful it seems, becoming a mere mass of dirt and rock.

Mt. Fuji looks far better from a distance. What's more, the stark ruggedness of the mountain is fortunately broken up by a series of five distinctly different lakes on its north and east sides which provide excellent

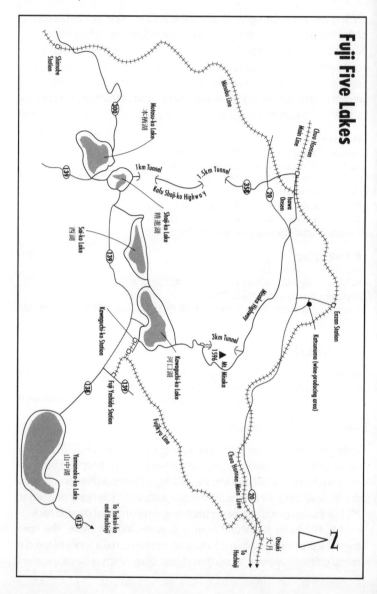

Fuji Five Lakes

Shimobe Station

Minobu Line

Chuo Honsen Main Line

300

Motosu-ko Lake 本栖湖

139

1km Tunnel

1.5km Tunnel

Kofu Shoji-ko Highway

358

20

Isawa Onsen

Shoji-ko Lake 精進湖

Sai-ko Lake 西湖

139

Kawaguchi-ko Station

Misaka Highway

Enzan Station

Katsunuma (wine-producing area)

3km Tunnel

1596 ▲ Mt. Misaka

Kawaguchi-ko Lake 河口湖

139

Fuji Yoshida Station

138

Fujikyu Line

Chuo Honsen Main Line

20

Yamanaka-ko Lake 山中湖

To Tsukui-ko and Hachioji

413

Otsuki 大月

To Hachioji

N

riding around their perimeter. If you have dreams of scaling Mt. Fuji on your bike, keep them in mind while enjoying a relaxing ride around one or all of the Fuji Five Lakes.

Yamanaka-ko Lake, the largest, is within a hard day's ride from Tokyo, naturally most of it uphill. For those so inclined, take the Koshu Kaido from Shinjuku, through Hachioji to Sagami-ko Lake. Go left on Route 412, which runs along the east side of the lake then goes over a hill into the town of Tsukui. About six kilometers past the lake, turn right onto Route 413, also known as the Doshi Kaido.

This road goes uphill for over forty kilometers, with a few downhills here and there, the most notable a long, sizzling downhill to a bridge over the Doshi-gawa River. After you cross the river, the road gets steeper as it climbs back up through the canyon, turning into a steady climb through a series of straight sections, each of which gives you the impression that the pass is just around the bend. It isn't, so keep riding. When the road gets steeper again, and the curves become tighter, Yamabushi-toge Pass (through a short tunnel) is near. After the pass, the road takes a long, slow landing into the Yamanaka basin.

After reading this description, you may decide to take in the Doshi Kaido on the way back to Tokyo and, of course, this makes for a particularly fast return. I once rode this route, taking only four hours from Yamanaka-ko Lake to Shibuya via Sagamihara, Machida, and Setagaya Dori.

To get to the lakes by train, take the Chuo Line from Shinjuku to Otsuki (about one hour by express), then change to the Fujikyu Line for Kawaguchi-ko Station (about one hour) at Kawaguchi-ko Lake. (There are also a few direct trains from Shinjuku and Tokyo stations each day.)

If you're planning to ride around Yamanaka-ko Lake, get off at Fuji Yoshida, two stations before Kawaguchi-ko, and take Route 139, then Route 138 about ten kilometers southeast to the northwest edge.

In order to stay closest to the water, you will want to ride around these lakes in a counterclockwise direction, as traffic travels on the left. Also realize that each lake is unique in terms of size, road configuration, and character, so you might want to skip a few. There are places to stay at all the lakes and, depending on your schedule, you might want to stay one or two nights in the area. You may also wish to head down to the Kofu area via the Kofu–Shoji-ko or Misaka-toge Pass highways (see page 121), both of which offer fast, hair-raising downhill stretches.

⇨ Yamanaka-ko Lake

Yamanaka-ko is the largest, and its proximity to both the Tomei and Chuo expressways makes it the most touristy, although Kawaguchi-ko runs a close second, being the second largest and right at the end of the Chuo Expressway. The road around Yamanaka-ko is largely flat and straight, and since the lake is almost oval-shaped, the distance around is about the same as Kawaguchi-ko: a bit under twenty kilometers. A bike trail follows the water's edge around most of the lake, but the proliferation of unsteady riders on rental bikes and tandems makes it somewhat of an obstacle course on weekends. There's a small climb through a heavily forested area on the north shore, but it's over before you know it. Since this lake has the most traffic around its shores, and it's set apart from the other four lakes, it's the one to avoid if you don't have time to cycle all five.

❶ Field Information
Fuji Yoshida Minshuku Association ☎ 0555 23-7514
Yamanaka-ko Tourist Information ☎ 0555 62-3100

⌂ Lodging Log
Cottage Nu (Fuji Yoshida) ☎ 0555 23-7514
Lake Yamanaka-ko Inn ☎ 0555 62-0218

⇨ Kawaguchi-ko Lake

Kawaguchi-ko is intensely touristed, with gift shop after big hotel after restaurant along the lower half of its eastern shore. There's even a bridge across a corner of the lake, so take it if you decide to loop the lake a second time. From Kawaguchi-ko Station, go north on Route 137. A few kilometers after it leaves the shore, turn left at Oishi and you'll soon be back along the lake. (Or, go straight for Kofu via Misaka-toge Pass, detailed later.)

Although this stretch is a ways above the water, it is the nicest part of the lake, continuing on for about eight kilometers. A little over halfway is a small coffee shop that simply announces "Food Drink" in English on a small sign. The food may not be better than the big touristy places, but the atmosphere is a lot nicer. I had a good-sized salad and a large plate of spaghetti, while enjoying some great jazz music and a panoramic view of the lake.

❸ Field Information
Kawaguchi-ko Tourist Information ☎ 0555 72-2460
Kawaguchi-ko Minshuku Association ☎ 0555 76-6400

♠ Lodging Log
Petit Hotel Ebisuya ☎ 0555 72-0165
Hotel Sunnyside Village ☎ 0555 76-6004

⇨ Sai-ko Lake

At the junction at the west end of Kawaguchi-ko you can go on to Sai-ko, or turn left to continue around the southern half of the lake. It's a nice ride, but you can do this stretch on the way back to Kawaguchi-ko Station if you plan to return from there. On the south shore, the road forks at the Hotel Yesterday; turn left to stay on the lake's edge. Total distance around the lake (if you don't take the bridge) is nineteen kilometers.

Sai-ko is smaller and a bit more beautiful, but only ten kilometers around. From Kawaguchi-ko, go over a low hill and you'll soon be on its eastern edge. Go straight, past a heavily treed trailer park (of all things!) and enjoy the winding but flat road. After a small bridge you'll see a gas station in which the pumps have been replaced by vending machines (this no doubt creates interesting thoughts in the minds of cyclists); turn left and continue along for several kilometers until the road rejoins the shore. When you come back to where you started, ride the north shore again—it's worth it—but go straight past the "vending station" and over a gradual hill. About three kilometers later you'll be at the eastern edge of Shoji-ko Lake.

❸ Field Information
Sai-ko Minshuku Association ☎ 0555 82-2148

⇨ Shoji-ko Lake

Shoji-ko is the smallest lake by far and best characterized as a large pond. It's also the most deserted. It's only a few kilometers around, the exact figure doesn't matter because you'll circle it before you know it. On the north side, take the turnoff on the left near a large "family restaurant" to continue around the lake. (Or, go straight for Kofu via the astonishing downhill stretches of the Kofu–Shoji-ko Highway, detailed later.)

The road leaves the shore on the peninsula on the southwest side, tucks through a little tunnel, then continues on to Route 139. You could go left at the junction to finish the Shoji-ko circle, but it never goes near the water and the distance is too short to bother. Instead, turn right and head for Motosu-ko Lake about three more kilometers down Route 139. Don't miss the turnoff on the right, just past the striking sight of two old thatched-roof buildings.

❶ Field information
Shoji-ko Tourist Information ☎ 0555 87-2321

⌂ Lodging Log
Minshuku Fumito Shoji-ko (also has good rental bikes) ☎ 0555 87-2215

➪ Motosu-ko Lake

Motosu-ko Lake somehow reminds me of a miniature version of Shikotsu-ko Lake in Hokkaido. Steep mountainsides plunge down to meet the lake, with a flat road hugging the shore. There's also a deserted feeling, like at Sai-ko Lake, in spite of the increased activity. Best of all, there's some real distance around the lake, a little over twelve kilometers of very pleasant riding, with none of the strenuous grades that usually accompany mountain scenery.

On reaching the northeast edge of Motosu-ko, turn right onto Route 300 and go straight with the lake to your left, and pass through a short tunnel that features a nice walkway, although traffic is so light you may want to just stay on the road. At the northwest edge of the lake, turn left just before the long tunnel to continue around the lake. There's a nice rest area here with picnic tables, making it ideal for a lunch break. From here, the road follows the shore closely, becoming narrower with sharper curves. As you roll along the downhill stretches, use the road mirrors to avoid any oncoming surprises. The road later straightens out and widens near what is called a motorboat research center, where there's a large complex on the right and a lot of little speedboats on the waterfront to your left. Further along, just past the totem-poled campground, the road narrows again as it curves around the jagged shore under a thick canopy of trees. As you move around to the other side of the lake, you'll notice a proliferation of little rowboats for fishermen. The scene is so perfect it makes you want to trade in your wheels for a fishing rod.

Back at the junction, you can turn back toward Kawaguchi-ko or turn left to retrace your route around the lake and stay on Route 300 for a wild, downhill ride into the hot-spring town of Shimobe. From Shimobe Station, you can take the Minobu Line south (seventy minutes by express) to Fuji Station on the Tokaido Line, or north (forty-five minutes by express) to Kofu Station on the Chuo Line.

❶ Field Information
Shimobe Tourist Information ☎ 0556 36-1616
Kamabitai Minshuku Association (10 km west of Motosu-ko) ☎ 0556 38-0201

➪ The Roads Down to Kofu

From the Fuji Five Lakes area, the broad plain centering around Kofu can be reached easily by two different routes, the Misaka-toge Pass Highway and the Kofu–Shoji-ko Highway, both offering spectacular downhill stretches.

To get onto the Misaka-toge Pass Highway, from the north end of Kawaguchi-ko, stay on Route 137 northbound. The road climbs up a stiff grade for about five kilometers, then levels out onto a toll road that quickly plunges into a three-kilometer tunnel. The shoulder is very narrow, so you'll want to have good lights for this one. (If you want to avoid paying the ¥30 toll charged for bicycles, you may continue climbing for another eight kilometers or so to go over Misaka-toge on a road that is said to be narrow and poorly paved in stretches.) Once out of the tunnel, pay your toll and prepare to enjoy a wild, swooping downhill with gentle curves for the next ten kilometers. Continue on straight, under the Chuo Expressway, to reach Route 20. Turn right for the prefectural seat of Kofu, or left for the wine country of Katsunuma.

The Kofu–Shoji-ko highway is even easier because there is no climbing as you leave the north side of Shoji-ko. Just enter the one-kilometer tunnel and enjoy a long, spectacular downhill to the toll booth, where bicycles are charged ¥30. Several kilometers later, the road climbs a bit and then levels and continues through a 1.5-kilometer tunnel. After the tunnel, there are several more kilometers of downhill riding to the next toll booth, where you'll have to put out another ¥30. You'll soon pass through Nakamichi and, after going under the Chuo Expressway, the road heads straight into Kofu. Before you reach the city center, you may want to turn right on Route 20 to head for Isawa Onsen, followed by the wine country of Katsunuma.   🖎 BH

🏠 **Lodging Log**
Kofu: Higashi Yanagi-ya ☎ 0552 35-3731; Sansui-kan ☎ 0552 52-8541
For information on Katsunuma lodgings, see page 127.

Yamanashi Wine Country

Route: A meander around a major wine-producing area with visits to one or several wineries and afterward to Oku Tama-ko Lake via the scenic Tamba Gorge.
Start: Katsunuma Budo Kyo Station (Chuo Line)
Goal: Ome Station (Ome Line—for central Tokyo take the Ome Line to Tachikawa and change to the Chuo Line)

Universally, the most romantic vision of a bike tour involves a carefree ride through rolling hills with lunch out of the proverbial picnic basket, washed down with a good bottle of wine. Those who take wine even halfway seriously have extrapolated this scenario, even in daydreams, into the great wine regions of France and possibly even the Napa and Sonoma valleys of California. The tour actually occurs within a fine wine glass, enjoyed in a series of grand tasting rooms, all connected by hazy memories of having ridden a bicycle between them.

Those considering a similar type of laid-back tour in Japan could possibly direct themselves to a route of sake breweries, but the romanticism just doesn't seem to carry over. Nor does the reality, where sake is produced nearly everywhere, and informal drop-in tasting bars are a rarity.

Just as Japan has insurmountable difficulties in re-creating the great wines of the world, cycle tourists will have a hard time re-creating the scenario for a great wine tour. For those not willing to give up so easily, however, salvation is at hand in the form of a tour round the wine country of Yamanashi.

Yes, "wine regions" do exist in Japan, although none are really as notable as Katsunuma in Yamanashi Prefecture. Providing aficionados with forty percent of the total wine produced in Japan, Katsunuma covers the low hillsides on the eastern edge of a large, flat valley which centers on the

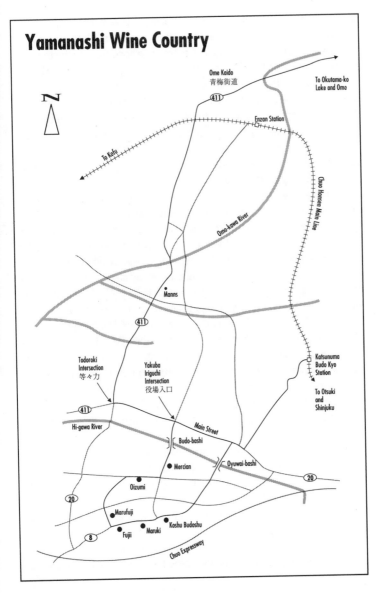

Yamanashi Wine Country

N

Ome Kaido
青梅街道

411

To Okutama-ko
Lake and Omo

Enzan Station

To Kofu

Chuo Honsen Main Line

Omo-kawa River

Manns

411

Todoroki
Intersection
等々力

Yakuba
Iriguchi
Intersection
役場入口

Katsunuma
Budo Kyo
Station

To Otsuki
and
Shinjuku

411

Hi-gawa River

Main Street

Budo-bashi

Mercian

Oyuwai-bashi

20

Oizumi

Marufuji

Maruki

Koshu Budoshu

20

8

Fuji

Chuo Expressway

prefectural capital of Kofu. The rich volcanic soil is well drained , with the area as a whole enjoying good southwestern exposure. Most importantly, the days are quite warm and the nights are quite cool, creating the temperature extremes said to be an essential ingredient in good wine grapes.

Although such classic grape varieties as Cabernet Sauvignon, Merlot, and Riesling have been planted in small quantities in recent years, the predominant variety in the region is the Koshu grape, which is said to be originally a European variety that arrived over a thousand years ago via the Silk Road. However, it wasn't until the Meiji period that wine was produced in Japan. Other popular varieties are invariably table grapes or varieties thereof, such as Berry A and Muscat.

Enthusiasts will find these wines rather undistinguished, though, in some cases, to mutate a computer phrase, "boozer friendly." Those looking for a more authentic wine experience should seek out the few wines made from Cabernet, Chardonnay, and Merlot—occasionally a hundred percent, but more often in blends. The Merlot wines, in particular, are among the best.

But even without the wine, Katsunuma would still be a prime destination for some wonderfully relaxing backroads cycling. The best times to go are from late March through mid-June and from mid-September through December. Mid-winter, though clear, is very cold, while summers, because of the surrounding mountains, are even hotter than Tokyo.

In keeping with the spirit of a wine country tour (which is to go no place in particular), it would be best to arrive in Katsunuma and just ride round and explore. The most common sights are, of course, the vineyards. During grape season in early fall, many farmers allow you to pick your own grapes for a small fee. Also, here and there, are peach and apple orchards.

Rising abruptly on the west side of town is a set of mountains which tumble into the foothills comprising Katsunuma town. The foothills gradually level out past the east side of town, just before Isawa, a razzle-dazzle hot spring town on the way to Kofu. Throughout Katsunuma, the roads are pleasant, traversing rolling hills. This continues all the way north to Enzan, a quiet hot-spring town at the foot of the mountains, and all the way south to the Chuo Expressway.

Getting to Katsunuma from Tokyo is easy. Although one could possibly ride out from Shinjuku on either Koshu Kaido or Ome Kaido, it would take most riders more than a day, half of which would be in heavy traffic anyway. Needless to say, this is not the way to start a wine tour. Instead, leave Shinjuku on the Chuo Line, taking an express to Otsuki (one hour) and then change to a local train that takes another half hour to get to Katsunuma Budo Kyo Station. Or, if you're really laid-back, the Kofu-bound local train from Shinjuku stops at Katsunuma exactly two hours later.

At Katsunuma Budo Kyo Station, check out the wine pub operated by the town of Katsunuma. There's a good selection here and prices are reasonable. On your return to Tokyo, you may want to drop in while waiting for your train, but be careful not to get carried away and miss it.

Before you leave the station, pick up the Katsunuma Kanko Route Map (in Japanese) from the tourist information counter. Along with a rough sketch of the town is a list of vineyards, wineries, and *minshuku*. I recommend reserving accommodations in the center of town, in the vicinity of the post office and the town hall (*yakuba*), where you'll be able to continue touring wineries on foot as the day progresses.

From the station, facing west, go left and head south on a winding road that eventually intersects with the main road through town. Turn right and ride for about three kilometers to the second signal, at the Yakuba Iriguchi (town hall entrance) intersection, where you turn left and head down the hill to the Hi-gawa River, crossing the famous Budo-bashi (grape bridge) and then head up the hill to the Mercian Winery complex, which includes a rather large tasting room and a wine museum up the hill in the back.

While you'll probably be more interested in visiting the smaller Mom and Pop–style family wineries, the Mercian tasting room is a good place to start your Katsunuma wine tour. Their knowledgeable staff is familiar with the wines and production techniques of Europe, while their large section of locally produced wines will give you some idea of what to expect as you attempt to ferret out smaller wineries off the beaten track.

After Mercian, continue up the short hill. At the top take the first right onto a narrow road. A few hundred meters later, on your left, is the Oizumi Winery, a spirited little operation which sells wine directly to customers from its small office, with the "tasting room" a small table to the right of the entrance. When I arrived, I was waved over to the table and told to help myself. After Oizumi, continue on this small road, turn left at the next intersection, and go straight down this winding country road. At the Fujii intersection, cross the busy four-lane Route 20 and continue on this road for a few hundred meters as it winds up a little hill. On your left is the Marufuji Winery, a charming little family-style operation which offers surprisingly dry and interestingly flavored wines. Founded in 1890, Marufuji is one of the oldest wineries in the region, and is currently run by the fourth-generation owner.

After Marufuji, continue up the hill, turn left at the next intersection, and trundle along Route 8, a scenic road lined with grape farms. You'll also pass the Fujii, Maruki, and Koshu Budoshu wineries before you cross Route 20 again. After the second set of stoplights, head downhill and cross the Hi-gawa again at Oyuwai-bashi, then go up the hill to reach the main street running through the center of town.

If, at this point, you've reserved a place to stay in the center of town, and can't readily recall how many wineries you've visited, it might be a good idea to ride to your lodgings, check in, and park your bike for the day. Within walking distance from here are nearly twenty wineries where you may continue your research. Besides, a brisk walk may do you some good by now.

The next morning, you and the weather permitting, you may want to forsake a continuation of your Katsunuma tour for the prospect of an exhilarating ride through the mountains and a seemingly endless dowhill stretch that takes you closer to Tokyo. Go straight along the main street of Katsunuma toward Kofu; about a kilometer past the Yakuba Iriguchi intersection is the Todoroki intersection, where the main street meets Route 411. Turn right here and go north on 411 toward Enzan. After the second bridge you'll see the Mann's Winery, the last one on the edge of town. If it's not too early, they may be open, and you can have one last taste of Katsunuma wine.

Ride through Enzan and continue on Route 411 as it climbs gently along a river. (This route is the start of the Ome Kaido, which finishes just north of Shinjuku Station.) In the upper reaches of the river, the road steepens and winds into the mountains. In less than five kilometers, however, you'll cross over Yanagisawa-toge Pass, and the road will suddenly lurch downhill, joining up with the upper reaches of the Tamba-gawa River that flows into Oku Tama-ko Lake. The road through the Tamba Gorge is scenic, but narrow, with oncoming traffic surprising you on the curves.

Along this stretch you'll do a lot of heavy braking, so it's a good idea to stop periodically to let your rims cool and your neck and shoulder muscles unwind.

About forty kilometers from Katsunuma, the road hits Oku Tama-ko Lake, hugging the shore and padding through an endless procession of short tunnels. Ride another seven kilometers or so to the dam, where there's a nice place to rest and have lunch. Afterward continue down Route 411, and I mean down, through a long, winding gorge that goes on for about twenty-five kilometers into Ome City.

From Ome you can take the train back to Shinjuku; direct trains leave about every half hour, and the trip takes a little over an hour. Alternatively, you can continue riding on Ome Kaido back into Tokyo. From here on, the scenery deteriorates and the traffic worsens. You may also choose to continue on Route 411 for another twenty kilometers into Hachioji, although on weekends this road is generally crowded as well.   ✍ BH

❶ Field information
Katsunuma Town Hall Information Section ☎ 0553 44-1111
Budo Matsuri (Wine Festival): first Saturday in October—eat grapes and drink wine to your heart's content and all for free
Katsunuma Wine Pub ☎ 0553 44-2827
Oizumi Winery ☎ 0553 44-2872
Marufuji Winery ☎ 0553 44-0043
Mercian Winery ☎ 0553 44-1011

⌂ Lodging Log
Katsunuma: Daisen-ji (unique national treasure *minshuku*) ☎ 0553 44-0027

The Chikuma-gawa River Path

Route: A civilized meander along the banks of the Chikuma-gawa River: beautiful scenery with the minimum amount of effort
Start: Ueda Station (Shinetsu Line from Ueno)
Goal: Nagano Station (Shinetsu Line from Ueno)

The Nagano Prefectural Road Construction Department has done the local citizenry as well as the members of the Flat Earth Society a good turn by laying down a stretch of mostly bicycle-use-only pavement along the Chikuma-gawa River in Nagano Prefecture. The Ueda-Nagano Bike Path is a narrow country road which extends the forty or so kilometers between Ueda City and Nagano City. Running mostly on the dike along the west

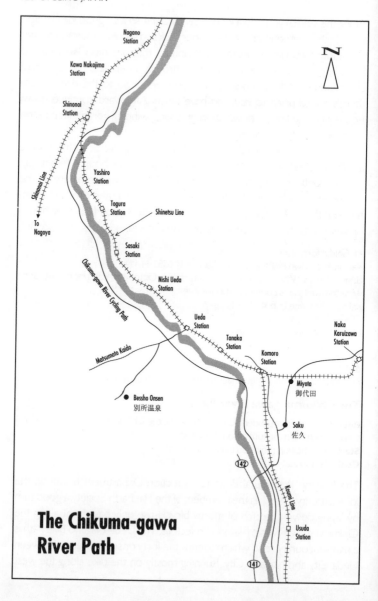

The Chikuma-gawa River Path

side of the river, the route traverses parks, community gardens, and a tremendous amount of natural river floodplain fauna as it meanders along flat as a pancake from Ueda to Nagano. The path is not particularly broad, averaging about 2.5 meters in width, but there aren't a lot of other riders out there to distract you from the scenery, which is really picturesque. The lack of major roads nearby means that there are no car exhausts or road noise to bother you—just one postcard scene after the other meandering by.

The Ueda to Nagano path is downstream, so over the course of the trip you will descend approximately ninety meters in elevation, adding to the relative ease with which this ride can be accomplished. One weekend plan would be to combine the river path with a trip to Bessho Onsen, an old hot-spring town with the reputation of being the "Kamakura of the North" because of its numerous temples.

The bike path runs parallel to the Shinetsu Line, a major rail line between Tokyo (Ueno Station) and Niigata on the Japan Sea. The route can be easily accessed from any of the several stations along the way, for example Komoro, Togura, Ueda. Whichever station you happen to get off at, simply head for the west bank of the Chikuma-gawa via the closest bridge. If you are anywhere between Ueda and Nagano, the path will be just lying there waiting for you. Herein lies the beauty of this trip: The route can easily be lengthened or shortened depending on the time, the weather, or your personal energy level. It can be cut as short as the ten or so kilometers between the towns of Togura and Koshoku or expanded to a multi-day journey between Karuizawa and the Japan Sea. A little creative map work will keep you off all the main arteries while not on the bike path, and since you never actually do leave civilization, foodstores, bike shops, *onsen*, and all the other cyclists' comforts are available in the towns along the way to keep the show on the road.   ✍ HB

❶ Field Information
Komoro Tourist Information ☎ 0267 22-0568

⛩ Lodging Log
Ueda: Mizuno Ryokan ☎ 0268 22-1017; Nokura Sanso (traditional *minshuku* 15 km southwest of Ueda with *irori*) ☎ 0268 38-2735; Uematsuya Ryokan ☎ 0268 38-2300
Bessho Onsen: Mahoroba Youth Hostel ☎ 0268 38-5229

Komoro: Komoro San-so ☎ 0267 22-6524; Nakadana Onsen Ryokan ☎ 0267 22-1511

Nagano: Nagano-shi Cycling Terminal (see page 263) ☎ 0262 21-1731

A Slow Boat to Boso

Route: Another world of winding country lanes and rolling hills offering a variety of interesting rides only a short ferry ride away from the central Tokyo area
Start: Tokyo Station (Uchibo, Sotobo lines) or ferry to Kisarazu from Kawasaki Ferry Terminal
Goal: Ohara Station (Sotobo Line) or Kisarazu for ferry back to Kawasaki

The southern half of the Boso-hanto Peninsula is one of my favorite cycling destinations in Japan. It is far less rugged than the Izu-hanto, where many of the "skyline" toll roads are closed to bicycles. Boso also has more quiet country roads suitable for cycling, too. It's odd that in such a paradise of charming roads and lanes winding around rolling hills, over small mountains, and through short tunnels, one sees so few cyclists, particularly considering its proximity to the Tokyo metropolitan area.

Getting there is rather easy compared to other places. You can bag your bike and take JR's Uchibo (bay side) or Sotobo (ocean side) lines from Tokyo Station, and in two hours you'll be there. The lines follow the coast all round the peninsula so you can easily choose which part of the peninsula you wish to explore. The best choice, however, is to bike over to the ferry landing in Kawasaki and take a one-hour cruise to Kisarazu across the bay. From 6:30 A.M. boats leave about every half-hour, the last boat leaving Kisarazu at 8:00 P.M. The fare is ¥1,030 plus ¥300 for your bicycle as is and free if you bag it. Another possibility is to hop onto one of the express trains on the inexpensive Keihin Kyuko Line and ride to Kurihama, then assemble your bike and ride over to the ferry terminal and take the 35-minute boat ride across to Kanaya, just north of Tateyama at the end of the peninsula.

While the coastal highways are loaded with vehicles on weekends, most roads in the scenic interior of the peninsula are invariably quiet. Connecting farm villages, these roads are mostly ignored by tourists since, for them, they don't go anywhere. With a good map in hand, you'll see that the stretches of road between major intersections are

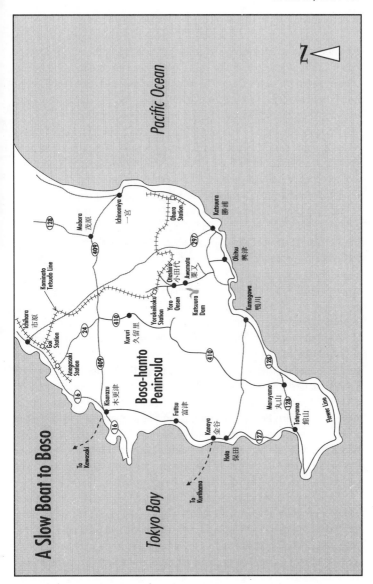

A Slow Boat to Boso

Pacific Ocean

Tokyo Bay

Boso-hanto Peninsula

To Kawasaki

To Kurihama

Kisarazu 木更津

Futtsu 富津

Kanaya 金谷

Hota 保田

Tateyama 館山

Maruyama 丸山

Flower Line

Kamogawa 鴨川

Okitsu 興津

Katsuura 勝浦

Ohara Station, Ohara 大原

Ichinomiya 一宮

Mobara 茂原

Awamata 粟又

Onstshiro 小田代

Yoro Onsen

Yorokeikoku Station

Katsuura Dam

Kururi 久留里

Goi Station 市原

Ichihara 市原

Anegasaki Station

Kominato Tetsudo Line

16

409

24

410

410

128

128

127

128

297

409

128

short, allowing you to make a good route as you go along.

The riding is at its best south of Futtsu on the west side facing the bay, and south of Ichinomiya on the east side facing the Pacific Ocean. From south of Ichinomiya the route becomes very scenic; local fishing villages seem to have escaped development as resort areas for Tokyo-ites. The road also runs up bluffs overlooking the ocean, bends inland with some ups and downs, and cuts through the odd tunnel.

Roughly between Futtsu and Ohara, there's a small mountain range running from east to west across the peninsula. A number of major roads run north-south through this area, snaking through the mountains along creeks, and usually peaking through tunnels at the top of passes.

All of these stretches offer great riding, but one that really stands out is the run from Otashiro, just south of Yoro Onsen at the edge of the Yoro Keikoku Gorge to Katsuura Dam and on to the village of Ueno on the headlands above Okitsu, just west of Katsuura. A short ways along this road is Awamata, a wide spot in the road with a restaurant/hotel overlooking a scenic gorge on the Yoro-gawa River. A series of inviting swimming holes are connected by a chain of waterfalls, the famous Yoro no Taki Falls, after which the chain of *yakitori* pubs is named. In the warmer months the water feels just fine—when there's enough of it.

Another good stretch is the part of Route 410 (which runs north-south up the spine of the peninsula) from Kururi to Maruyama at the southern end of the peninsula northwest of the rather large town of Tateyama. Best taken from south to north, it's roughly fifty kilometers of abrupt scene changes and some rough climbing. It also provides a good view of Southern Boso, from the rolling hills in the south, to the plain around Kamogawa, to the rugged hills in the center. After you cross Route 34, the main highway linking Kamogawa with Hota on the Tokyo Bay side, Route 410 climbs steeply through tall trees. Be quiet and look carefully—if you're lucky you may see groups of wild monkeys.

The section from Ichinomiya to Tateyama along Route 128 is about eighty kilometers in length; the additional loop of about fifty kilometers around the tip of the peninsula a good scenic ride and warm most of the year, well deserving its title as the Flower Line. In summer, try to ride it on a weekday as it's a popular tourist destination for drivers from the cities.

All in all, the main point in riding through the Boso-hanto Peninsula is to get slightly lost, preferably with a good map. In this regard, it's like Shikoku—just meander around, and turn off on smaller roads that look inviting—there's almost always something interesting to see.

Boso can be done in a day, though you'll feel far less rushed if you plan to spend the night out there. However, although the best riding is inland, away from the coast highways, most of the places to stay are on the seaside. It's a good idea to arrive at a *minshuku* by mid-afternoon if you haven't reserved in advance.

Also keep in mind that the area is usually several degrees warmer than central Tokyo in the winter, and several degrees cooler in the summer. Once you explore some of the small inland roads, you'll wonder why more people haven't discovered this cycling paradise. ✎ BH

⦿ Field Information
Tateyama Tourist Information ☏ 0470 22-2531
Shirahama Minshuku Association ☏ 0470 38-2656
Kamogawa Tourist Information ☏ 04709 3-4995
Okitsu Tourist Information ☏ 0470 76-0800
Ichinomiya Minshuku Association ☏ 0475 42-2866

☉ Lodging Log
Ohara: Minshuku Marukaku ☏ 0470 62-0026
Shirahama: Go-so ☏ 047038-2795

Nasu Highlands Hot Springs ⮂

Route: A fairly level route around the Nasu Highlands via Yumoto hot springs and Itamuro Gorge
Start: Nasu Shiobara Station (Tohoku Shinkansen Line)
Goal: Kuroiso Station (Tohoku Honsen Main Line)

The appeal of these wide-open highlands is in both the simplicity of their pleasures and their proximity to Tokyo. Only eighty minutes from Tokyo by shinkansen, Nasu Shiobara is a pleasant starting point for exploring this broad plain that inclines to the northwest. In fact, it is this orientation which will determine the direction of your riding, and the main roads run in a corresponding grid pattern. Generally, riding northwest is uphill, downhill is southeast. For a break on the level, go either northeast or southwest.

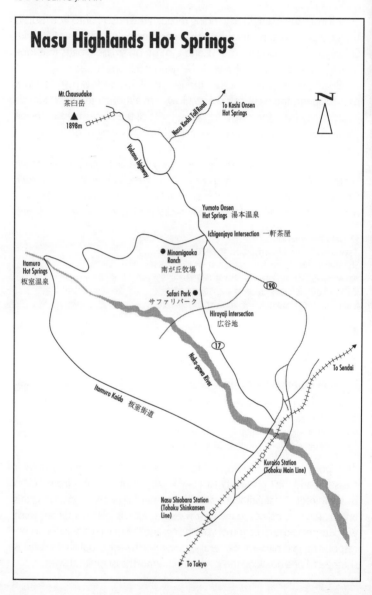

Nasu Highlands Hot Springs

Mt.Chausudake
茶臼岳

▲
1898m

To Koshi Onsen
Hot Springs

Nasu Koshi Toll Road

Volcano Highway

Yumoto Onsen
Hot Springs 湯本温泉

Ichigenjaya Intersection 一軒茶屋

Itamuro
Hot Springs
板室温泉

● Minamigaoka
Ranch
南が丘牧場

● Safari Park
サファリパーク

Hiroyaji Intersection
広谷地

190

17

Naka-gawa River

Itamuro Kaido 板室街道

To Sendai

Kuroiso Station
(Tohoku Main Line)

Nasu Shiobara Station
(Tohoku Shinkansen
Line)

To Tokyo

The best way to enjoy the Nasu Highlands is not to aim for anywhere in particular, but ride around its big grid of farm roads to discover everything from hidden ponds and streams to large ranches to (you guessed it) tourist attractions.

From the south side of Nasu Shiobara Station, turn left onto Route 4 and head north to Kuroiso, the largest town on the plain. At the fork in the road about two kilometers later, go left off the highway and take the main road through the center of town. Just after the bridge that crosses high above the wide Naka-gawa river, turn left and head northeast (uphill, remember?) for about thirteen kilometers. After the Hiroyaji intersection, turn left and head on the mostly level road (well, a few ups and downs) for about three kilometers to the lunch spot.

The place is Minamigaoka Ranch and yes, it's a tourist trap, falling squarely into the "dude ranch" category. Nonetheless, the main dining room serves good food in hearty portions. Try a big bowl of borscht with some thick slices of their heavy brown bread and a piroshki on the side. If you're visiting on a weekend, make sure you show up for lunch before noon so you don't have to wait for a table. The ranch also makes their own ice cream and cheesecake for those who need a little extra sustenance before setting off. After a heavy dinner you might consider a little stroll over by the horse pens and trout ponds. There's also an interesting rock garden with over two thousand varieties of wild flowers.

When you feel ready to mount your steed again, backtrack to the Ichigenjaya intersection, turn left, and continue on what is fast becoming a challenging grade. A few kilometers later you'll find yourself in the middle of Yumoto, a hot spring town with quite a number of places to stay. Those willing to brave the brutal climb up the mountain can enter the toll road (¥50 for bicycles) and be rewarded with a stay at some of the nicer places further up. They're few in number, so reservations are recommended. Although it's a little on the expensive side, I recommend Omaru Onsen, where the outdoor bath is a small river that's dammed up to hold the hot water bubbling down from the rocks above.

The following day, those hungry for more elevation can continue up a small road that approaches the summit of Chausudake (1,915m), the highest peak on the ridge. Normal people, however, may want to putter around the back roads and make their own discoveries. A good map of the area is recommended, although with a little confidence in your sense of direction, there should be no difficulty in negotiating the general grid pattern of the area's roads.

Between the Ichigenjaya and Hiroyaji intersections, about a half kilometer from the main road, is a safari park, where wild animals roam. Those not wanting to take any chances should steer clear of this area, take the left fork at Ichigenjaya, and enjoy a beautiful stretch of downhill that's largely unmarred by the ticky-tacky tourist atmosphere of road you came up on.

A good return route is to go back to the Minamigaoka Ranch and continue on the same road to Itamaro hot springs. The road rolls up and down for about ten kilometers, with good views off to the left as it hugs the side of the mountain. Finally, the road plunges into the Itamaro Gorge near the hot springs turnoff. Cross the bridge and continue around the gorge and head downhill. The road will take you right into Kuroiso.

In Kuroiso there are any number of places where you can enjoy an early dinner before returning from Kuroiso Station to Tokyo on the Tohoku Honsen Line. (Most trains take between two and a half to three hours and some go directly to Shinjuku and Ikebukuro.) Or, if you're in a hurry, you can ride the six kilometers or so back to Nasu Shiobara Station and take the shinkansen back to Tokyo. ✍ BH

🏠 Lodging Log

Yumoto Onsen: Ishikawa-so ☎ 0287 76-2214; Tomioka-ya ☎ 0287 76-2244; Hillside ☎ 0287 78-0073; Omori ☎ 028776-3736; Sunvalley Nasu ☎ 0287 76-3800
Nasu Kogen (Highlands): Minamigaoka Ranch ☎ 0287 76-2150; Takabochi ☎ 0287 76-2441; Asagiri-so ☎ 0287 76-3670; Mayunosato (has rental bikes) ☎ 0287 78-1061
Omaru Onsen (from ¥12,000) ☎ 0287 76-3050

Alpine Riding 🚲 🚲 🚲 🚲 🚲 🚲 🚲 🚲 🚲 🚲 🚲 🚲 🚲 🚲

Japan's Shangri-la 🚲

Route: After meandering along the Chikuma-gawa River, the route creeps up to Mikuni-toge Pass at 1,740m and ends with a stunning descent into Chichibu
Start: Nobeyama Station (Chuo Line from Shinjuku Station to Kobuchizawa Station, change to Koumi Line for fourth stop, Nobeyama Station)
Goal: Mitsumineguchi Station (Seibu Chichibu Line)

Near where the prefectures of Saitama, Nagano, and Gunma meet is a little known Shangri-la, seemingly built specially for cycle tourists. The Nobeyama plain just inside Nagano, over 1,000m in elevation, is a wonderful place in summer, with brisk, cool air and an open, endless sky. Start your trip from Nobeyama, which has the distinction of having the highest rail station in Japan as well as a large radio observatory—a huge ranch of parabolic antennas pointing up toward the sky. Apart from cattle ranches, a few *minshuku*, and a small ski resort/golf course complex, there's not a lot happening in Nobeyama. Maybe that's its appeal. Crowds don't seem to make it up to Nobeyama as Kiyosato, a tourist nightmare just down the hill rivaling Karuizawa with its waves of kitschy, cutesy gift shops, seems to siphon off most of the visitors. Avoiding it is all the more reason to carry on further up to Nobeyama. For excitement, head over to the dude ranch on the other side of Route 141 (the main highway through town), located one block behind the large discount vegetable stand. Admission is free and there's good coffee in the coffee shop up front.

The Nagano side of Mikuni-toge, the pass leading down into Chichibu, tends to look more like Hokkaido. Follow the signs from Nobeyama Station for Kawakami-mura, a village seemingly stuck in time. The road crosses the railway tracks several times; when you reach an intersection, turn left to discover the main part of the village huddled around a tiny rail station. If you turn right, you'll be in for a memorable experience of Japan. Winding its way along the Chikuma-gawa River, the road passes long stretches of fields and seems to be traveled more by tractors than by cars, making it perfect for cycling.

When we last cycled this route, there was little traffic all the way from

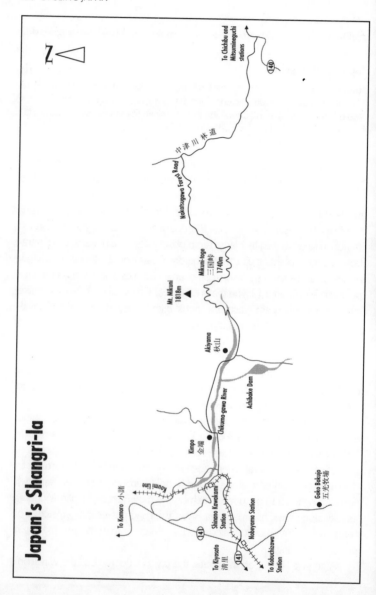

Japan's Shangri-la

Kawakami to Mikuni-toge, a pass about 1,800 m. in elevation. We do recommend this road, which poses a reasonable challenge—particularly in the rain.

All thoughts of an easy downhill coast into Chichibu, where a hot bath would be waiting, turned out to be wishful thinking. We arrived at the top of the pass only to find twenty kilometers of a rocky sea of mud that would have challenged even a 4WD vehicle. For our 1-1/8" bicycle tires, the fastest speed was a medium walk. Despite the pain of squeezing brake levers with cold, wet hands for three hours, we felt absolutely no desire to prolong the misery by walking the bikes.

Worse was to come: About halfway through the unpaved portion, my wife slowed down to just above stall-out speed. Having suddenly less control of the bike, but not wanting to ask why, she just slowed down and kept going, exercising even greater care. Finally reaching paved road and the start of the first sunshine in two days, we discovered she had a flat tire. The tire was in shreds and, for the grand finale, the tire tube exploded when I tried to inflate it. So, with Chichibu about forty kilometers off, we started walking.

After about an hour and a half of walking through what would have been great cycling, I flagged down a pickup truck. The sympathetic driver not only drove us into Chichibu, but also invited us to stay the night in his brand-new home equipped with every electronic device known to man. The next morning, we packed up the bikes and took the Seibu Red Arrow *Tokkyu* back to Tokyo. The nearest station on the line when coming down from Mikuni-toge is Mitsumineguchi. The next time you're suddenly stricken with Tokyo's summer disease, consider a trip out to the cyclists' Shangri-la. *Minshuku* are available in Nobeyama, Kimpo, Kawakami, and Akiyama, but note that most are closed in the winter months.　　✍ JK

⌂ Lodging Log
Nobeyama: Goko Bokujo (open year round) ☎ 0267 98-2468
Kawakami: Ryuen-so ☎ 0267 99-2573; Tosa-ya ☎ 0267 99-2069
Kimpo: Chikuma ☎ 0267 99-2625; Kimpo ☎ 0267 99-2050
Akiyama: Iwane-sanso ☎ 0267 99-2200

The Old Post Road ☗

Route: An alpine route following part of the Nakasendo, one of the two post roads linking Tokyo and Kyoto during the Tokugawa shogunate. Starting either in the wine-producing town of Shiojiri, or Matsumoto, the city famous for its sixteenth-century "black" castle, the route heads through lacquer-producing villages to Kiso-Fukushima, where a toll barrier was maintained during the Edo period. Continuing through stunning scenery, the route crosses Seinaiji-toge Pass, dropping down dramatically into the town of Iida.

Start: Shiojiri or Matsumoto stations (Chuo Honsen Main Line express from Shinjuku Station)

Goal: Iida Station (Iida Line to Okaya and change to the Chuo Honsen Main Line for Shinjuku Station)

"Road through the Mountains" is perhaps the best interpretation of the name Nakasendo. Once one of the two main routes connecting Kyoto and Tokyo, the Nakasendo is now a sparsely trodden route winding through the Chuo Alps. This old post road offers panoramic views of alpine scenery laced with wildflowers, wooden bridges, hot springs, waterfalls, and a series of small post towns which still retain the flavor of old Japan.

The Nakasendo trail offers many challenges for the energetic adventurer. The natural surroundings provide a clean break away from Tokyo; you can enjoy beautiful mountain scenery, bathe in outdoor hot springs, and lodge at an old-fashioned Japanese *minshuku*. There are plenty of temples, gardens, and historical landmarks along the way. Rental bikes are available at some of the post towns, but their condition is not guaranteed.

Since Nagano Prefecture is much higher in elevation than Nagoya, it makes sense to start there. Although the city of Matsumoto features many attractions, including one of Japan's finest castles, the roads leading out of the city are generally crowded and cluttered. If you can resist the attractions of Matsumoto, I recommend starting at Shiojiri, where the Chuo Line from Nagoya meets the Chuo Line from Shinjuku before going into Matsumoto. From Shinjuku, there's at least one express train leaving each hour, with the trip to Shiojiri taking just under three hours. From Nagoya, trains are just as frequent, but it takes only three hours.

From Shiojiri Station, head west through town a few kilometers until you reach Route 19, the Nakasendo, at an intersection called Kikkyogahara. Here

The Old Post Road

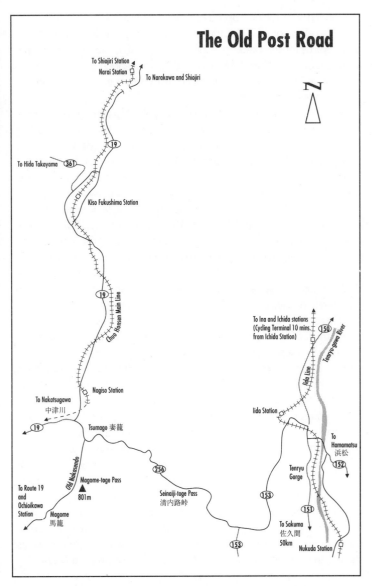

To Shiojiri Station
Narai Station
To Narakawa and Shiojiri

N

19

To Hida Takayama 361

Kiso Fukushima Station

19

Chuo Honsen Main Line

To Ina and Ichida stations
(Cycling Terminal 10 mins.
from Ichida Station)

150

Tenryu-gawa River

Iida Line

Nagiso Station

To Nakatsugawa
中津川

Iida Station

19

Tsumago 妻籠

To Hamamatsu
浜松

256

152

Old Nakasendo

Magome-toge Pass

Seinaiji-toge Pass
清内路峠

Tenryu
Gorge

▲
801m

153

To Route 19
and
Ochioikawa
Station

151

Magome
馬籠

To Sakuma
佐久間
50km

153

Nukuda Station

you can find two of Shiojiri's biggest attractions: the Hayashi and Izutsu wineries.

At an elevation of 700m, the plain surrounding Shiojiri has been home to vineyards for the better part of a century. While table grape varieties such as Concord, Muscat, Berry A, and Niagara abound, there are a few plantings of Chardonnay and Merlot in these parts. Seek out these varieties in the wines you choose to taste.

From the Kikkyogahara intersection, cross the Nakasendo and continue on for a few hundred meters. First on your left is the brand new, spanking clean Izutsu Winery tasting room and gift shop. (Take the door to the right for a direct entrance to the tasting area.) Founded in 1933, Izutsu produces some moderately sturdy (if a bit sweet) wines for the table, with whites outshining reds somewhat. From Izutsu, you can practically walk across the street to the Hayashi Winery, more of a down-home family operation that dates back to 1911. Hayashi's Go-ichi Wines are largely stupefyingly sweet rose and white vintages—one large bottle proclaims "Economy," while others are boldly marked "Sweet" in large letters. They also produce wine from locally grown apples and kiwi fruit, though I didn't have room to taste them. Hayashi's Chateau Go-ichi wines, however, are notable efforts with both red and white produced from local Merlot grapes.

There are three other wineries in the area and though one could easily spend most of a day cruising among them and tasting their products, the Nakasendo does await the cyclist with long, easy downhill stretches and rapid changes in scenery as the road curves up through the Narai-gawa River canyon, through the Torii tunnel and down through the Kiso-gawa River canyon to Nakatsugawa and points beyond.

As you continue south, the road climbs gently, with short steep stretches in some places. Approaching Narakawa, you'll notice an increasing number of shops selling lacquerware, a specialty of the region. Just past the turnoff for Naraijuku, the river widens—during summer the swimming must be great. You can't help but notice the large, curved, arch bridge that crosses the river at one point. From here the road enters the Torii tunnel. It's over a kilometer long but there's a wide walkway separated from the traffic by a railing, which makes passage more pleasant. You may have noticed by now that despite its remote location, the Nakasendo carries more than its share of truck traffic. This becomes all the more obvious in the tunnels.

After the tunnels, it's mostly gradual downhill riding into the town of Kiso Fukushima. There's the short 500m Fukushima tunnel, but for a while afterward there are bike paths on both sides of the road. The river widens around Kakehashi Onsen, where there's a wide bridge crossing the river.

The Nakasendo forks at the turnoff for Route 256, so go left to stay on it. (If you stay on Route 19, the road follows the river all the way into Nakatsugawa some thirty-five kilometers later.) Go up Route 256 for two kilometers, then turn right onto a small road. A few meters down on the left is a large billboard map showing a number of *minshuku* where you can stay; overall, the area has quite a historic emphasis. Tsumago is one of the largest of the post towns and features narrow alleyways bordered by old wooden lattice structures, a sake brewery, a folk museum, and village craftsmen reknowned for their country hospitality. The local cuisine is filling, fresh, and fishy. Typical are a variety of trout, vegetables, sake, and the local specialty, fried *sawagani*, a freshwater mountain crab, served and eaten in the shell.

You won't be thinking much about the past, though, as you climb the steep eight kilometers on the harrowingly narrow road to Magome. To get the feel of life in Meiji Magome and Tsumago, have a look at *The Family* by Shimazaki Toson, whose family home in Magome is now a museum. This area is also a good place to spend the night and prepare yourself for the next day's healthy climb over part of the Chuo Alps.

The following day, say good-bye to the Nakasendo, go back to Route 256, and begin the long climb to Seinaiji-toge Pass. The road climbs steadily for about six kilometers, then rewards you with a small downhill. Then it's straight up for another ten kilometers or so to an extremely steep and winding road. The views are tremendous and you may find yourself enjoying them with increasing frequency as the grade slowly wears you down.

As you pass through a short tunnel at the top, you'll be rewarded with a spectacular view of a large, broad canyon that you'll no doubt be at the bottom of within an hour of brisk, downhill riding. From Seinaiji-toge, the downhill is almost letter perfect: not too steep, with broad, sweeping turns connecting longish straight stretches. This goes on and on until Route 256 dead ends at Route 153. Go right on 153 toward Iida; the road continues its descent practically all the way to the edge of the city some ten kilometers later. From Iida you can get a train back to Nagoya (via Toyohashi) or

Shinjuku (via Okaya). An alternative is to cycle up to Ichida Station, five stops up from Iida, and stay in the cycle terminal located very conveniently about ten minutes from the station. Ichida is also one of the places from where boat cruises on the Tenryu Gorge begin—enjoy a leisurely cruise down the river and try out the wildflower cycling course later in the day.

⇨ Route Extension

If you have another day or two, a good continuation would be to head west from Iida Station on Route 151 (Route 153 becomes Route 151 in town); stay on Route 151 by turning left at the intersection with Route 153. Head south a kilometer or so, then turn left onto Route 152. Continue for about three kilometers, and after crossing the wide Tenryu-gawa River about six kilometers later, turn right. The river gorge is beautiful and worth dismounting for a short hike around the area.

Here, you can cross back over the river and get back on Route 151 heading south, or continue on this road and enjoy more rugged cycling as the road negotiates a number of small mountains on its way southward. About twenty kilometers later the road rejoins the river just before Nukuda Station, where it crosses over the river and hugs the west bank for a good fifty kilometers into the town of Sakuma. The mountains get very rugged toward the end of this stretch, and the road passes through what seems a million short tunnels.

At the intersection before Sakuma, keep left and continue for another seven kilometers through a steep gorge to the junction of Route 152. Turn right onto 152 and follow the river gradually downward on its journey to the Pacific Ocean. At the fork just before the bridge, turn left and get onto the less traveled road on the other side of the Tenryu-gawa from Route 152. You can stay on this road for another twenty kilometers or so until it runs into Route 152 near a bridge. Go right across the bridge, take the first left, then continue along the river opposite the highway.

The road finally crosses the river again, rejoining Route 152, which leads you into the middle of Hamamatsu City about twenty-five kilometers later. South of Hamamatsu, there are good cycling paths that follow the coast for over fifty kilometers in each direction. Explore them if you have time, or return to Tokyo from Hamamatsu Station by shinkansen.   ✍ BH

❶ Field Information

Matsumoto Tourist Information ☎ 0263 32-2814
Narakawa-mura Tourist Information (also Narai) ☎ 0264 34-2001
Kiso Fukushima Tourist Information ☎ 0264 22-2001
Tsumago Tourist Information ☎ 0264 57-3123
Magome Tourist Information ☎ 0264 59-2336
Toson Kinenkan ☎ 0264 59-2047

⚓ Lodging Log

Matsumoto: Nishiya Ryokan ☎ 0263 33-4332; Marumo Ryokan ☎ 0263 33-3586; Matsumoto Tourist Hotel ☎ 0263 33-9000

Shiojiri: Akita-so ☎ 0263 56-2615; Yamabiko ☎ 0263 56-2645; Shikura ☎ 0263 52-6935; Sasayabu ☎ 0263 52-0947

Narai: Iseya ☎ 0264 34-3051; Ejimaya ☎ 0264 34-2609; Kojimaya ☎ 0264 34-3176; Machida ☎ 0264 34-3202; Nagai ☎ 0264 34-2624; Hoihoi ☎ 0264 34-3225; Shimada ☎ 0264 34-2678

Kiso Fukushima: Kurokawa-so (traditional wooden three-storied building) ☎ 0264 27-6103; Kiso Yado (known for wild boar, pheasant, and bear meat served at the traditional *irori*) ☎ 0264 22-3177

Tsumago: Sakamoto-ya ☎ 0264 57-3111; Yuya ☎ 0264 57-3233; Izutsu-ya ☎ 0264 57-3109; Shitachoji-ya ☎ 0264 57-3222; Daikichi ☎ 0264 57-2595

Magome: Toge Shimizu-ya ☎ 0264 59-2141; Marukitano-ya ☎ 0264 59-2408; Sawaya ☎ 0264 59-2046; Magome Chashitsu ☎ 0264 59-2038; Tsutaya ☎ 0264 59-2407; Iroribata ☎ 0264 59-2026; Oshima-ya ☎ 0264 59-2441

Tenryu Gorge: Takamori-machi Cycling Terminal ☎ 0265 35-8260; Yoshino-ya Ryokan ☎ 0260 32-2160; Sakamoto Ryokan ☎ 0260 32-3131; Tokura ☎ 0260 32-2775

Hamamatsu: Hamamatsu Sago Hotel ☎ 053 452-1181

The Oku Shiga Forest Road   🚲

Route: Via Nozawa Onsen hot springs, the route climbs through verdant forests to a height of 1,700m at Shiga Kogen, finishing at the small town of Yamanouchi
Start: Yokokura Station (Iyama Line)
Goal: Yudanaka Station (Nagano Dentetsu Line)

This route is for neither the faint of heart nor the unprepared. The Oku Shiga Forest Road is basically an unimproved fire road which ascends the mountains of the Joshinetsu National Park and runs through forests, along ridgetops and generally traverses the highlands of this sparsely populated region of northern Nagano Prefecture. The Oku Shiga Forest Road originates in Sakae-mura, a small village along the Chikuma-gawa River right at

The Oku-Shiga Forest Road

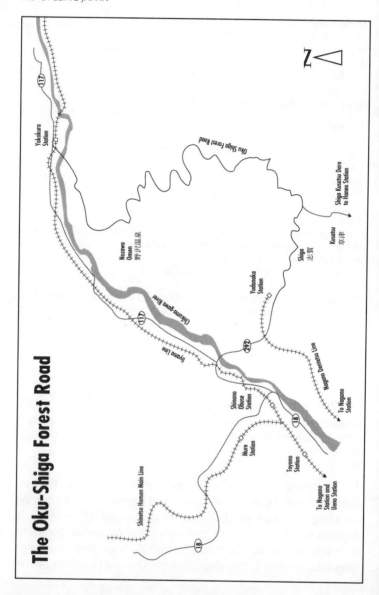

the Nagano-Niigata border. The nearest station is Yokokura Station on the Iyama Line, about an hour and a half from Nagano Station. Head west out of the station for about half a kilometer until you come to a bridge. Cross the Chikuma-gawa River and turn right and head off on the Oku Shiga Rindo. From an elevation of about 250m, the road moves south into the mountains, gradually gaining elevation. At Nozawa Onsen ski area some twenty kilometers to the south the road levels out at about 1,000m. From here it bounces and weaves between 800 and 1,700m elevation, with the high point occurring in Shiga Kogen. Shiga is a world-famous ski area and you'll find snow up here all year around. Watch the weather—it can change quickly and usually for the worse. The other news is that Shiga is the southern terminus of the forest road. From here there is a well-paved but thoroughly insane descent into a town called Yamanouchi. From Yudanaka Station (the terminus of the Nagano Dentetsu Line) it's a short ride back to civilization.

For the most part, this is utterly unpopulated highland territory. And while the distances are not great as the crow flies, this is perhaps the closest you can get to true wilderness on the island of Honshu. There are mountains, valleys, whitewater rivers, and seemingly untouched tracts of forest. It is not at all unreasonable to expect to see all manner of flora and fauna while negotiating the coarse gravel which makes up all but a few of the roads. The climbs are grueling, the downhills crazy, and the experience thoroughly worth your while.

It is possible to do the trip in two days, but three days are recommended. This is simply gorgeous territory and there is just no reason to blindly rush through it. A well-made mountain bike with two water bottles, two racks, camping gear, and food are, well, essential. There are no towns along the way and therefore precious few places to buy anything at all. A southerly route, from Sakae-mura to Yamanouchi, is recommended. The climb out of Sakae-mura is far more gentle than the one you would face heading north out of Yamanouchi. Riding up toward Shiga from Yamanouchi is akin to climbing Tokyo Tower with the likes of Godzilla on your back. No reason to do that to yourself. Go the other way. It's easier. Besides that, the ten-kilometer, supersonic Mach 2.0+ descent is definitely something not to be missed.

Looking at the map, the route would not necessarily have to be cut at Shiga Kogen. It could quite naturally be continued further south to Shirane-san (an active volcano), Manza Onsen, and on along the Asama Shirane Volcano Route. However, south of Shiga Kogen, although the views are very scenic, one might be forgiven for believing that the descent into the underworld is about to start when faced not only with a barrage of fumes from the traffic but an onslaught of sulfurous emissions from the volcanoes. ✍ HB

❶ Field Information
Nozawa Onsen Minshuku Association ☎ 0269 85-2068

♠ Lodging Log
Shiga Kogen (3 km east of Yudanaka Station): Kanemoto ☎ 0269 33-2030; Shiga ☎ 0269 33-2304; Izumi-so ☎ 0269 33-4733; Miyama ☎ 0269 33-2260; Tachibana ☎ 0269 33-0106; Seki ☎ 0269 33-3444; Kutsu no Kan ☎ 0269 33-2048

Water, Fire, and Earth

Route: A meander along the Naka-gawa River, a detour to the pottery town of Mashiko, and gradual ascent through the mountains and forests of Nikko are the mere preliminaries to the breathtaking climb to Yumoto Hot Springs and Katashina Ski Resort
Start: Mito Station (Joban Line Super Express)
Goal: Shibukawa Station (Joetsu Honsen Main Line)

To enjoy the traditional Japanese fall pastime of viewing the russet and golden foliage, try a trip to the areas immediately before and immediately beyond the tourist town of Nikko. You could take a whole week to do justice to this route, but if you only have a free weekend consider doing the different parts separately.

Picking up Route 123 just beyond Mito, we turned right onto Route 118, crossed the Naka-gawa River, and then went left onto a side road which parallels the river and rejoins Route 123 at Gozenyama, where the surrounding countryside is especially scenic. Cross the river at the Noguchi intersection and continue along the banks of the river until the road again meets up with Route 123. From this point it's about twenty kilometers to the pottery town of Mashiko, where over a hundred kilns produce the local utilitarian ware made famous by Hamada Shoji. Have a ride round the town and surrounding area; sometimes sales are held and the display of

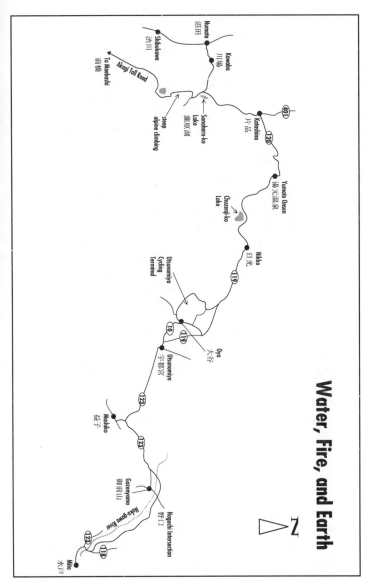

Water, Fire, and Earth

Numata 沼田
Shibukawa 渋川
Kawaba 川場
To Maebashi 前橋
Akagi Toll Road
steep alpine climbing
Sonohara-ko Lake 園原湖
Katashina 片品
40
120
Yumoto Onsen 湯元温泉
Chuzenji-ko Lake
Nikko 日光
119
Utsunomiya Cycling Terminal
Oya 大谷
10
119
Utsunomiya 宇都宮
123
Mashiko 益子
123
Gozenyama 御前山
Haka-gawa River
Noguchi Intersection 野口
123
118
Mito 水戸

N

Hamada's collection of folk arts at the Mashiko Sankokan is worth a look. To get back to Tokyo, take the Moka Line from Mashiko Station to Shimo-date Station and change to the Mito Line for Oyama Station on the Tohoku Shinkansen Line. *Minshuku* are available in the town.

If you still have the energy and courage to continue on to Nikko, take Route 123 from Mashiko to Utsunomiya. An alternative to staying overnight in Mashiko would be to drop in at the Cycling Terminal in Fukuo-ka-machi. Cross the train tracks and turn right toward Utsunomiya Station. Take the road (Route 70) directly in front of the station and stay on it. On the way you'll pass the Tohoku Expressway and the turn for the Oya quar-ries. At the entrance to the Shinrin-koen Park you'll find the cycling terminal on your right. The terminal offers a fascinating ten-kilometer course around the Oya area. Not to be missed are the Buddhist rock carvings said to date from the Heian period. The Oya stone became particularly popu-lar in the Edo period, but now many of the quarries are exhausted, causing periodic landslides and the disappearance of homesteads into huge craters. Some parts are open to the public; the cold subterranean air gives the quarry an atmosphere more suited to a Greek temple—indeed perfor-mances of avant-garde plays are often held in the subterranean depths of the quarry. The following day, retrace your steps back to the junction with Route 293 and turn left until the road joins up with Route 293.This road first crosses Nikko Utsunomiya Doro and then Route 119; turning left here will take you right into Nikko. The scenery is beautiful, and the road good with little traffic.

West of Nikko, Route 119 becomes 120, and the climbing changes from gradual to horrendous. In a series of twenty-two switchbacks the road rises to Chuzenji-ko Lake. The views are spectacular and well worth the effort. Our primary suggestion for future riders is to choose a day when it's not raining. Also, even in early May, warm clothing is a must at these altitudes. A lot of cars we saw had loaded ski racks.

Upon reaching Chuzenji-ko, the road levels for a few kilometers before it starts climbing viciously again. With this sort of climbing plus the rain, we didn't get quite as much distance in as we had originally hoped, and checked in early at a *ryokan* in Yumoto, well-equipped with a strong heater that we used to dry our shoes, socks, and riding shorts. At ¥10,000, it was our most expensive stay, but the excellent dinner included was highly appreciated. A specialty of Yumoto is the rainbow trout raised in the nearby dammed-up streams. Some friends who stayed in Yumoto were so enthusiastic about the trout that the *minshuku* owners organized a "Rocky Mountain" breakfast consisting of trout fried in butter with eggs, toast, and hot coffee instead of the more usual fermented soybeans and rice.

The next morning was fortunately sunny, and we continued the seemingly endless uphill on Route 120 until we finished our climb at the summit's tunnel. The views, especially with the improved weather, were breathtaking.

On the downhill leg toward Numata along Route 120 we passed some frozen ponds and then stopped for lunch at a ski lodge just shy of Katashina. The rest of the ride to Numata was generally downhill, but there were a few unexpectedly sharp climbs that we didn't feel we deserved. That's life. The total distance was about a hundred kilometers. Just before Numata there's the very friendly hot-spring village of Kawaba surrounded by paddy fields where you can soon find a farmhouse *minshuku* and soak your aching body. The owners are very friendly and make an effort to show the traditional methods handed down over the years, from the secrets of making tasty *konnyaku*, a local specialty, to the intricacies of planting rice.

In Numata, an old castle town built on a plateau overlooking the valley, we found a competent bike mechanic who replaced several spokes and sold us a few new tires. We then took Route 17 south, through some stunning scenery along the east bank of the Tone-gawa River to Shibukawa. Don't let the sometimes busy highway mar your enjoyment of the ravines, cliffs, and rushing waters: simply cross the river and take the narrow, winding road on the opposite side that parallels Route 17.   ✐ JK

✧ Route Extension

For some bracing air and a chance to race along with professional cyclists. try the following route across Mt. Akagi, a conical double volcano. The mountain is particularly beautiful during autumn when the bright pink azaleas growing wild all over it are in full bloom.

From Kawaba, turn onto Route 21 and head eastward along the Katashina-gawa River. Alternatively, if you're coming from the direction of Katashina, turn left for Sonohara-ko Lake around the village of Takatoya.

This road eventually drops down to Route 21. Cross over the river and backtrack for nearly two kilometers, then turn left at the Aoki intersection onto a road which meanders along the Akagi-gawa River before joining the Akagi Doro for the steep, twisting climb to Onuma-ko and Konuma-ko lakes at the top of Mt. Akagi. By this time you'll probably have had enough of cycling; limp around the lake past Akagi-jinja Shrine to the *kokumin-shukusha* at the southeastern corner of the lake. A little further on the left is the ropeway to the top of Mt. Akagi. The next morning, continue past the ropeway and turn left onto the Akagi Toll Road for the twenty-four-kilometer breeze down through silver-birch trees to an enormous *torii* at the end of the road; go through the gate and head toward Fujimi-mura and the city of Maebashi. After about six kilometers the road ends up at Chuo Maebashi Station on the Jomo Dentetsu Line. Turn right at the junction in front of the station; at the junction with Tokyu Inn on your left, take the pleasant, tree-lined boulevard with the gas station on the corner to Mae-bashi Station from where you can take a train on the Ryomo Line to Takasaki to change to the shinkansen for Tokyo.   ✍ KS

❶ Field Information
Nikko Tourist Information ☎ 0288 54-2496
Chuzenji Minshuku Association ☎ 0288 55-0648
Katashina Tourist Information ☎ 0278 58-3222
Kawaba-mura Tourist Information ☎ 0278 52-3412

⛺ Lodging Log
Mashiko: Furusato (offers pottery instruction) ☎ 0285 72-3156; Yamaji (offers a bar-becue) ☎ 0285 72-2525; Yamabiko ☎ 0285 72-1829; Toki ☎ 0285 72-3393; Higeta ☎ 0285 72-2559; Furuki ☎ 0285 72-3866
Utsunomiya-shi Cycling Terminal (see page 262) ☎ 0286 52-4497
Yumoto Onsen: Wakaba-so ☎ 0288 62-252; Pension Katsura-so ☎ 0288 62-2571; Hotel Echigo-ya (wooden bathing hall) ☎ 0288 62-2325
Mt. Akagi: Kokuminshukusha Akagi Ryokufu-so ☎ 0272 87-8111
Shibukawa: Hotel Tatsumi (3 min from Shibukawa Station) ☎ 0279 22-2443

Northern Japan 🚲🚲🚲🚲🚲🚲🚲🚲🚲🚲🚲🚲🚲🚲

Far from any of the major urban centers of Japan is Tohoku, another side of the country much less known and developed. Minutes from the coast and hills, and a few more minutes from full-scale mountains, the roads are good and the people are even better. Many main roads have bike paths running alongside them, and there is an intricate web of local roads meandering through traditional rural scenery: thatched-roofed houses, fences of rice drying in the sun, and elderly women dressed head to toe in black, working the rice fields.

The geography here is compressed enough to offer a large variety of good riding loops, from fifty kilometers and longer. Coast along the seashore, jaunt through rice paddies, cruise along the contours of wooded hills, race down broad river valleys and narrow gorges, and, of course, climb mountains.

Discovering the Back Side of Japan 🚲

Route: A fairly flat route along the Japan Sea coast past rocky seascapes to the Squid Capital of Japan with ample opportunities for swimming and camping, and rest stops at hot springs
Start: Nakajo Station (Uetsu Honsen Main Line from Niigata Station)
Goal: Atsumi Onsen Station (Uetsu Honsen Main Line)

Last spring a friend and I took a three-day trip along the rarely traveled Japan Sea coast. Starting in Nakajo, about forty kilometers from Niigata, we headed for Route 345, but soon discovered unmarked roads that took us through freshly planted rice paddies. We decided to stick with these, enjoying the way the bright green shoots contrasted with the muddied water.

We turned left at the Ara-kawa River, and soon crossed Route 345. Just after the bridge, we turned off onto a local road that parallels the national highway. At a soft drink and porno mag vending area we merged into Route 345, and immediately turned left toward the ferry terminal for boats to the island of Awa-shima. Here, the scenery changed to include groups of pines precariously anchored in sandy soil. A long curve around these trees took us to the Japan Sea.

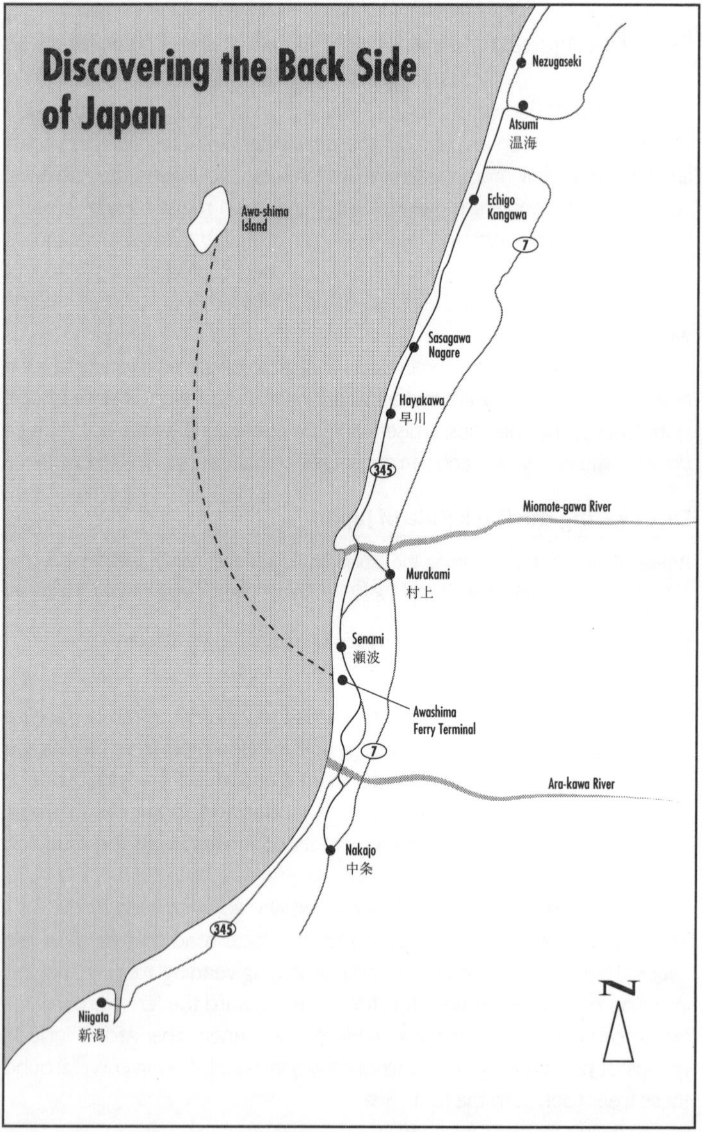
Discovering the Back Side of Japan
Nezugaseki
Atsumi
温海
Echigo Kangawa
7
Awa-shima Island
Sasagawa Nagare
Hayakawa
早川
345
Miomote-gawa River
Murakami
村上
Senami
瀬波
Awashima Ferry Terminal
7
Ara-kawa River
Nakajo
中条
345
Niigata
新潟
N

We passed by the ferry and cut back to Route 345 in the next town. The smell of salt air was soon tinged by the acrid smell of sulfur as we approached the hot springs at Senami Onsen. The roadside was cluttered with the usual tourist shops, so just after entering the town we took a hard left and cut down to a side road that parallels the beach. We came to a slight grade where the road turns right and rejoins Route 345 just before it crosses the Miomote-gawa River.

This brought us to our only big hill of the trip. We shifted into low gear and puffed up to the top of the headland. Here, the Japan Sea seemed to change its character; no longer a dull grey-green mat, it now sparkled blue in the sun. Ahead of us lay Sasagawa Nagare, a coast of rocky pinnacles, and white sand beaches with eye-opening snorkeling.

As we coasted down the other side of the hill we could see Route 345 continuing ahead of us, a narrow ribbon of concrete twisting between jutting rocks and verdant hills. Every five or six kilometers, we left the highway and passed through small towns on roads not quite wide enough for two bicycles abreast. Often we would negotiate a sharp turn and come face to face with local people, who would gasp in surprise and, registering our bicycles, smile and offer a hearty *gambatte*.

Later we began to think about dinner, and looked for a store to buy food to cook. After passing only small shops selling inedible household goods, we finally spotted a liquor store in Hayakawa. We were not really looking for a liquid dinner, but were aware these places often carry a large variety of snacks and canned food.

What we found was a smiling face and interest. The elderly owner commented on our bicycles and asked about our activities. After buying some crackers and instant noodles, we told her we were going to Sasagawa, and planned to cook dinner and camp out on the beach. Saying it would be difficult to do that, she motioned us into the back, sat us down in her kitchen, and started preparing some noodles. While we were waiting we had pickles, grilled fish, ham, oranges, and then finally the noodles for dessert. After the meal she brought out a *shikishi*, a square piece of decorative cardboard, that we signed and left as a memento.

As we backtracked to the beach, it occurred to me that in Tokyo, an area supposedly internationally minded and rife with Westerners, I had been refused entrance to bars and restaurants because I wasn't Japanese, and had rarely been invited into the homes of Japanese because they were "too small." Yet here, in rural Japan, we were being mothered, fed, and, on top of everything, asked for an autograph.

We set up camp on the beach behind a primary school. Surprisingly, a Japanese family was also camped there, unusual for May. We built a small fire and sipped the beer we had bought back at the liquor shop.

The next day we set out on the fifty-kilometer ride to Atsumi, a smaller and less commercial spa than Senami. We had another fine day curving in and out of tunnels, stopping to check out potential swimming spots, and exploring small towns. Hanging from windows, decorating the embankments, and scattered over the road were clumps of seaweed drying in the sea breeze. Cycle carefully to avoid flattening the seaweed and the old women laying it out.

Right after the town of Echigo-Kangawa, Route 7 joins up with Route 345 and we passed into Yamagata Prefecture and on to Nezugaseki, which we immediately dubbed the Squid Capital of Japan. Squid was omnipresent, drying from lines and on the road, alive in tanks and sinks, and sold in countless varieties in the many specialty restaurants. For lunch it was grilled squid on a stick.

About ninety minutes further up Route 7 we saw a sign for Atsumi Onsen, and the traffic became heavier and the riding not so pleasurable. We cut inland, gently ascended into the village and looked for the public bath. One of the most pleasurable aspects of cycling in Japan is submerging aching muscles in hot mineral waters after a day on the road. We washed and soaked for a good hour. Through the steam wafting from the pool we could just make out the blue sky and mountains beyond.

Feeling totally refreshed after the bath, we backtracked to a beach we'd spotted on the way up, set up our tent, and made a fire with driftwood. We lay back on the beach and watched the sun set over the sea, slowly diffusing into the horizon as the first stars made their appearance. The next day we would leave for home.

✍ PL

ⓘ Field Information

Sasagawa Nagare Minshuku Association ☎ 0254 77-2259

⌂ Lodging Log
Senami: Suzuki Minshuku ☎ 0254 52-1223; Wakabayashi ☎ 0254 52-5881; Kotobuki ☎ 0254 52-2616; Miomote ☎ 0254 532480
Atsumi: Sango ☎ 0235 44-2215

Lake and Samurai

Route: A trail around the deepest lake in Japan ending in the old castle town of Kakunodate with its samurai houses and old merchant homes
Start: Tazawako Station (Tazawako Line from Morioka)
Goal: Kakunodate Station (Tazawako Line to Morioka or Akita)

Last summer a friend and I packed our bikes and headed north. We were looking for a nice, uncrowded mountain area with clear lakes, unspoiled evergreen scenery, and crisp, pine-scented air.

We found it. We found Tazawa-ko Lake.

Getting there by train may be a bit expensive, but it is certainly worth it. We took the Tohoku shinkansen from Ueno all the way to the end at Morioka, then changed to the Tazawako Line and got off at Tazawako Station. After assembling our bicycles, we rode from the station up a very slight three-kilometer grade to the shore of the lake. Then it was smooth, level riding (broken only by one hill) around one of the clearest lakes in Honshu. It was a weekday, and there were very few cars. The road around Tazawa-ko is about twenty kilometers in total, with only one hardly challenging hill. There was also a toll gate where bicycles were charged a miniscule sum.

We stopped at the Prince Hotel on the south shore and had cool drinks and ice cream in the restaurant that overlooks the lake. We had eaten earlier and we regretted not splurging there on a hotel lunch instead. In fact, since we had to be in Akita the following night, we couldn't even have the luxury of staying at the lake.

Late in the afternoon we left the lake on the south exit road and enjoyed a glorious downhill with wide, scenic curves that seemed to go on for over fifteen kilometers. After much more riding in a long, flat valley surrounded by rice fields, we arrived at Kakunodate. A quiet little town with a section of straight, tree-lined streets, Kakunodate has an impressive collection of old houses where samurai once summered, and most are open to the public.

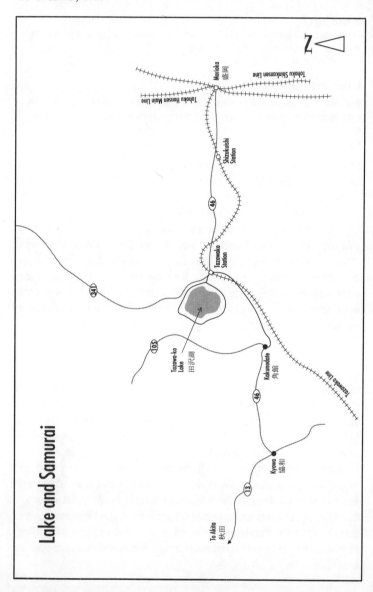

Lake and Samurai

Tazawa-ko Lake
田沢湖

Tazawako Station

Kakunodate
角館

Kyowa
協和

To Akita
秋田

Morioka
盛岡

Shizukuishi Station

Tohoku Shinkansen Line

Tohoku Honsen Main Line

Tazawako Line

The town also features a cozy little restaurant called Fuga. The son of the owner studied cooking in Italy for several years and returned to build a very pleasant little Italian restaurant. Prices are reasonable, and the food is great. Restaurant guests used to be able to stagger from the restaurant to the *minshuku* on the upper floors but the owners have unfortunately now given up the *minshuku* side of the business.

The next day we rode to Akita, and then went down the Japan Sea coast to Yamagata. However, we really enjoyed most the first two days of our trip at Tazawa-ko Lake and Kakunodate.　　　📖 BH

❶ Field Information
Tazawa-ko Information Center ☎ 0187 43-0307
Kakunodate Information Center ☎ 0187 54-2700
Fuga Italian Restaurant ☎ 0187 54-2784

⌂ Lodging Log
Tazawa-ko Lake: Kuroyu Onsen (rustic hot springs) ☎ 0187 46-2214; Tsurunoyu Onsen (rural hot springs) ☎ 0187 46-2814
Kakunodate: Watanabe ☎ 0187 54-3244; Hyaku Suien (traditional building) ☎ 0187 55-5715; Shimokawara (traditional building) ☎ 0187 53-2357; Sakura no Sato ☎ 0187 55-5652; Sozan-so ☎ 0187 55-1640

Osore-zan: The Gateway to Hell　　

Route: Coastal routes around the Shimokita-hanto Peninsula head for the other-worldly Osore-zan, home of departed spirits, and another type of hell, Rokkasho-mura, the home of Japan's first low-level radioactive waste storage facility. For refreshment the route continues to Towada-ko, a deep volcanic lake
Start: Oma (ferry from Hakodate)
Goal: Towada-ko Lake

A tour of Hokkaido last summer left us in a good position to explore northern Tohoku. It was, after all, on the way back to Tokyo.

We got an early-morning start from Hakodate and headed to the ferry landing. The boat to Oma on the Shimokita-hanto is cheap and takes only an hour and a half. Route 338 down the west coast of the peninsula is rather rugged, but if you have time and energy the area has some excellent views and interesting rock formations. If you're coming from the south, an interesting approach would be to get a boat from Aomori to Wakinosawa on the south-western corner of the peninsula and continue the ride into Mutsu from there.

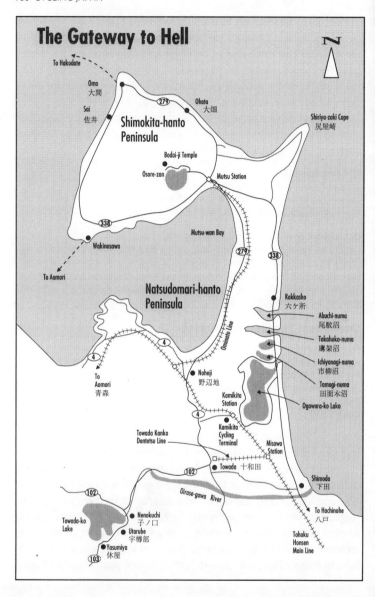

The Gateway to Hell

N

To Hakodate

Oma
大間

Sai
佐井

Ohata
大畑

(279)

Shimokita-hanto
Peninsula

Shiriya-zaki Cape
尻屋崎

Bodai-ji Temple

Osore-zan

Mutsu Station

(338)

Mutsu-wan Bay

Wakinosawa

(279)

(338)

To Aomori

Natsudomari-hanto
Peninsula

Rokkasho
六ヶ所

Abuchi-numa
尾駮沼

Takahoko-numa
鷹架沼

Ominato Line

Ichiyanagi-numa
市柳沼

Tamogi-numa
田面木沼

(4)

Ogawara-ko Lake

(4)

Noheji
野辺地

To
Aomori
青森

Kamikita
Station

Towada Kanko
Dentetsu Line

Kamikita
Cycling
Terminal

Misawa
Station

(102)

Towada 十和田

Shimoda
下田

Oirase-gawa River

(102)

To Hachinohe
八戸

Towada-ko
Lake

Nenokuchi
子ノ口

Utarube
宇樽部

Tohoku
Honsen
Main Line

(103)

Yasumiya
休屋

Even if you don't take Route 338, rather than staying in the slightly drab town of Oma, one idea is to ride about fifteen kilometers down the coast to the beach area of Sai, where *minshuku* are available. The next day, we rode along the northeastern coast, taking Route 279, which was lined with shellfish farms on one side and fishing boats strung with lanterns for night fishing on the other. Despite the strong headwinds we decided to push on to Mutsu instead of staying around Ohata. After getting used to finding camping sites relatively easily in Hokkaido, we didn't have much luck finding places to camp in Mutsu and we ended up camping in the city park. Later we were to experience the same difficulties throughout Tohoku.

Apart from the desolate, windswept hills and the stunning coastal scenery of the Shimokita-hanto, one of the major attractions of this area is to see one of the few places in Japan where local beliefs rooted in animism are still very much in evidence. The word *osore* literally means dread, and Osore-zan is known as a gathering spot for spirits to communicate with the living. On hand to facilitate the communication between the living and the dear departed are blind shaman women known as *itako*. You may run across *itako* at any time of the year, but during festival periods (July 20–24 and October 9–11) it's possible to see over twenty *itako* in action. Even if your Tohoku dialect is a bit rusty, the sessions offer an interesting and rare glimpse into the religious life of old communities.

After about two hours' ride from Mutsu, the overpowering smell of sulphur that assaulted our senses made it quite obvious that we were nearing the rim of the crater. The road began to go down, and gradually the whitish blue water of Usori-ko Lake came into view. We first rode over to Bodai-ji, a temple founded in the ninth century on the northeast shore of the lake, where the *itako* gather to communicate with the spirits during the two major festivals. Attached to the temple is an inn which can be very crowded during the festivals. But in August there were fewer than twenty visitors and we were given a big room overlooking the lake. The inn prefers guests to arrive by five in the afternoon, so try and get there early or call in advance to make sure of a room.

After dinner we wandered down to Sai-no-kawara, the river dividing heaven and hell. We gazed at all the small tombs, monuments, and Buddhist statues in the area, ruminating on the meaning of life. Wandering souls desperate for a last chance to enter heaven are said to be responsible for the piles of stones at Sai-no-Kawara. Protecting the efforts of the departed are a battalion of *jizo* statues; the smaller *jizo* festooned with colorful bibs, toys, and sweets are in memory of deceased children. As it grew dark the atmosphere became more and more eerie—sinister streams of vapor well up from the steaming ground, stunted trees and grasses punctuate the land, and all of a sudden flocks of screeching crows sweep down onto the tombs. All in all we were glad to be able to escape to the bath houses in the grounds of the temple, which are open to the public regardless of whether you are staying at the inn. The bath houses are small, about sixty meters square, made of wood, and all cater for mixed bathers. We entered one of the baths and found two people already enjoying a long soak. One was a college student traveling by scooter who had set up a tent just by the main gate of the temple. Curiously enough, the other bather was not a tourist but a resident of Mutsu who regularly used the hot spring bath instead of going to the public baths in the city. However, as the night wore on, we began to suspect that he came to the baths merely to amuse himself by scaring unsuspecting strangers with his sinister stories. One night in summer, so the story went, he took a bath as usual in one of the bath houses and remembers very clearly the bangings and clatterings and high-spirited chatter coming from the neighboring bath, signifying that several people were enjoying the waters. He finished his bath and as usual set off on the path back to his car. However, he was astonished to find there were no lights in the next bath house and indeed no sign of anybody leaving the bath. Summoning up courage, he went forward and pushed open the door. Nobody was inside and the floor was completely dry. That he had interrupted the shades' bathtime was, he insisted, the only possible explanation for his strange experience.

The next day, a morning prayer was held in one of the temple buildings. Although the ceremony was nothing out of the ordinary, what *was* different was the display in the temple. Set up all around the building were typical Japanese dolls, which were all clad in white. It seemed that they were dedicated to people who had died young and single, in the hope that they would find their perfect match in paradise. To complete the rather sinister image, clothes belonging to the departed were draped here and there around the room. It's hardly any wonder that the people of the Shimokita-hanto believe that the area is an important destination for departed spirits—it's also very interesting for the living, but we weren't sorry to be cycling away from Osore-zan the next day.

From Mutsu you have two choices of routes, both involving lakes. To continue the theme of riding into hell, take Route 338 to Ogawara-ko Lake. This area is another kind of eerie wasteland as it involves riding through Rokkasho, the town made famous for its storage facility capable of storing three million drums of nuclear waste. With plans afoot to make Rokkasho into a vast "nuclear toilet" with the construction of a high-level radioactive waste storage facility and plants for uranium enrichment and reprocessing of nuclear waste, you can be sure that dinner conversation will not be dull.

There is pleasant cycling around Ogawara-ko, a lake sixty-two kilometers in circumference. On the southwestern corner is the Ogawara-ko Cycling Terminal, a convenient if rather impersonal place to put up for the night. The terminal is located about ten minutes from Kamikita Station on the Tohoku Honsen Main Line, with direct trains to Tokyo and other stations on the main shinkansen line. Spring is a particularly good time to visit the lake to see the water lilies; in winter the lake is frozen over and fishermen sit huddled up brooding over their holes in the ice.

From Mutsu it's possible to make Towada-ko Lake in a day, as Route 279 meanders along the coast like a route across the English fens. From Noheji, a transportation hub for the Shimokita-hanto, turn left onto Route 4 and head for Towada. There are plenty of *minshuku* in this area, but we were lucky to run into some members of a Tenrikyo temple who offered to put us up in exchange for a brief appearance at an English class.

The next day we rode up to Towada-ko on Route 102, which winds its way along the scenic Oirase-gawa River. From Towada Onsen there is a special bike path leading down into the small town of Nenokuchi. Turn left and the road follows the shore of the lake to the largest town, Yasumiya. Despite its reputation as the biggest tourist attraction in northern Honshu, the area is pleasant and also has a number of campgrounds.

Yasumiya is the transport center of the area; buses leave from here to all corners of Tohoku, such as Aomori, Morioka, and Hirosaki. From Morioka you could take the route to Tazawa-ko Lake , as described on page 157.

⇨ Route Extension

From Aomori, try heading for the Japan Sea coastline. From west of Goshogawara and Aomori, Route 101 follows the coast south for about a hundred kilometers to Noshiro, near the Oga-hanto Peninsula. This stretch is highly recommended for its outstanding scenery—melon fields, inviting beaches, and small villages. There are few tunnels and traffic is light because of the wider Route 7 that runs inland and takes all but the local traffic. Judging from the reactions of the locals, particularly when we were looking for a *minshuku*, this area sees few foreigners. The town of Iwasaki is suggested as a convenient stopover. *Minshuku* are available on the Oga-hanto, many of which offer bicycles for hire, and there's also a well-equipped campground facing the ocean.   ✍ NGH

❶ Field Information

Boats: Three daily runs from Hakodate to Oma; trip takes 90 minutes; one departure daily to Muroran (extra runs during summer); trip takes 5 hours. Aomori to Wakinosawa once a day; trip takes an hour

Sai-mura Minshuku Association ☎ 0175 38-2225
Wakinosawa Tourist Information ☎ 0175 44-2217
Ohata Tourist Information ☎ 0175 34-2111
Mutsu Tourist Information ☎ 0175 22-1111
Rokkasho-mura Tourist Information ☎ 0175 72-2332
For reservations in the Towada City area, call Nambu-so ☎ 0176 23-5655
Towada-ko Information Center ☎ 0176 75-2506
Towada-ko Minshuku Association ☎ 0176 75-2805
Oga Tourist Information ☎ 0185 37-2122

⌂ Lodging Log

Ohata: Ryokan Muraki ☎ 0175 34-5698; Minshuku Matsunoki ☎ 0175 34-2467
Wakinosawa: Sugiura-so (fishing boat available) ☎ 0175 44-2357
Rokkasho-mura: (Tomari area) Benten-so ☎ 0175 772142; Ueno ☎ 0175 77-2472; Kawachi House ☎ 0175 77-3038
Towada-ko: (Yasumiya area) Sugiyama ☎ 0176 75-2713; Kaede-so ☎ 0176 75-2126; (Utarube area) Momiji-so ☎ 0176 75-2613; Mizuumi ☎ 0176 75-2712; (Nenokuchi area) Kumoi-so ☎ 0176 75-2537; Negishi-ya ☎ 0176 75-2903
Iwasaki area: Shichinohe ☎ 0173 77-2203; Juniko-kan ☎ 0173 77-2228; Shirakami-so ☎ 0173 77-2227

The (Summer) Cycling Paradise of Hokkaido

Hakodate: The Jewel of Hokkaido   🚲

Route: A meandering route from Hakodate around the Kameda-hanto Peninsula with glorious views of unspoilt fishing villages and mountain lakes
Start: Hakodate Station (JR Tsugaru Line from Aomori, ferry from Northern Honshu ports of Oma, Noheji, and Aomori)
Goal: Hakodate

Situated near the southern tip of Hokkaido, Hakodate serves as a gateway to the island, and the perfect place to start or end a tour of Hokkaido. You may want to put aside a few days to stay in town, making day trips out in each direction. Although Hakodate may not be as interesting as it must have been, say, a hundred years ago, evidence remains of its cosmopolitan past, with strong western influence in both the architecture and layout of the city. Hakodate has far more charm and character than any other city in Hokkaido, although Otaru comes a close second.

The best time to start your exploration of Hakodate is at sunset; the place is atop Hakodate-yama, a 333m high mountain that overlooks the city on its southern edge. The road to the top is a speedway of taxis and tour buses, so it's best to cycle to the tram station at the foot of the mountain and ride to the top for a look at the city. What unfolds in front of you as the sun goes down is a compact city on a narrowing peninsula that gradually becomes lit up with strands of lights.

After you descend, enjoy a *sushi* or seafood dinner in one of the many good restaurants in town. The next morning get up early and ride the waterfront along Hakodate Harbor to check out the fish market. The old center of the city is quite small and colorful, with a combination of influences that make it seem a little bit American, a little bit European and a little bit Japanese. The small collection of foreign cemeteries overlooking the ocean on the far west side of town gives a clue as to how cosmopolitan Hakodate must have been when it was a major port of call in the Far East in times past.

A recommended *minshuku* in town, located near Hakodate City Hall, is Akai Boshi, somewhat Western-style with reasonable prices. The owner is very friendly, flexible about a lot of things, and very helpful; reservations

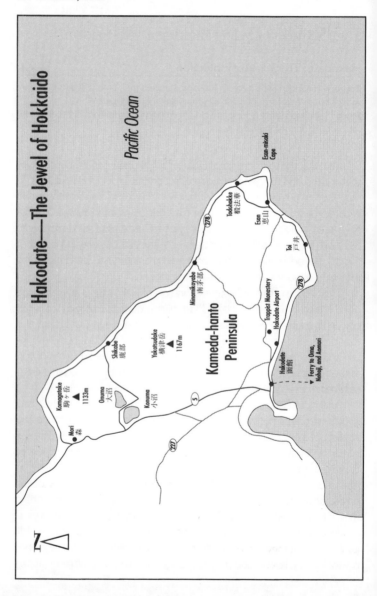

Hakodate—The Jewel of Hokkaido

Pacific Ocean

Kameda-hanto Peninsula

Mori
森

Komagatake
駒ヶ岳
1133m

Onuma
大沼

Konuma
小沼

Shikabe
鹿部

Yokotsudake
横津岳
1167m

Minamikayabe
南茅部

Todohokke
椴法華

Esan
恵山

Esan-misaki
Cape

Toi
戸井

Trappist Monastery

Hakodate Airport

Hakodate
函館

Ferry to Oma,
Noheji, and Aomori

5

227

278

278

should be made at least three days in advance. An interesting alternative is Toshogu-jinja, an unpublicized Shinto Shrine, which charges ¥500 if you have a sleeping bag or ¥1,000 if you borrow a *futon*.

The coast east of Hakodate and some nearby lakeshores make for excellent riding. A circle starting from Hakodate takes riders along the coast east of Route 278 to Shikabe, a distance of about eighty kilometers. Route 278 is generally easy riding with beautiful scenery and special character, featuring one fishing village after another. About six kilometers from Hakodate is Yunokawa Onsen; the hot springs not only feed the big hotels but also the village's public bath. This is a good destination after a swim, or perhaps before a flight leaving Hakodate Airport a few kilometers further along Route 278. *Minshuku* are also available in Toi further along the coast.

When we rode round the peninsula, it seemed that the whole population was either in boats pulling in long strips of seaweed, or on the shore laying them out to dry. In the early morning hours, this section must be a photographer's paradise. Between villages, there are some hills, none of which are very steep. There are also some tunnels, maybe three of which are a kilometer or so long with no sidewalks, though traffic is light.

From Shikabe Onsen, turn left toward Onuma-koen Park, about fifteen kilometers inland, which has several lakes. The smaller of the two lakes is Konuma-ko, around which Route 5 runs, but Onuma-ko is much nicer to ride around. If you're interested in spending the night in this area, there are hot-spring *minshuku* at Yamamizu Onsen on the north side of Konuma-ko and Higashi Onuma Onsen on the far side of Onuma-ko. Leaving the park, Hakodate is less than thirty kilometers away.   ✍ BH

❶ Field Information
Hakodate Tourist Information (in Motomachi Park) ☎ 0138 23-5440
Hakodate Minshuku Association ☎ 0138 26-1126
Onuma-koen Tourist Information ☎ 0138 67-2170

⚓ Lodging Log
Hakodate: Akai Boshi ☎ 0138 26-4035; Toshogu-jinja ☎ 0138 32-2221; Hotel New Hakodate (interesting modern hotel with surprising touches in converted Meiji period bank) ☎ 0138 22-8131
Near Hakodate Station: Hakodate-so ☎ 0138 23-6431; Kumachi ☎ 0138 22-3437
At the foot of Hakodate-yama: Karamatsu-so ☎ 0138 22-7759; Hijikata ☎ 0138 22-2839;

St. MC Rider House ☎ 0138 22-6841; Meet Rider House ☎ 0138 23-3327
Yunokawa Onsen: Kita no Yado ☎ 0138 59-2092; Sumire ☎ 0138 59-2092; Yamaoyaji ☎ 0138 59-0512; Chishima Ryokan ☎ 0138 59-0087
Toi: For *minshuku* reservations call Drive in Toi ☎ 0138 82-2198
Esan: For *minshuku* reservations call ☎ 0138 85-2851
Onuma-koen: Onuma Minshuku ☎ 013865-2511; Tome no Yu ☎ 0138 67-3345

Tomakomai Two Lakes Route 🚲

Route: A pleasant run around two lakes in Southern Hokkaido with high-altitude adventures for the energetic, finishing with a sweep along the coast back to Tomakomai or round Uchiura-wan Bay to Hakodate
Start: Tomakomai (ferry from Tokyo, Nagoya, Oarai, Sendai, and Hachinohe, JR Chitose Line to Sapporo, and JR Hakodate Honsen Main Line to Hakodate
Goal: Tomakomai or Hakodate

From Tokyo's Ariake 4-chome wharf, we caught a ferry for Hokkaido late Saturday night, arriving in Tomakomai the following Monday about 5:30 A.M. on a drizzling, overcast morning.

A good ride starting from the Tomakomai ferry terminal is along National Route 276 northwest to Shikotsu-ko, a scenic lake surrounded by several volcanoes. For just over twenty kilometers from Tomakomai to Morappu there is a very pleasant cycling road. Once at Shikotsu-ko cyclists can ride around the lake on mostly good, level road. Starting from Poropinai at the northern edge of the lake there is a thirty-one kilometer cycling road to Sapporo. We enjoyed climbing the steep and varied peak of Eniwadake (1,320m), the most interesting of the dozen mountains we climbed in Hokkaido. Those wanting a more challenging hill might try Route 512. We, fortunately, coasted down this grade, which was steep and maybe three or four kilometers long, ending at lake level. If time affords, the loop around Eniwadake can be enlarged by taking the route over the hill with some fantastic riding into Sapporo. From Sapporo the route to Shakotan can be followed as described on page 171, looping round to Toya-ko via the Raiden Kaigan Route and across to Rebun.

From Shikotsu-ko, continue west for about thirty-five or forty kilometers on Route 276 and then turn left onto Route 723, which leads to Toyako, another lake. Route 276 has generally good shoulders and more gradual climbs. Tunnels usually have good sidewalks, although one tunnel about 1.5 kilometers long didn't. From that particular tunnel the remaining

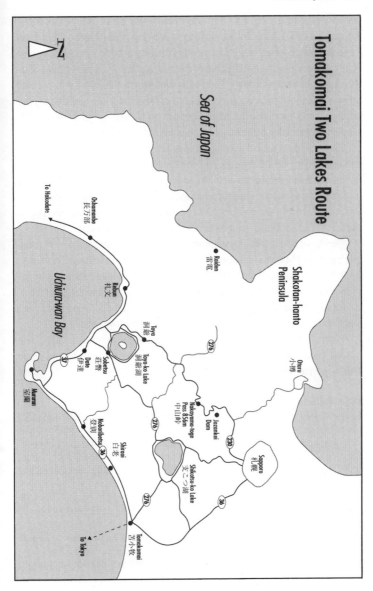

Tomakomai Two Lakes Route

Sea of Japan

Shakotan-hanto Peninsula

Otaru 小樽

276

Uchiura-wan Bay

To Hakodate

Oshamambe 長万部

Rebun 礼文

Reiden 雷電

Toya 洞爺

Toya-ko Lake 洞爺湖

Sobetsu 壮瞥

Date 伊達

37

Muroran 室蘭

36

Noboribetsu 登別

Shiraoi 白老

276

Nakayama-toge Pass 856m 中山峠

Jozankei Dam

230

Sapporo 札幌

Shikotsu-ko Lake 支こつ湖

276

36

Tomakomai 苫小牧

To Tokyo

N

portion of Route 276, and the entire thirty-five or so kilometers along Route 723 to Toyako Onsen, is pretty much downhill. There is lots of volcanic activity to observe in this area, particularly around Toyako Onsen. I highly recommend a few days here: the ride up the hill to see Showa Shinzan, a volcano born during 1943–44, is well worth the effort and we also enjoyed the Abuta volcanology museum in Toyako Onsen—especially the volcano simulation room. Both Toya-ko and Shikotsu-ko have a wide range of hotels and *minshuku*; campsites are also available.

Early the next morning we did the entire thirty-five kilometer circuit of the lake and found it delightful. Looking for cycling challenges, we left Toya-ko via Route 5 heading toward Noboribetsu, over the Orofure-toge Pass (930m). The view from the top is supposed to be spectacular, but visibility was only 25m in the dense fog. After a cold ride down, we warmed up in the sun at Noboribetsu, an area famed for its *onsen* and volcanic terrain.

Next, we spent two days at Shiraoi, famous as an important Ainu center; the Ainu Minzoku Hakubutsukan Museum is worth visiting. To make a circle back to Tomakomai and the ferry, retrace the above route or, alternatively, ride back along the coast on Route 36. While the area around Muroran looks like good riding on a map, much of the ride back to Tomakomai is along routes 36 and 37, which sometimes feature heavy traffic.

From Toyako Onsen, the sea is only about five kilometers away. Climb the hill separating Toya-ko Lake from the southern coastline, and circle around Uchiura-wan to Hakodate.   ✍ JK

❶ Field Information

Ferries: Tokyo to Tomakomai 4 sailings a week, departing 11:30 A.M. arriving 5:30 A.M. two days later. Depart Tomakomai 11:45 A.M. arriving Tokyo 5:00 P.M. two days later; from ¥11,840; for reservations call Nihon Enkai Ferry ☎ 03 3573-1911

Oarai to Tomakomai departing 11:59 A.M. arriving Tomakomai 8:00 A.M. 2 days later. Depart Tomakomai 11:45 A.M. arrive Oarai 7:00 P.M. 2 days later; for reservations call Blue Highway Line ☎ 03 3578-1127

Oarai to Muroran, 3 sailings a week, departing midnight arriving Muroran 7:20 P.M. the next day. Departs Muroran midnight arriving Oarai 6:50 P.M.; for reservations call Higashi Nihon Ferry ☎ 03 5561-0211

Hachinohe to Tomakomai, daily; contact Silver Ferries ☎ 03 3502-4838 or Higashi Nihon Ferry ☎ 0178 28-3985

Nagoya to Tomakomai via Sendai, one sailing every other day; for reservations

contact Taiheiyo Ferries ☎ 052 203-0227
Shikotsu-ko Tourist Information ☎ 0123 25-2404

🏠 **Lodging Log**
Tomakomai-shi Cycling Terminal ☎ 0144 35-1800
Shikotsu-ko: Tamura Minshuku ☎ 0142 38-2001
Toya-ko: Kawata Minshuku ☎ 01428 2-5503; Pension Toya ☎ 01428 7-2529
Shiraoi area: For reservations call Kurotake Minshuku ☎ 0144 87-2333

The Back Way to Hokkaido   🚲

Route: A scenic coastal route halfway round the rugged Shakotan-hanto Peninsula
to Nozuka. dropping into the wineries and whiskey distillery at Yoichi and exploring
the craggy Shakotan-misaki Cape
Start and Goal: Otaru (ferry from Niigata)

One of the few remaining travel bargains in Japan is the ferry that sails from
Maizuru/Tsuruga (opposite Osaka on the Japan Sea), stops at Niigata, and
continues to Otaru in Hokkaido. The ferry leaves at 11:30 A.M. and docks in
Otaru at 5:00 the next morning. If you leave on one of the first shinkansen
from Ueno, you can get to Niigata in time to board. This beautiful 1,200
kilometer cruise costs only ¥6,500, though unbagged bikes are ¥2,500 extra.

My wife and I took this ferry to Hokkaido last May. We stayed at the
youth hostel in Otaru and hiked up Mt. Tengu for a great view of town, and
the nearby snowy mountains. Otaru has a lot of old Western style buildings;
it's just starting to get touristy, so see it soon. In Otaru, we bought Shobunsha's compact but accurate *Two-Wheel Touring Mapbook of Hokkaido*.

Though summer is the time when the mountains are at their best, it's
also the best time to ride the coast. We left Otaru and headed for the
Shakotan-hanto, a rugged peninsula currently lacking a through road
around its coastline. (The tunnel connecting Route 229 with the road on
the other side of the peninsula is scheduled to be completed in 1995)
Cool breezes take the edge off the summer heat, while a quick ocean dip
always waits appealingly around the next bend.

This ride around the Shakotan-hanto can be done in a full day, but over
two days you can better savor the sights. Take Route 5 east out of town to
Yoichi. This area is quite interesting; the road runs almost at water level, with
rugged rock cliffs sprouting straight up here and there and short tunnels in

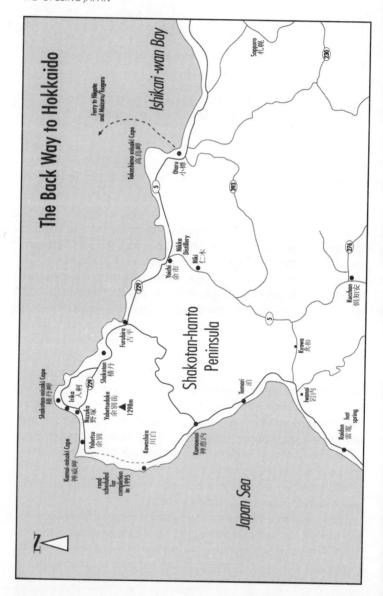

abundance. If you have time, stop at the Nikka distillery in Yoichi (follow the signs or ask) where whiskey and apple wine are dished out free to bus-loads of tourists, and various Hokkaido food items are on sale. The restaurant is reasonable and tasty, and there's also a nice lawn to stretch out on and nap on afterwards. You can also ride south a ways on Route 5 where fruit is sold at roadside stands. Cherries are in season until early August; the chilly Yoichi summer mornings make the fruit firm and tasty.

At Yoichi, turn onto Route 229 to Furubira. Go through Furubira, and ride on straight toward Shakotan-cho. There's bit of a climb, then the road straightens out and simmers slightly downhill through some very un-Japanese scenery with grassy rolling hills and scattered stands of trees. You'll be off the coast now, but you'll rejoin the sea where Route 229 meets the coast road at Nozuka. We found a fabulous beach campground there and liked it so much we stayed three nights. The road to the left at Nozuka leads to Hizuka and Yobetsu, where *minshuku* are available. If time is running out, turn right at Nozuka and ride along the water's edge through villages where seaweed and abalone are king toward Shakotan-misaki Cape. You can hike to the lighthouse and explore tidepools. Accommodation is available in the village of Irika near Shakotan-misaki. The road rolls up and down along the coast, and finally turns inland to join back up with Route 229, the road you came in on. Turn left and head back to Otaru.

Alternatively, you can take Route 998 for thirty kilometers over a 800m-high pass to the opposite side of the peninsula. In Raiden, a *ryokan* up on a hill let us camp in a pretty spot and use their wonderful *onsen*. We experienced this sort of hospitality almost every day we were in Hokkaido.

We then camped at the small village of Rebun, where the man at the *sento* let us take showers for free since we had come so far. It rained for thirty hours straight, and our seven-year-old tent couldn't stand such heavy weather, so, for the second night, we slept comfortably in an abandoned railroad tunnel, thinking of the movie *Stand By Me*. If you have time, Toya-ko and Shikotsu-ko lakes (see page 168) are tantalizingly close.   ✍ BH

❶ Field Information
Niigata to Otaru Ferry, from ¥5,150; for reservations call Shin Nihonkai Ferries ☎ 06 348-1120
Otaru Tourist Information Center (in Otaru Station) ☎ 0134 33-1661

Yoichi Tourist Information ☎ 0135 23-2141
Shakotan Tourist Association ☎ 0135 44-3715

🏠 **Lodging Log**
Central Otaru: Ponpon ☎ 0134 27-0866; Fukuhara-so ☎ 0134 22-9906; Ohara ☎ 0134 22-4648
Irika (just before Shakotan-misaki): Ginrinkaku ☎ 0135 40-6323
Hizuka (2km west of Nozuka): Hizuka-so ☎ 0135 45-6548
Yobetsu (the end of the road): Hamanasu Minshuku ☎ 0135 46-5111

The Lake District

Route: A scenic route exploring the numerous lakes of Eastern Hokkaido, finishing up on the wild and remote peninsula of Shiretoko
Start: Kushiro (ferry from Tokyo)
Goal: Utoro on the Shiretoko Peninsula

For a trip around some of the most stunning scenery in Japan, the town of Kushiro serves as a convenient gateway. Accessible by ferry from Tokyo, the town has the feel of a major fishing port in Northern Europe. The thirty-two hour cruise provides ample time for relaxation before the rigors of cycling around Japan's Lake District. If the cruise is too relaxing, consider a trip around Hidaka, the coastal horse ranching region on the way to Erimo-misaki Cape, which is flat and provides some nice cycling.

We headed up to Akan National Park, leaving the cold and fog of Kushiro for welcome sun and warmth. From Tsurumi-bashi Bridge in Kushiro to Akan-machi there is a pleasant twenty-six kilometer cycling path following the Akan-gawa River. From the path it's easy to get onto Route 240 for Akan-ko Lake by heading left. Just after Akan-machi is the Akan-ko Cycling Terminal, located near Tancho no Sato, a well known wintering spot for the red-crowned crane. Hundreds of cranes can be seen here from November through March, unfortunately not times when you're likely to be cycling through the area, although some cranes are kept in captivity here.

Akan-ko Lake was so pleasant we stayed for five days and climbed three high volcanoes in the vicinity; O-Akandake, Me-Akandake, and Akan-Fuji. The road from Akan-ko to Kussharo-ko Lake, Route 241 and Route 243 from the Teshikaga intersection, was another fantastic one. Teshikaga is not only the meeting point of the main roads in the area, but is also, bizarrely enough, the location of the European Folkcrafts Museum.

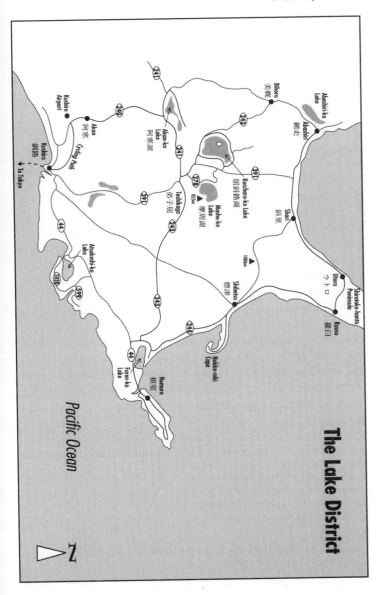

The Lake District

Kussharo-ko was beautifully green, but infested with mosquitoes. Mashu-ko is another beautiful lake, shrouded in mist for most of the year, earning it the name of Lake of the Gods among the Ainu people. All these lakes are pleasant to cycle around with the exception of Mashu-ko, which is a steep-sided crater lake with no roads around it.

Our next destination was Nemuro, the easternmost city in Hokkaido. There is a new, free campground here, but in July the weather is generally cold and wet. We would have been better off heading north instead. On a rainy, foggy day we hitch-hiked to Nosappu-misaki Cape and caught a glimpse of the Habomai-shoto, some of the islands seized by the Soviets in 1945. A museum illustrating the history of the troubled islands, the Hopporyodo-kan near Nemuro Station, is worth a visit.

In cold weather, we turned north along the Sea of Okhotsk to Shibetsu. We splurged on our wedding anniversary and stayed at the very friendly youth hostel there. The next day was cold and drizzly, but we rode out on Nokke-hanto Peninsula to the end of the road. In the mist it was pretty, and in the afternoon it warmed up a bit for our ride to Rausu, on the Shiretoko-hanto Peninsula.

Shiretoko-hanto is very rugged, and most of it is only accessible on foot or by boat. The campground at Rausu has a great, free *rotenburo*, and was crowded with motorcycle tourists, but good fun and highly recommended. We headed up the long and nicely graded hill to Shiretoko-toge Pass (730m). The weather kept improving and we could see all around, even to Kunashiri, another Soviet-held island. Going down the other side was great; something like fourteen kilometers without pedaling a single stroke.   ✍ NGH

❶ Field Information

Ferry Info: Depart Tokyo 11:00 P.M. arriving Kushiro two days later at 8:30 A.M.; ferry departs Kushiro 12:30 P.M. arriving Tokyo thirty-two hours later at 7:40 P.M.; for reservations call Kinkai Yusen toll-free ☎ 0120 154946
Akanko Tourist Information ☎ 0154 67-3200
Nemuro Tourist Information ☎ 01532 3-6111
Nokke-hanto Tourist Information ☎ 01537-5-3651
Utoro Minshuku Information Center ☎ 01522 4-2207

🏠 Lodging Log

Kushiro: Charanke-so (in front of Youth Hostel) ☎ 0154 41-2386; Taiki-kan (near Kushiro Station) ☎ 0154 25-1934

Akan-ko:Yamagoya ☎ 0154 67-2557; Kiri ☎ 0154 67-2755; Ryogoku ☎ 0154 67-2773 (all onsen); Akan-ko Han Rider House Mumin ☎ 0154 67-2727

Nemuro: Furen (run by birdwatcher for birdwatchers; closed Oct. and Nov.) ☎ 01532 5-3919; Jiyu no Ie Noto (rider house) ☎ 01532 3-3335

Central Rausu: Shiretoko House ☎ 01538 7-2225; Marumi (Yagihama-machi) ☎ 01538 8-2923; Kannari ☎ 01538 7-3338, Ishibashi ☎ 01538 7-3222 (Yunozawa-machi); Marumi Shokudo ☎ 01538 8-2146, Fuji ☎ 01538 8-2776 (Azabu-machi); Rider House Shirakaba (Sakai-machi) ☎ 01538 7-2506; Rider House Akai Yane (Kasuga-machi) ☎ 01538 8-2271; Ippen Kite Mina Ya (rider house, Rebun-machi) ☎ 01538 7-2235

Utoro: Rider House Kitsune no Ie ☎ 01522 4-2656; Rider House Kabochiya-en ☎ 01522 3-1651

Shibetsu: Sencho no Ie ☎ 01538 2-3051; Hamanasu ☎ 01538 2-3139; Minato-ya ☎ 01538 2-2676

Arctic Loop

Route: Get away from it all by taking this leisurely route through desolate scenery in one of the most sparsely populated regions of Japan, spiced up with side-trips to a Yosemite lookalike gorge and short hops to offshore islands
Start: Asahikawa or any of the other stations along the Soya Honsen Main Line, eg Kenbuchi, Shibutsu, Nayoro
Goal: Sapporo

Deciding on a start in the city of Asahikawa leaves a variety of routes open to you. Those who crave the heady atmosphere of high altitudes can take Route 39 and head toward Saroma-ko Lake on the east coast. At the intersection in Kamikawa turn left on to Route 273 and go straight ahead, the road following the river. When Route 273 turns off to the left toward Monbetsu, go straight on Route 333, the road gradually climbing up to the Sekihoku-toge Pass (1,050m), which is actually rather easier than it looks on the map. Route 333 winds down toward Engaru with a final flourish of a series of stunning curves—turn on to Route 242 to Monbetsu. From Monbetsu you can explore the area around Saroma-ko Lake. Alternatively, head up the coast toward Hamatonbetsu and Wakkanai.

Those with time to spare might like to consider a side-trip to Sounkyo Gorge, a great place to cycle and hike and generally while away a few days. From Asahikawa, turn on to Route 39 and at the Kamikawa interchange, turn right where the road forks with Route 273 and you'll soon find yourself

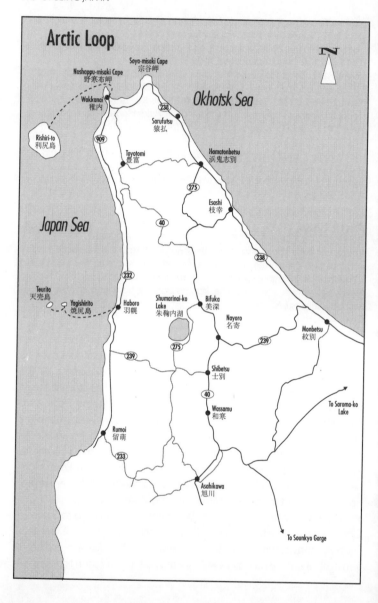

Arctic Loop

Soya-misaki Cape
宗谷岬

Noshappu-misaki Cape
野寒布岬

Okhotsk Sea

Wakkanai
稚内

238

Sarufutsu
猿払

Rishiri-to
利尻島

909

Toyotomi
豊富

Hamatonbetsu
浜鬼志別

275

Japan Sea

Esashi
枝幸

40

238

232

Teurito
天売島

Yagishirito
焼尻島

Haboro
羽幌

Shumarinai-ko
Lake
朱鞠内湖

Bifuka
美深

Nayoro
名寄

Monbetsu
紋別

239

275

239

Shibetsu
士別

40

Wassamu
和寒

To Saroma-ko
Lake

Rumoi
留萌

233

Asahikawa
旭川

To Sounkyo Gorge

riding through a gorge like a miniature Yosemite Valley with steep cliffs and thundering waterfalls. One of the best things about the area is the cycling path with great views of the gorge; rental bicycles are available. The area is simply a pleasant place to spend a few days hiking and cycling around. For example, we attempted the highest mountain in Hokkaido—Asahidake (2290m) with supposedly great views of the surrounding area, but, unfortunately, were turned back one kilometer from the summit by fierce winds, heavy fog, and smothering snow.

The third route from Asahikawa heads up north toward Wakkanai, the northernmost town in Japan. The main attraction of this area is its bleakness and lack of tourists: the ideal place to go to get away from it all and get rid of stress at the same time. The light is very attractive, too, giving the area a golden northerly feel, an atmosphere peculiar to northern towns, reminding one of Beijing or Oslo. From Asahikawa head north on Route 40 to Otoineppu and then turn right onto Route 275 for Hamatonbetsu. If you like cycling in winter and have a pair of snow tires, Hamatonbetsu is a great place for iceberg watching. From Hamatonbetsu, follow the coast road through desolate fishing villages up to Soya-misaki Cape, the most northerly point of Japan since the end of the war, when the Soviet Union occupied Japan's northernmost islands. From the cape it's just over twenty kilometers to the town of Wakkanai, where many *minshuku* and rider houses are available. From Wakkanai, take a boat for the two and a half hour hop over to the island of Rishiri. For more information, see page 250.

After a night in Wakkanai with a cycling friend, we headed south along the coast in the direction of Sapporo. Route 909 to Teshio is very quiet, passing through marshy land studded with knots of reeds and grasses and there are stunning views of Mt. Rishiri-Fuji on the island of Rishiri. From Teshio, the coast road becomes Route 232. From Haboro we took a ferry for a three-day side trip to Yagishiri and Teuri islands. Both are small, about ten kilometers in circumference, and offer great swimming in the warm summer seas. ✍ NGH

❶ Field Information
Wakkanai Tourist Information ☎ 0162 22-2384
Sounkyo Minshuku Information Center ☎ 01658 5-3841
Yagishiri Tourist Information ☎ 01648 2-3348

Teuri Tourist Information ☎ 01648 3-5401
Wakkanai Minshuku Association ☎ 0162 23-2845

⚓ Lodging Log

Asahikawa: Echigo-ya Ryokan ☎ 0166 23-5131; Asahikawa Bike-mura (rider house) ☎ 0166 54-6458; Bike-ya Ride (rider house) ☎ 0166 54-7442
Sounkyo: Pension Yukara ☎ 01658 5-3216
Monbetsu: Hokkaido Rider Charida Kyowakoku (rider house) ☎ 01582 3-2942
Esashi: Akiaji Banya ☎ 01636 2-4088; Rider House Esashi You ☎ 01636 2-2999; Rider House Touring Hinangoya ☎ 01634 2-2001
Hamatonbetsu: Totsuka Minshuku (for iceberg watching) ☎ 01634 2-2836
Soya-misaki Cape: Kashiwa-ya ☎ 0162 76-2152; Soya Misaki ☎ 0162 76-2422; Saihoku no Yado (the northernmost *minshuku* in Japan) ☎ 0162 2408
Noshappu-misaki: Noshappu Misaki ☎ 0162 23-5729; Minshuku Matsumoto ☎ 0162 23-2845; Rider House Sagaren ☎ 0162 23-2021
Wakkanai center: Nakayama ☎ 0162 22-8868; Satsuki ☎ 0162 23-3566; Soya-kan ☎ 0162 22-3939; Rider House Asahi ☎ 0162 23-2867; Saihokutan Mitsuba no Ie (rider house) ☎ 0162 22-1705; Rider House Domingo Gumi ☎ 0162 24-0787
Wakkanai Onsen (Japan's most northerly hot springs): Kita no Yado ☎ 0162 28-1137; Rider House Miyuki-so ☎ 0162 28-1065; Rider House Friend ☎ 0162 28-1107
Haboro Port: Misaki Yokoyama ☎ 01646 2-2134; Kiri Kiri ☎ 01646 2-3480
Teuri: Minshuku Kurosaki ☎ 01648 3-5722
Rumoi: for reservations call Kawabara ☎ 01644 2-2756

Beyond Kyoto and Osaka

Cycling in the Kyoto and Osaka area seems to involve rather a lot of time spent avoiding homicidal taxi drivers and shortsighted housewives on bicycles laden with enough supplies to see them through a nine-week tour of Patagonia. However, with a bit of creative map work, it is possible to discover routes with nary a pachinko parlor or vending machine in sight, where the only other road users are lone hikers, wild boar, skiers, and sunbathers. And all less than two hours from Kyoto Station.

Bicycling Beautiful Biwa-ko

Route: A loop tracing the perimeters of the beautiful Biwa-ko Lake
Start: Maibara Station (Kodama trains on JR Tokaido Shinkansen Line) or Kyoto Station (JR Tokaido Shinkansen Line)
Goal: Maibara Station

As autumn slowly moves from north to south, one wants to linger in its presence for as long as possible. For observing the unrestrained rainbow hues of fall foliage and the romantic autumn moon, no place in Japan is better than Biwa-ko Lake. And, naturally, the best way to experience fall the Japanese way is by circling the lake on a bicycle.

Located less than ten kilometers northeast of Kyoto in Shiga Prefecture, Biwa-ko is Japan's largest freshwater lake, with a circumference of about two hundred kilometers. So wide that you cannot see the other side, the lake seems to continue forever. An occasional ferry crossing the lake on the horizon adds a romantic finishing touch. Best of all, it is only, at worst, slightly industrialized at its southern tip, leaving the rest in a lush, almost primitive state.

Biwa-ko is easily approached from Kyoto (see below for more information); however, our trip around the lake began at Maibara on the eastern shore. We could have taken the shinkansen there in just a few hours, but to save lodging costs, we took a night train leaving from Tokyo Station at 11:25 P.M. Make sure you get there a couple of hours early, as getting a seat makes all the difference between an agonizing ride and a restful overnight to Maibara. Reserved seats cost an extra couple of thousand yen.

Arriving at Maibara Station around 7:50 the next morning, we rode west for less than half a kilometer before running into the lake. The best advice on

Bicycling Beautiful Biwa-ko

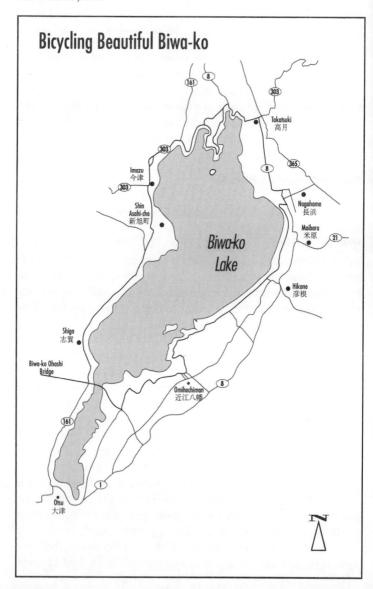

how to get around the lake is also the simplest: Keep the water on your left. This way, you will make a circle in a counterclockwise direction, starting out northward along the eastern shore and heading south along the western shore. This direction lets you spend most of your time in the more heavily forested northern part of the lake, and away from much of the industrialization in the south. You can also avoid the southernmost part by crossing a bridge that spans the lake at its narrowest point some three-fourths of the way down.

As you travel north from Maibara, you'll be right next to the lake on a road that has a wide shoulder for cyclists and pedestrians. Follow this lakeside roadway until you get to Nagahama, where you have the choice of staying along the shore or moving inland towards Dogan-ji Temple and its exquisitely carved eleven-faced Kannon dating from the early Heian period, Located after Nagahama in the town of Takatsuki, the Dogan-ji Temple Kannon-do is open from 9:00 A.M. to 5:00 P.M. from April to October, and from 10:00 A.M. to 5:00 P.M. from November to March. There are numerous other shrines and temples in Takatsuki, and if you're not careful you could end up spending several days here.

Leave Takatsuki on Route 303 or weave along side roads back to the lake. If you stay on 303 you'll run into some pretty mountainous country, with some of the most difficult climbs around the lake. In either case, Route 303 merges with the lakeside road at the lake's northern tip, and the road continues south around the west side. This part is the least populated, and features dense forests which should be quite colorful even into December.

In Shin Asahi-cho we stayed at Fushamura Minshuku, which had fairly large rooms and a very relaxing *ofuro*. The next morning we continued along the lakeside on excellent roads enjoying the clear lake view and almost effortless riding. Some three-fourths of the way down the west side we passed through the town of Shiga, and crossed Biwa-ko Ohashi, the large suspension bridge mentioned earlier. The trip across the bridge with its spectacular view of the water and the mountains to the west will set you back ¥20 per bicycle, and starts with a short climb followed by a downhill with delicious views.

If you're approaching Biwa-ko from Kyoto, try Route 367, a beautiful, lightly traveled road which follows a creek, heading northeast. For the most part, the road rises gradually until turning east and leading downhill to Biwa-ko and the Biwa-ko Ohashi Bridge rising high over the lake. From the eastern end of the bridge, the generally flat road leads to the lake's edge. Keeping the lake to your left, the road passes through multicolored forests trimmed with bamboo. There is also a good path alongside most of the road that can be used if traffic gets bad. While the road generally follows the lake, it sometimes ends, causing you to detour on unmarked farm roads until finding it again along the lakeside. In one particularly pleasant stretch, the road narrows to a single lane running between trees.

The road crosses a few short bridges over some lush river deltas, passing through Omihachiman and Hikone before returning you to Maibara. Alternatively, you might wish to break your trip, particularly if you've cycled from Kyoto—a distance of about eighty-five kilometers—in Hikone, a small pleasant town with one of the few original castles in Japan; *minshuku* and *ryokan* are readily available.

If you're leaving from Maibara, you might want to bag your bicycle, lock it to some immovable object, then relax for a leisurely dinner. The station has a good, cheap noodle stand with beer, and there's a discount supermarket behind the station where you can buy treats for the trip home. If you are returning to Tokyo by night train, you might think about taking an earlier train to Ogaki since the night train that leaves later in the evening will stop at Ogaki anyway and you'll have to transfer. By getting to Ogaki early, you'll greatly increase your chances of getting a seat on the train to Tokyo. The last train from Maibara/Ogaki arrives in Tokyo about 5:00 the next morning, and you'll have no trouble getting a seat on another JR train to take you home.

Biwa-ko is said to contain the eight wonders of the Japanese world; to experience them you have to see them—photos alone are incomplete and a car will merely transport you around the lake. Only on a cycle trip round the lake can you fully experience the wonders of the wilderness that surrounds it. ✍ SLC

⌂ Lodging Log
Shin Asahi-cho area: Fushamura ☎ 0740-25-5588
Imazu-hama area: Kanroku ☎ 0740 22-2278; ES ☎ 0740 22-1539; M Club ☎ 0740 22-3276

Hikone (2 km northwest of Hikone Station): Yoshihara Minshuku ☎ 0749 22-6702
Nagahama-shi Cycling Terminal (see page 264) ☎ 0749 63-9285

Tokobashira Country

Route: From ancient temples to deep gorges to gushing rivers, this route covers a
variety of scenery, running through the more remote areas of northern Kyoto
toward a region thickly forested with trees used to make *tokobashira*, the traditional
alcove pillars in Japanese houses
Start: Kurama Station (Eizan Kurama Line)
Goal: Hozukyo Station (JR Sanyo Line)

Kyoto City is easily seen by bicycle and public transportation, but for a real
taste of rural Japan, the rolling hills and beautiful mountain scenery, fresh air,
and clear waters of Kitayama just north of the city should not be missed.
Throughout Kitayama are numerous temples, particularly in the Kurama
and Takao area. With its cooler temperatures and abundant foliage, the
area is a great weekend retreat, especially during the summer and autumn.

Getting there is easy: From the north end of Kyoto, look for signs to
Kurama and the Eizan Kurama train line which winds up through a deep
gorge, ending eight kilometers later in the village itself. Kurama-dera Temple,
home of the Tengu mountain spirits, was established in 770 and served to
guard the capital of Kyoto from northern spiritual intrusions. It also serves
as a pleasant space to catch your breath, stretch your legs, and visit the
temple grounds for a cup of tea. Just over the pass at the bottom of the hill
is Hanase; from here continue down to Ofuse, cross the bridge that spans
the Katsura-gawa River and turn left. If you have time, the eight-hundred-
year-old temple of Daihizan Bujo-ji, a miniature Kiyomizu lookalike, is just
six kilometers to the right up the quiet river valley. The thirty-minute hike
from the temple gate to the main hall on the peak is through virgin hard-
wood forest and gives you the idea of what the area must have looked like
before Kitayama was first logged in the Edo period.

The road west from Ofuse to Keihoku travels alongside the little creek
that will grow to be the Katsura-gawa. Changing its name three times
before it joins the mighty Yodo-gawa River below Kyoto, the river is best
known for the rapids in Hozu Gorge near Arashiyama. The source of the
Katsura-gawa is just eight kilometers behind you in the canyons around

Tokobashira Country

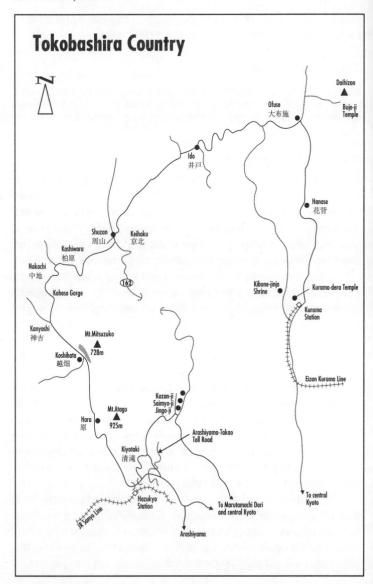

N

Daihizan

Ofuse
大布施

Bujo-ji
Temple

Ido
井戸

Hanase
花背

Shuzan
周山

Keihoku
京北

Kashiwara
柏原

Nakachi
中地

162

Kohoso Gorge

Kibune-jinja
Shrine

Kurama-dera Temple

Kurama
Station

Kanyoshi
神吉

Mt.Mitsuzuko

728m

Koshihata
越畑

Eizan Kurama Line

Kozan-ji
Saimyo-ji
Jingo-ji

Hara
原

Mt.Atago

925m

Arashiyama-Takao
Toll Road

Kiyotaki
清滝

To central
Kyoto

Hozukyo
Station

To Marutamachi Dori
and central Kyoto

JR Sanyo Line

Arashiyama

Hirogawara, beyond which there are no villages until well into Fukui Prefecture. Slow down in the valley and drink in the tranquility. In the villages, check out what's drying in the sun—onions in the late spring, grapes and plums in the summer, persimmons in the fall, *daikon* (white radish) at any time. I had the finest *soba* and freshest vegetables I have ever tasted at one rustic restaurant on this stretch. I knew it was fresh as I watched the owner kneeding the dough and his grandmother pulling the greens from the garden. The few foreigners that pass through the area, particularly those on bicycles, attract attention, but the smiles are honest and the people friendly.

Follow the main road along the river past Ido as it straightens out. Keihoku, the midway point, is just four more bridges away in a wide valley with a reputation for relentless afternoon winds coming off the Japan Sea to the north. Where the road meets Route 162 is Shuzan, Keihoku-cho. You'll see both names on the signs, but don't get confused—the names are synonymous. If you're not feeling up to the rest of the trip, or if you want more time to explore, here is where to bail out onto Route 162 back to Kyoto, or to find a room for the night (ask at the town office 75m up the road).

Turn left onto Route 162 and take not the first but the second right just 600m down the road. Cross the small Hatcho-bashi Bridge over the Katsuragawa and follow the road along the river. Leading to the same village, Kashiwara, as the other road, this road is level and more scenic. Three kilometers ahead at Nakachi turn left (south) across the Hiyoshi-bashi Bridge to head up into the lovely, cedar-forested Kohoso Gorge. In late spring when the *ayu* fish are around, such bridges are elbow to elbow with anglers. The wide shores below are ideal for camping and a dip. However, a better place to swim is two kilometers further up the Kohoso-gawa, where there are great swimming holes you can scramble down to from hiking trails.

The road continues up, up, up, but gently. Moss and ferns flourish; waters dribble across the road from slopes up to 60° steep. In the unearthly quiet come echoes of splashing waters from the cataracts below. Blocking out much of the light, the canopy of cedar trees gives one the feeling of entering a natural cathedral. Planted very close together, the trees form a wall of towering trunks. Woodcutters frequently strip off the lower branches to force them to grow ever higher with what little photosynthesis capacity there is left in the sun-seeking crown.

Watch the mirrors at sharp corners for any traffic, especially for the ten-ton trucks taking the shortcut to Yagi and Kameoka. With the aid of ice and water, the surface is regularly chewed up by these clowns, so watch out for potholes.

This is *tokobashira* country, the birthplace of the alcove pole forming the ceremonial and spiritual center of the Japanese house. The standard pole is chopped from the center of a 10–15m trunk. Fewer knots mean more money, so branches are regularly pruned. The bark is hydraulically stripped and the pole hand-sanded to a fine smoothness. Many homes have poles with unusual patterns and indentations in the wood that come from having been pressed in while growing. The tree is wrapped in strips of nylon fabric that have hard plastic forms glued to the sheet (wavy tubes, tear drops, bars). Then a steel mesh is wrapped around the tree and wired in place. As the trunk grows the patterns are pressed in. Many of the finest poles in Japan come from the Kitayama region, and individual patterns are registered and origin can be determined by them. A simple, cheap pole costs ¥40,000, and prices can go well past ¥400,000 for exotic species of wood, special patterns, and top grades of finish.

At the pass you'll find a few small groves of bamboo and some ponds, and then all of a sudden you burst into sunlight at Kanyoshi village with its wide mountain plateau of rice fields, somewhat startling for such a mountainous place away from obvious water sources. It's a gentle descent to the lake under Mt. Mitsuzuko—a great site for a picnic. At the end of the lake, head left uphill, a short grind of a climb into the beautiful village of Koshihata. The vistas across the broad Kameoka Valley far below are stunning. This five-kilometer stretch along the south flanks of Mt. Atago (925m) to the pass is mostly level, passing through groves of cedar and spruce. The next village, Hara, is a jumpoff point for the hike to the peak. Enjoy the well-deserved descent, but watch the curves, as the road drops dangerously fast to the Hozu-gawa River and the Hozu Gorge, 300m below. Just across the river is the JR Sanyo's Hozukyo Station, where many hikers disembark from Kyoto to hike the hills. Watch for the boats from Kameoka filled with tourists running the rapids, a twenty-kilometer ride of two hours. Less than a kilometer ahead is a short tunnel and a short but killing climb over the ridge. If you want to try something different, don't go up that hill:

instead, take off on the hiking trail to the left, the one that follows the river to Kiyotaki, just over a kilometer upstream. This delightful route is part of the Tokai Shizen Hodo (Tokai Hiking Trail) that eventually winds up in Kyoto, and this section is half cycling, half walking next to the Kiyotaki-gawa River with its great swimming holes. Stop for tea and cakes at the teahouses in Kiyotaki; to return, cross the bridge and head up a killer hill to the first intersection.

If you really want to have fun, the ancient Buddhist mountain retreat of Kozan-ji is another three kilometers past Kiyotaki on the trail. There is a solemn air at this ninth-century complex, and hikers often rest here before the next stretch. There'll also be many tourists coming from the bus stop on Route 162 just ahead, your escape to town should you choose this exit.

Just over that wicked climb is a larger intersection where the Arashiyama–Takao Toll Road starts—bikes are not allowed on this road. You'll now be in Sakyo-ku, on the northwestern edge of Kyoto. The road heading straight sails into town becoming Marutamachi Dori, the road that passes Nijo Castle. The road to the right heads off to Sagano and Arashiyama—worth a day's tour in their own right for their temples, beautiful gardens, creaking bamboo groves, old architecture, and teahouses. ✍ MS

❶ Field Information
Keihoku-cho Town Office ☎ 07715 2-0300

⌂ Lodging Log
Ido: Kami Katsura ☎ 07715 3-0925
Keihoku-cho: Pension Atagomichi ☎ 07715 2-1177; Oshio Minshuku ☎ 07715 3-0433

Cycling the Echizen Coast

Route: Few places in Japan offer so much scenery for so little effort as this laid-back route along the Echizen Coast to the famous suicide spot at Tojimbo rocks, curving inland to the temple complex of Eihei-ji, head of the Soto sect of Zen Buddhism
Start: Tsuruga Station (Hokuriku Honsen Main Line, Obama Line)
Goal: Awara Yunomachi Station (Keifuku Dentetsu Mikuni Awara Line) or Awara Onsen Station (Hokuriku Honsen Main Line)

While mountain bikes and wider gear ratios have made it easier to head for the hills on a bicycle trip, many still prefer the coastal routes for some of the loveliest scenery around. And nowhere is the scenery better than on

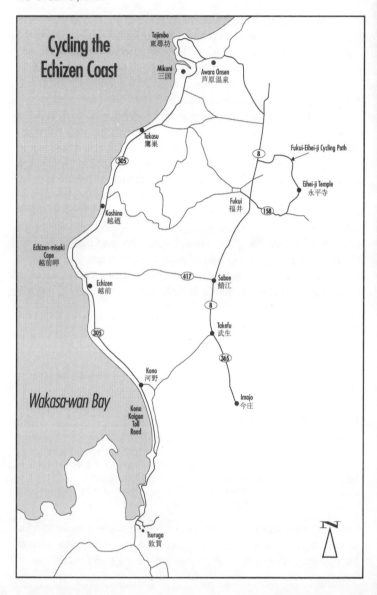

Cycling the Echizen Coast

Tojimbo
東尋坊

Mikuni
三国

Awara Onsen
芦原温泉

Takasu
鷹巣

305

Fukui-Eihei-ji Cycling Path

8

Eihei-ji Temple
永平寺

Koshino
越廼

Fukui
福井

158

Echizen-misaki
Cape
越前岬

Echizen
越前

417

Sabae
鯖江

8

305

Takefu
武生

365

Kono
河野

Imajo
今庄

Wakasa-wan Bay

Kono
Kaigan
Toll
Road

Tsuruga
敦賀

N

the Nihonkai—the Japan Sea coast. From Kansai, this coastline is the ideal destination, since it's a complete change: more relaxed, much less developed, filled with beautiful scenery, and—most importantly—there's wonderfully clear water you can actually swim in.

The Japan Sea is also convenient for other reasons: from Osaka, *tokkyu* (limited express) trains leave almost every half hour for Tsuruga, the nearest starting point for a coast tour. The ride takes only an hour and a half; from Kyoto it's even faster and cheaper. Once you get there, you can go either west past Obama and other beaches to Amanohashidate (see page 209), or east along the beautiful Echizen coast.

I recommend the latter—Echizen has to be one of the easiest bike trips in Japan and one of the most scenic—offering rocky coastlines, unexpected waterfalls, quiet little fishing villages, and an incredible huge stone arch across the road.

From Tsuruga, you can be on the coast within fifteen minutes of leaving the train station. Go out of the station and head left on Route 8, then follow the signs to the Kono Kaigan Yuryo Doro (toll road). This road goes a considerable way up the Echizen coast. Before you reach the toll road, you will pass through two short tunnels and there will be a lot of traffic, mostly trucks bound for Fukui. Once you turn onto the toll road, though, traffic is light all the way round the coast. The ride is best from Tsuruga to Tojimbo, a major tourist attraction that consists of steep cliffs overlooking the sea, a famous spot for suicides. Taking a thirty-minute sightseeing boat gives you an even better view of the cliffs than from the road. You can also take an elevator to the top of Tojimbo Tower to an observatory located 100m above the ground for a great view of the surrounding area. The ride to Tojimbo is an easy day or even half-day ride—on my last trip I left Tsuruga at 9:30 A.M. and made it almost to Tojimbo by 2:00 P.M. But it's much nicer to stay in one of the many *minshuku* in the area. Note that many are open only during the summer from the end of June to mid-September. The town of Takasu, just before Tojimbo, is a nice little beach town and has one *minshuku*, Yamane-ya, that's open year round. When you decide to leave, depart from Awara Yunomachi Station on the Keifuku Dentetsu Mikuni Awara Line to Fukui.

Alternatively, you could ride to Fukui and then take a bike path east of Fukui for about sixteen kilometers that takes you all the way to Eihei-ji, founded in 1244 and one of two head temples of the Soto sect of Zen Buddhism (the other is Soji-ji Temple in Tsurumi near Yokohama). The complex, consisting of over seventy buildings, is home for more than two hundred monks. Accommodation is available, but notice in advance is necessary.

If you're heading back to Tsuruga, you can make a loop through the countryside on Route 8, turning onto Route 365 at Takefu, to Imajo where there is a cycling terminal, conveniently located five minutes from the station. The terminal offers over seven courses, which meander through forests and hamlets of thatched cottages. When you run out of time, simply bag your bike and take the Hokuriku Main Line from Imajo back to Tsuruga. ✍ DT

❸ Field Information
Echizen-machi Tourist Information ☎ 0778 37-1234
Koshino Tourist Information ☎ 0776 89-2210
Awara Station Tourist Information ☎ 0776 77-2279
Mikuni Tourist Information ☎ 0776 82-5515
Takasu Tourist Association ☎ 0776 87-2704

⌂ Lodging Log
Takasu: Yamaneya ☎ 0776-86-1727
Eihei-ji Temple: Sanzenkei, Eihei-ji, Eiheiji-cho, Yoshida-gun, Fukui-ken ☎ 0776 63-3102; Eihei-ji Monzen Yamaguchi Youth Hostel ☎ 0776 63-3123; Kokuminshukusha Green Lodge ☎ 0776 63-3126
Imajo: Imajo-cho Cycling Terminal ☎ 0778 45-0073 (see page 264)

High on Hiei

Route: Forget about the normal restraints of asphalt, gravity, and sanity and enjoy a breathtaking descent from the top of Mt. Hiei down to the temple of Shugakuin

This route, which includes two of Japan's most famous historical sights, takes you away from the noise and pollution of Kyoto's urban sprawl, is eighty-five percent downhill, and brings you inevitably into contact with nature. As it turned out, it nearly brought me into fatal contact with nature, in the shape of an untold number of very large trees.

I bundled my bike into a *rinko* bag in front of Kyoto Station and took the Kosei Line for the thirty-five minute journey to Eizan Station on the shores of Biwa-ko Lake. The lake was shrouded in mist and the station platform crowded with teenagers in high-heels and short skirts heading

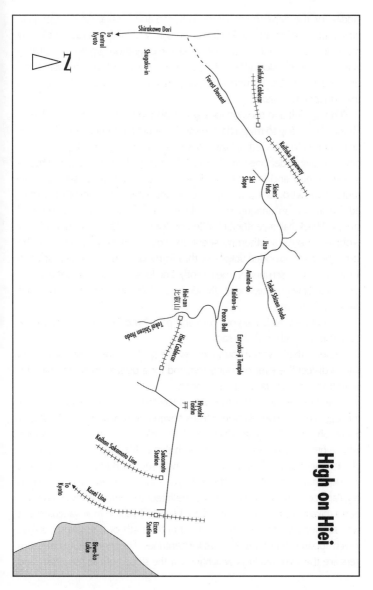

High on Hiei

Shirakawa Dori

To Central Kyoto

Shugaku-in

Forest Descent

Keifuku Cablecar

Keifuku Ropeway

Ski Slope

Skiers' Huts

Jizo

Tokai Shizen Hodo

Amida-do

Kaidan-in

Peace Bell

Enryaku-ji Temple

Hiei-zan 比叡山

Tokai Shizen Hodo

Hiei Cablecar

Hiyoshi Taisha

Keihan Sakamoto Line

Sakamoto Station

Kosei Line

To Kyoto

Eizan Station

Biwa-ko Lake

N

giddily for the department stores in Kyoto and Osaka. An octagenarian newspaper seller and a kindergarten girl watched me assemble my machine, casting their critical eyes over the operation, giggling as I tried in vain to stuff the balloon-like *rinko* bag into my tiny rucksack. In frustration I simply clutched the humongous bag to my side and pedaled away from their disapproving gaze.

I hung a left and took off for my first planned stop, the Hiyoshi Taisha Shrine. According to my guide, the shrine should have been just a few hundred meters to the west of Eizan Station, so I soldiered on still clutching the billowing bag under one arm. So much for the guide. The road soon began to rise steeply and I climbed and climbed and climbed, passing a video rental store, a bookshop, a dilapidated shrine gate, and an equally dilapidated farmer on an antique tractor. In the space of 300m it seemed I'd stepped back half a century. I battled on for over a kilometer until I finally wobbled into the southernmost entrance of the Hiyoshi Shrine. From the stronghold of a wooden ticket booth, a formidable shrine maiden, seventy if she was a day, scrutinized me intently. She looked at the bike, at my purple, sweat-stained face, and finally her eyes rested on the enormous scarlet bag under my arm.

"You'll have to leave your bike and parachute here, but don't worry, they'll be safe with me," she said.

At least that's what it sounded like. She spoke in the most convoluted Kansai dialect I've ever encountered, and for a bizarre moment I had the sensation that I was talking to a Geordie.

I paid the entrance fee and walked toward the Higashi Hongu shrine, through a dark grove of ancient trees covered in moss. Hiyoshi Taisha, or Sanno Shrine, or Hie-jinja, whichever you prefer to call it, is a Shinto shrine whose history is inextricably linked with that of Mt. Hiei's Enryaku-ji Temple and Saicho, the founder of the Tendai sect of Buddhism. When the warrior monks of Mt. Hiei attacked Kyoto, as they were wont to do on regular occasions between 993 and the fifteenth century, they always carried a *mikoshi*, or portable shrine, from Hiyoshi Taisha in their vanguard as it was sacrilege for the enemy to stand in the path of the *mikoshi*, a ruse which apparently proved effective for centuries. The shrine deity's messengers are the wild monkeys which inhabit the slopes of the mountain, and their images may be seen dotted throughout the sprawling shrine buildings. Hiyoshi Taisha is still a popular Shinto shrine where ceremonies are frequently held. In one part of the grounds, a priest in blue, white, and gold ceremonial robes and giant black wooden shoes was intoning prayers for the safety and well-being of a brand new Toyota Corolla and its occupants, all the while dusting the vehicle with what appeared to be an oversized African fly-swish. Considering the hazards of cycling in Japan, I inquired at the shrine office whether the safety blessing was available for bicycles too. Although the cost is ¥5,000, the same as for cars, you might consider it money well spent, particularly if you spend much time on roads in the Kansai area.

I walked back down to the entrance, where the ancient shrine-maiden was guarding my gear with bulldog-like determination. According to her, the shrine can get very crowded in fall when crowds pack the narrow avenues to see the *koyo*, the autumn foliage, but at other times the shrine is usually deserted. The shrine festival takes place between April 12 and April 15, when it's best to leave your bicycle at home.

Much rested after the steep climb from Enzan Station, I turned right out of the shrine exit and continued past a group of intriguing stone *jizo* and up the main road. After 500m, I turned right up the short incline to the antiquated waiting room of the Hiei-zan Sakamoto Cableway. Once again I stuffed my bike into its bag. The woman at the ticket booth was friendly but adamant—I could take the bike up the mountain but there wouldn't be anywhere to ride once I got there as there were no roads. (There were plenty, as it turned out.) I tried to explain that mountain-bikers don't need roads, but getting nowhere, I promised that I'd go up by cable car and go down by bus with my bicycle safely in its bag. To my amazement, this seemed to satisfy her completely and seconds later, I was clutching the ¥810 ticket that would take me to the top of arguably Japan's second most-famous mountain. But already I was beginning to have doubts about how I was going to get down again.

The cars to the summit depart every thirty minutes, and as I'd just missed one I killed time by reading the wanted posters until a portly, bored taxi driver came over to chat. It turned out he was from Niigata Prefecture, so I mentioned that I'd once cycled from Niigata to Kyoto. His eyes grew as round as *ramen* bowls.

"Niigata to Kyoto? You foreigners are incredible. Mind you, it's the diet, of course. All that steak. How can we compete with you when we're a bunch of feeble rice-eaters?"

As the bell started to ring to announce the arrival of the next cablecar, the taxi driver wondered aloud whether Sakamoto would ever get its own McDonald's. Telling a white lie for the second time in five minutes, I said that I hoped that it would.

I boarded the cable car along with twenty factory workers from Otsu, who, judging from their varying shades of scarlet, had been celebrating Christmas early. The reddest of them all slung my bicycle across his shoulders and bundled it effortlessly into the car. The driver locked us all in and the rickety machine began to clank and wheeze its way up the mountain. After five minutes we passed the mountain cave at Horaioka which contains a stone Buddha. Continuing its ascent, the car groaned and creaked even more, and, as we cleared the first tree-line, Biwa-ko Lake appeared in the distance, reduced to the size of a large pond. The air became noticeably cooler and Biwa-ko dwindled to a distant, if sparkling, puddle. The mountain dropped away dramatically on either side.

"We're all going to die," shouted a factory worker gleefully. "Better have another one," he added, pulling a beer can the size of a small depthcharge from his rucksack. A knot of fear gripped my stomach as I realized that somehow I'd have to cycle down this mountain. The cable-car reached its destination. As I passed through the ticket barrier, I noticed I was the only passenger with a one-way ticket.

At the cable-car station, I put the bike together, fortified myself with a bowl of noodles from the tiny refreshment stand, girded my loins, and boldly set forth on the paved road leading uphill to the right. (This is part of the Tokai Shizen Hodo, an extensive network of hiking and biking trails that cover the region. A saner alternative to the route I took would be to turn left from the cable-car station and follow the Tokai Shizen Hodo all the way down the mountain to the south as far as Otsu.)

After over a kilometer, the route comes to the main Kompon Chudo area of Enryaku-ji, the headquarters of the Tendai sect. This temple complex, numbering over three thousand temples at the peak of its power, was primarily the base for marauding bands of monks who regularly went on murderous forays into Kyoto, supposedly to protect it from evil influences. However, Enryaku-ji's power was severely limited in 1571 when Oda Nobunaga went on a slash-and-burn mission to Mt. Hiei.

However, there's still plenty to see and do at Enryaku-ji, though for my money Hiyoshi Taisha is more interesting. Cycle up the steep slope to the west of the Morinaga monument, to the Peace Bell. For a mere ¥50 donation, you can wallop the giant bell with what looks like half a railway sleeper suspended from an enormous rope; somehow it's deeply satisfying to announce your presence to the world from the top of a mountain. Keen to get on my bike and do some real work, I climbed the hill past a beautiful shrine building to the right, the Kaidan-in, weathered over the centuries from brilliant red to a more dignified ruddy brown. At the top of the hill, I walked through the courtyard of the more modern Amida-do, respectfully wheeling the bike until I passed beneath the walkway that connected the two temple buildings. Almost immediately the path dropped down a wooded decline, passing an abandoned prefabricated hut, covered in, of all things, religious graffiti—a spray-can painting of a Buddhist figure and some indecipherable characters. I idly wondered if it said "Kannon was here," until a nasty skid to the right drew my attention back to the more secular considerations of staying vertical. I passed a stone *jizo* statue in a splendid red balaclava, and a signpost told me once again that I was back on the Tokai Shizen Hodo, climbing a brief rise in the direction of the Sancho area and the artificial ski slope. A whole host of inviting trails led off the beaten path here, beckoning exploration, but as the afternoon was wearing on, I resisted the temptation. After a short while, the terrain became quite tough going, and I shifted into the lowest gear to negotiate the fist-sized chunks of rock that covered the path at regular intervals. Bashing my ankle on such a stone brought forth a flood of language hardly suited to the refined ecclesiastical atmosphere of Mt. Hiei—sturdy footwear is recommended, not to mention puncture-repair equipment. Ten minutes later I dropped down to the artificial ski slope, where I was greeted with the slightly bizarre sight of hundreds of fluorescent-jacketed skiers speeding serious-faced down a very large lump of green plastic. No doubt I looked just as peculiar to them, liberally covered as I was in mud. Each to his own. I preferred to clatter down the gravel path to the west of the skiers' huts—take care not to overspeed here as the surface is very rough—to the adjoining stations of the Keifuku Railway and the Keifuku Cable-Car, your last chance to change your mind, swallow your pride, and ship yourself and your bike down the mountain to Kyoto sensibly and peacefully.

With open disbelief, a cable-car driver showed me in the direction of the path down to Kyoto. Passing the east side of the Keifuku Hiei Rope-way, the path twisted around the mountain, narrowed into what looked like elephant grass, and dipped into the black hole that was the forest.

I cycled for all of 10m along a path that was about as wide as my handlebars and came to logged steps which cut a zig-zag trail down into the forest and out of sight. There was no option but to carry my bike on my shoulders, which I did for about 20m until the path widened slightly into an area carpeted with leaves. where I got back onto the bike again. After less than a minute, the mountain fell away, taking me with it. Suddenly I was hurtling downhill, terrifyingly out of control, desperately trying to brake and not break my neck. I remember having the momentary illusion that I was standing still and hundreds of tree trunks were rushing uphill past me. Then a particularly large one appeared that wasn't rushing past. It was heading straight for me. I hit the brakes and went into a spectacularly terrifying skid. To the right was mountain; to the left was thin air; in front an oncoming tree. Then silence. I opened my eyes to discover a monstrous cryptomeria less than a foot from my front tire, that is to say less than two feet from my nose-end. But, I'd stopped moving and I was still alive.

I sat down to reconsider my riding style. Cycling as I was, the slope was far too steep for me to retain any semblance of control, and I was in danger of deforesting much of Mt. Hiei with my teeth. I tried a different riding technique which, ungainly as it was, proved the perfect way to get down the mountain, and probably saved a few cryptomeria trees into the bargain. I lowered the seatpost as far as it would go and hung my backside out over the rear wheel. I began carefully at first, worried that I might hang the aforementioned out too far and receive an unwarranted quantity of spinning Bridgestone rubber where I'd most notice it but least appreciate it.

In this undignified but essentially life-saving posture, I slipped, skidded, yelled, plummeted, and occasionally pedaled down the mountain. Much of the path is simply a steep-sided gulley carved out of the earth by rainwater, the loose, sandy soil more slippery than any politician. Gradually, I began to master the laid-back, sidewinding technique that might just get me down the mountain in one piece. After twenty minutes, with a hint of overconfidence creeping in, I rounded a blind corner only to be confronted with a steel hawser as thick as the shrine-ropes of Hiyoshi-jinja, strung across the path at neck height. I ducked and the rusty steel cable just missed giving me a new parting. This is the time to confess that I wasn't wearing a helmet—DO—it's essential. In retrospect, anything up to and including chainmail seems advisable for this route.

I rode on more gingerly for all of five minutes before the adrenaline cut in once more and I sped on down the mountain. Rounding a corner, I came face to face with a white-bearded old man striding purposefully uphill with what looked suspiciously like a shotgun. I hit the brakes and skidded to a halt, showering the old-timer with dust. I apologized profusely, all the more so when I realized that he was, indeed, carrying a shotgun. "No problem," he laughed and took off up the mountain once more, as sure-footed—and hirsute—as a mountain goat. I carried on and after a few seconds came across three very excited hunting dogs tied to a tree, with what appeared to be misshaped wire coat-hangers attached to their collars. As I stopped to stroke the hounds, a second bearded old man stepped from the trees clutching a radio transceiver and a gun. I enquired what he was hunting.

"Wild boar and cyclists," came the reply.

The old man went on to tell me about his quarry, the *sus scrofa leucomystax*, better known in Japan as *inoshishi*. Apparently these ferocious creatures grow to 140cm in length, weigh up to a hundred kilograms, and, "when they attack, they make almost as much noise as you did coming down the mountain."

The dogs had picked up a fresh scent, and his colleague had gone uphill to try and flush the boar down toward them. I asked him if he thought he'd be eating *inoshishi* steaks that evening.

"I doubt it," came the answer, "they make good eating but even better money." I wished him good luck and carried on down the mountain in my own two-wheeled version of a boar charge on a path which gradually became stony, twisting, and narrow as it moved through woodland toward thicker undergrowth. Eventually, however, the path widened out and the gradient lessened slightly. A small stream spilled across the trail, leaving the surface even more slippery, and the brakes that much less effective. I heard the party of hikers before I saw them. Unfortunately, I couldn't say the same for them. Japanese hikers carry enough tinkling objects to wake the mountain spirits from their ancestral slumbers. The two men and two women hulking refrigerator-sized backpacks were so deafened by their own clanking, plonking, and tinkling that they were completely oblivious of my approach. I coughed discreetly. I said *sumimasen*. All to no avail. Finally, I bellowed *sumimasen*. The effect was electrifying: The group launched themselves, still clanking, into the undergrowth. Apologizing, I pedaled on once again toward the city.

Almost immediately the path widened into a narrow paved road, still slippery, but delightfully smooth after the molar-loosening, vision-blurring terrain I'd been covering for the last hour or so. I returned to the normal riding position and flew down into Shugakuin Imperial Villa, exhausted, elated, and covered in mud. That evening I bored the customers at my neighborhood pub with tales of my exploits, over a sumptuous meal of, you've guessed it, *sus scrofa leucomystax*.   ✍ JA

Western Japan Days 🚲 🚲 🚲 🚲 🚲 🚲 🚲 🚲 🚲 🚲 🚲 🚲

In the Land of Lacquer 🚲

Route: Loop round the hot-spring resorts and lacquer-producing villages nestled along the stunning rocky coast of the Noto-hanto Peninsula
Start and Goal: Kanazawa Station (Hokuriku Honsen Main Line from Kyoto)

It's hard to believe there can be many places more charming and picturesque than Ishikawa Prefecture. Many seasoned travelers write glowingly of this historic, tranquil area in books and magazines. One of the best ways to explore this "other side" of Japan is on two wheels.

Ishikawa's major city is Kanazawa, a "little Kyoto" five to seven hours away from Tokyo by train through the Japan Alps. Kanazawa has a fine balance of the ancient and the modern, though the emphasis is on things traditional. Never bombed during the war, the city retains many splendid old houses, shops, and temples, all tucked away in a maze of tiny streets. Kanazawa Castle (now Kanazawa University) is in the center of town next to Kenrokuen, one of Japan's most beautiful and extensive landscaped gardens. And all over town are fine restaurants slicing up the freshest sashimi and sushi. Stay in one of Kanazawa's youth hostels, or better, at Murata-ya Ryokan, on a quiet alley in the middle of town.

Ishikawa's ultimate destination is the Noto-hanto Peninsula, a big "thumb" that sticks out into the Japan Sea. It's about seventy kilometers from Kanazawa to Wakura Onsen at the foot of the peninsula. By train it takes about one and one-half hours, perhaps the better part of a day by bicycle. Wakura is a very popular resort; try Kagaya Onsen, an unreal luxury city, boasting one of the fanciest giant hot-spring baths in Japan. However, next door is the Port Inn, run by the same management, where one can stay cheaply, and get free vouchers to troop over to Kagaya for a memorable soak in their opulent *onsen*. From Wakura, there's quick and easy access by bridge to Noto-jima Island, You can spend a leisurely day circling the island, taking in the scenic rolling hills along the coast dotted with fishing villages, temples, and rice fields. Take delight in the absence of flashy pachinko parlors and don't miss the attractive aquarium (*suizokukan*) located halfway round the island. Stay at a *mishuku* on the island or back at Wakura.

In the Land of Lacquer

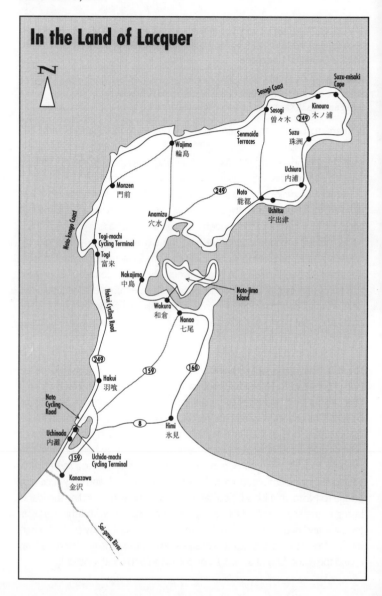

N

Suzu-misaki Cape

Sosogi Coast

Sosogi
曽々木

Kinoura
木ノ浦

249

Senmaida
Terraces

Suzu
珠洲

Wajima
輪島

Uchiura
内浦

Monzen
門前

249

Noto
能都

Ushitsu
宇出津

Noto-kongo Coast

Anamizu
穴水

Togi-machi
Cycling Terminal

Togi
富来

Nakajima
中島

Noto-jima
Island

Hakui Cycling Road

Wakura
和倉

Nanao
七尾

160

249

159

Hakui
羽喰

Noto
Cycling
Road

8

Himi
氷見

Uchinada
内灘

159

Uchida-machi
Cycling Terminal

Kanazawa
金沢

Sai-gawa River

If you have more than three days, by all means continue up the peninsula. The bay side is tranquil and green, and the ocean side is studded with rocky cliffs that take a constant beating from the pounding surf. There are a number of picturesque villages to cycle through, with pottery, glass, and lacquerware factories. Further along the Sosogi coastline is Senmaida, the "thousand paddy fields" on terraces snaking up the mountainside, looking much like those in the Philippines or Nepal.

From the famous lacquer-producing town of Wajima with its lively early-morning market, ride along the coast through stunning coastal scenery toward the Noto Kongo Coast. For an interesting change of pace, there are a couple of unusual accommodation possibilities in this area. Sojo-ji, the former headquarters of the Soto Zen Buddhism sect, accepts guests, but you must make reservations beforehand. Or, stay at the Togi-machi Cycling Terminal and the next day simply sit back and enjoy the more than eighty-kilometer bike path that stretches all the way along the coast from Togi-machi to Uchinada near Kanazawa. The path also hosts the longest bench in the world, so there are plenty of places to have a rest and just gaze at the view. Beyond the Uchinada Cycling Terminal is the Sai-gawa River with wide, clean grassy banks and a paved path along which you can ride, away from cars, all the way back to Kanazawa some twenty kilometers away.   ✍ SK

❶ Field Information
Nanao and Wakura Tourist Information Center ☎ 0767 53-1111
Noto-jima Information ☎ 0767 84-1087
Suzu Station Tourist Center ☎ 0768 82-4688
Oku Noto Reservation Center ☎ 0768 62-3234
Sosogi Tourist Association ☎ 0768 32-0408
Wajima Tourist Information Center ☎ 0768 22-1503

♨ Lodging Log
Kanazawa: Murata-ya ☎ 0762 63-0455; Irita-ya ☎ 0762 65-6700; Hinode Ryokan ☎ 0762 31-5224; Ikigame ☎ 0762 41-0306
Wakura: Kagaya Onsen ☎ 0767 62-1111; Port Inn ☎ 0767 62-4000
Wajima: Minshuku Tachibana-ya ☎ 0768 32-0147; Shimbashi Ryokan ☎ 0768 22-0236
Monzen: Sojo-ji Temple, Monzen-machi, Fugeshi-gun, Ishikawa-ken ☎ 07684 2-0005
Togi-machi: Togi-machi Cycling Terminal (see page 263) ☎ 0767 42-2303
Uchinada: Uchinada-machi Cycling Terminal (see page 264) ☎ 0762 86-3766

Coasting the Kii Peninsula

Route: An inland route through the heart of unspoilt countryside to the sacred shrines of Hongu, descending slowly to the quiet coastline of the Kii-hanto Peninsula
Start: Gojo Station (Kansai Line to Oji then Wakayama Line to Gojo)
Goal: Nachi-Katsuura (ferry to Tokyo)

The Kii-hanto Peninsula is definitely a highly recommended area for cycling. An inland route starting in Gojo or Nara carries you through some of the most unspoilt countryside in Japan, leaving the unappealing signs of urban life far behind. Fifty kilometers south of Osaka on Route 310 in the Kiso Valley, Gojo is surrounded by the towering peaks of the Izumi Range (Kongo-Ikoma National Park) to the north and the Nagamine Range to the south, the most prominent peak being Mt. Koya, another good ride in itself.

Route 310 soon turns into Route 168, heading through the Yoshino Kumano National Park and thoroughly living up to its reputation as one of Japan's cycling paradises. After Nishi-Yoshino the real countryside starts, so make sure your water bottles are full and that you have a few snacks on hand. There are three stiff climbs on this ride and just past Gojo is the first. Route 168 runs flat for three kilometers, then the second and hardest climb is upon you and the fun begins to start.

You might well wonder if you're on the right road. Only wide enough for a single car at some points, the so-called highway crawls over dwarf bridges, through raw rock tunnels, and through villages perched on hillsides above twisting rivers and roaring rapids. On the hills push smaller gears, hydrate well, and enjoy the views. Watch the speed on descents, for the unseen turns ahead can be tricky. After passing through the Shin Amatsuji Tunnel at 750m, the road drops down to the waters of the Kiso-gawa River, where the road starts to widen and the views get better and better.

Spanning a gorge twelve kilometers south of Oto in the village of Uenoji is a spectacular pedestrian suspension bridge, said to be the biggest in the world. The Tanise Tsuri-bashi Bridge leads to hiking trails in the mountains beyond and to a riverside campground in the larch forests along the stony riverbed below. Walking the bridge, which is 125m up in the air, can be exciting in a good wind. This area is about the halfway point and is a good area to stop for a rest or to camp. After Tanise no Tsuri-bashi there

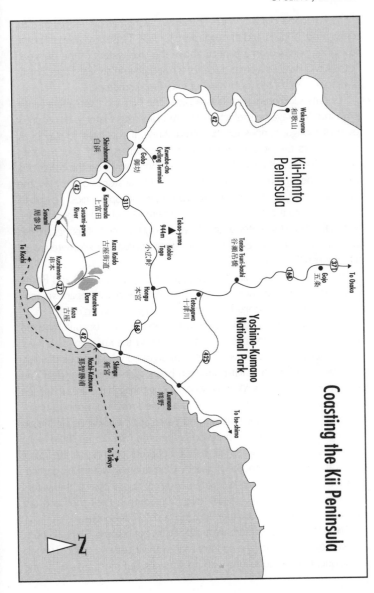

Coasting the Kii Peninsula

N

Kii-hanto Peninsula

Yoshino-Kumano National Park

Wakayama 和歌山

Gobo 御坊

Kawabe-cho Cycling Terminal

Shirahama 白浜

Kamitonda 上富田

Susami-gawa River

Koza Kaido 古座街道

Susami 周参見

Kushimoto 串本

Nanakawa Dam

Koza 古座

Tokoo-yama 遥尾山 944m

Kohiro Toge

小広峠

Hongu 本宮

Totsugawa 十津川

Tonise Tsuri-bashi 谷瀬吊橋

Gojo 五条

To Osaka

Shingu 新宮

Kumano 熊野

Nachi-Katsuura 那智勝浦

To Ise-shima

To Kochi

To Tokyo

42

31

37

168

425

is one last good climb toward Totsukawa along narrow ledges of cliffs, across more bridges, and through more tunnels. Totsukawa, a well-known hot spring perched on a plateau above the lake waters of the dammed Totsu-kawa River, is a great place for a hot bath and a meal. From Totsu-kawa to the end of the route is about sixty-five kilometers.

Twenty kilometers past Totsukawa is the Nitsuno Dam and a gentle climb into Wakayama Prefecture and ten kilometers later is the country town of Hongu, famous for its sacred shrine. If you have to stay over, Hongu offers the best accommodation possibilities, with over a dozen *onsen* in the area. Kawayu Onsen is a free hot springs on the banks of a small river near Hongu. Made with the smooth, flat stones of the river, the pools are great for an impromptu dip under the open skies. To get to Kawayu, turn right off Route 168 two kilometers south of Hongu and then right again after a kilometer or so. However, my favorite hot springs are the baths at Yunomine Onsen, located in a steep gorge three kilometers west of Hongu on Route 311.

From Hongu, there are two possible routes, Route 168 and Route 311, both offering stunning scenery. The next morning, prepare yourself mentally at Kumano Hongu Taisha in Hongu for your chosen route.

Route 168 toward Shingu is lightly traveled, and the beautiful scenery includes forests, hills, and river valleys. Past Hongu, the Kumano-gawa River widens, developing extensive beaches of polished white stones of every dimension. Fishermen in flat-bottomed boats glide across the clear and deceptively calm waters. When I was traveling through the area in the lee of a typhoon, fat droplets of warm rain lashed my face, ominous black clouds scurried across the horizon, and leaves and twigs danced in the air, creating an unforgettable impression. When the rains let up there were magical views: glorious waterfalls by the hundreds pouring off the lips of gorges and out of the mouths of ravines. One stunning waterfall in particular stands in my mind—ten kilometers south of Kumanogawa, the waters of Nariyuki no Taki fall vertically over 50m onto a rock shelf and are spewed out horizontally another 20m in a fan of white spray.

The last fifteen kilometers are anticlimactic, but relaxing. Some sections are like being on a one-lane country road with virtually no traffic. Tunnels are frequent, some quite long with no sidewalk, but most are well lit and with the light traffic and tail lights, they pose few problems. Running in a river plain up to two kilometers wide with flowers and ferns everywhere, the route has mostly gradual ascents but is still challenging in places. Shingu is a woodworkers' town and the fresh fish is good. From Shingu Station you can catch JR trains bound for Shirahama 105 kilometers to the west or Ise 130 kilometers to the east, both of which make delightful cycling destinations for the rugged coast, tailwinds, and fishing villages.

Back in Hongu, turning right on Route 311 offers dramatic scenery in return for a nineteen-kilometer climb uphill to Kobiro-toge Pass. Route 311 is also known as the Nakahechisendo, the Royal Road, which from the Nara period through the Edo period was traveled by rulers on pilgrimages to the principal Shinto shrines in the Kumano region. This route eventually leads down to the coast at Kamitonda and Shirahama Onsen. Turn left and head south along the coast on Route 42 to the southern tip of the peninsula and up the east coast toward Nachi-Katsuura for the ferry to Tokyo.

The ferry leaves at 1:40 A.M., a slightly inconvenient time, but there is a waiting room at the terminal with foam pads and blankets. The food on the ferry is uninspiring, so stash some goodies in your bag.   ✍ MS

↪Route Extension

If you have time, the coastal road from Nachi-Katsuura around the peninsula offers stunning views and glorious places to bathe en route. Last year we headed south from Nachi-Katsuura toward Kushimoto at the southern tip of the peninsula. Our idea was to follow the coast to Shirahama and back inland through *onsen* country, cycling about 210 kilometers in three days, .

Somehow the weatherman who had predicted nothing but sun for a week was slightly off as we headed into a drizzle at the start of our trip. The first thirty kilometers or so to Kushimoto were surprisingly not very hilly, but this changed beyond Kushimoto to Susami. Here, there was spectacular scenery with towering cliffs, hidden coves, and inviting beaches. The hills were there, one after the other, but fun to cycle and just long enough so you could enjoy the constant up and down. The only time we had to walk our bikes was when approaching the seaside *kokuminshukusha* in Susami. We must have been quite a sight, as our host lead us to the *ofuro* before showing us to our room! It was quite nice to be able to watch the rain from inside, but as the winds picked up we became more apprehensive.

The next morning, a combination of rain, strong winds, and a poor forecast made us change our course. Instead of continuing on to Shirahama we headed inland through beautiful country along the Susami-gawa River on the Koza Kaido. This part of the route is very picturesque, passing through rice fields and mountains, with no traffic. But unfortunately, we only lasted an hour in the rain before having to find shelter and wait for the heavy rains to become lighter, never mind them stopping or turning to a drizzle. The Koza Kaido eventually joins up with Route 371 at Nanakawa Dam—we had planned to turn onto Route 371, and then left along the picturesque Koza-gawa River down to the coast following a route recommended by several friends.

Instead we retraced our steps back to the same *kokuminshukusha* in Susami. The next morning we put on our wet shorts and shoes once again, but this time to go out in the sunshine to enjoy the same coastline back to Katsuura. We stopped many times to enjoy the cliffs and beaches, had a swim in the sea, and watched the waves pound the rocks of the southernmost tip of Honshu island. On the way back to the ferry at Nachi-Katsuura, don't miss Katsuura Onsen, a natural hot spring located in a rocky cliff overlooking the sea on the opposite side of Nachi-wan Bay from Nachi-Katsuura. The hotel on the peak above is reached by elevators through the cliffs. Bathing in a steaming pool in the bowels of a mountain with waves foaming at your feet after a long day in the saddle makes it all worthwhile.   ✍ GM

❶ Field information

Tokyo to Nachi-Katsuura ferry departs 18:20 P.M., arriving 7:40 A.M.; returning 1:40 A.M. arriving Tokyo 2:40 P.M.; for reservations call Blue Highway Line ☎ 03 3578-1127
Nachi-Katsuura Minshuku Association ☎ 0735 52-2318
Oto Tourist Information ☎ 0739 48-0301
Hongu Tourist Information ☎ 0735 42-0735
Koza-gawa River Tourist Information ☎ 07357 2-0180

⌂ Lodging Log

Hongu: Otonashi-kan ☎ 07354 2-0021; Zuiho-den ☎ 0735 42-0009
Shingu: Astro House (run by well-known amateur astronomer) ☎ 0735 22-4651
Susami: Kokuminshukusha Karekinada Susami ☎ 0739 55-3225
Shirahama: Aidoru ☎ 0739 43-5422; Kotobuki ☎ 0739 43-2916; Hamabei ☎ 0739 42-3686; Hagoromo ☎ 0739 42-2645; Hamayu ☎ 0739 42-3559

Cyclin' the San'in

Route: Tracing the northern coast, the route winds its way through the traditional town of Obama to Amanohashidate, one of the three wonders of Japan, around the Tango-hanto Peninsula to the sand dunes of Tottori, ending at Matsue and Izumo
Start and Goal: Route can be started from any of the major towns on the route described below, such as Tsuruga, Obama, Maizuru, Tottori, Matsue, or Izumo

Recently I took a nine-day break and cycled along the San'in Kaigan, the scenic coastline facing the Japan Sea and stretching from the Tango Peninsula in northern Kyoto-fu to the tip of Yamaguchi-ken. I started at Tsuruga and stopped over in Obama (both in Fukui-ken), visited Amanohashidate and Taisa (both in Kyoto-fu), Amarube (Hyogo-ken), Tottori City and Kaike Onsen (Tottori-ken), and Matsue and Izumo (Shimane-ken). The region had many sightseeing attractions, great ocean views, and more than its share of killer slopes.

The first day, I rode on Route 27 from Tsuruga Station. The highlight of the day was Mikata Go-ko, a series of five contiguous lakes with a very nice cycling path, which hugs the water's edge for much of the way. Turn onto the cycling path at Ikura—you can't miss a road sign with a picture of the lakes showing the way. I cycled around Kugushi-ko, Suigetsu-ko, and Mikata-ko lakes and skipped the other two for lack of time. There is also a "Rainbow Line" toll road from which there should be a good view of the lakes.

Although it's often busy, take the road on the southern side of Mikata-ko Lake to get back onto Route 27, which continues on to Obama. Stay at the Obama Youth Hostel on top of a steep hill and you'll have a bird's-eye view of Obama-wan Bay.

Early the next morning, I started off on a pleasant seaside road with nice views of the ocean and beaches. Whenever the seaside road disappears, simply switch back to Route 27. I always kept my eyes peeled for any seaside cycling/pedestrian paths and found a great one which went all the way to Aoto-hashi, from where Route 27 approached the water. I could have crossed this bridge and ridden on the cycling path (parallel to Route 27) on the other side, but I stayed on Route 27 and headed for the beach near Wakasawada Station. Wada-hama has a nice beachside path leading to Shiroyama-koen Park, a good place for a break. I continued on the beachside path a little further and then went back to Route 27 to climb the

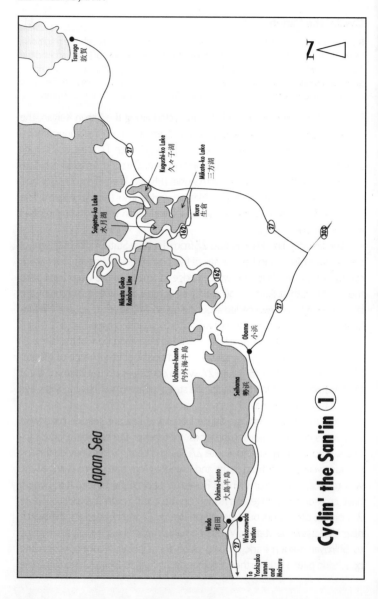

Japan Sea

Tsuruga 敦賀

Kugushi-ko Lake 久々子湖

Mikata-ko Lake 三方湖

Suigetsu-ko Lake 水月湖

Ikura 生倉

162

Mikata Goko Rainbow Line

303

27

Obama 小浜

Uchitomi-hanto 内外海半島

162

Seihama 勢浜

Oshima-hanto 大島半島

Wada 和田

Wakasawada Station

27

To Yoshizaka Tunnel and Maizuru

N

Cyclin' the San'in ①

slope leading to the Yoshizaka tunnel, entering Kyoto-fu.

After lunch in Higashi-Maizuru, I left Route 27 and went to Naka-Maizuru. Careful you don't make any wrong turns here or you could find yourself, as I did, in the middle of the Japan Self-Defense Force naval ship-yard—a real dead end. Pass through Nishi-Maizuru and cross the Yura-kawa River to ride on Route 178 all the way up to Yura-hama. The scenic route around the Kunda-hanto Peninsula featuring picturesque white sand beaches was a worthwhile detour except for the killing grades. From the western side of the peninsula, you can see Amanohashidate in the dis-tance, a sandbar more than three kilometers long studded with pine trees.

Along the entire eastern length of Amanohashidate facing Miyazu-wan there is a long swimming beach, and along the western side facing the enclosed Aso-kai, just a low stone wall. You can ride your bicycle on the dirt road running across the bridge from end to end, but you won't be alone since rental bicycles abound. I reached Monju (the town facing the southern end of Amanohashidate) late in the afternoon. Ride over to the northern end and you'll find the town of Fuchu. For a picture-postcard view of the bridge take a cable car to Kasamatsu-koen Park. Having cycled 110 kilometers, I checked in at the hospitable and cheap Amano-hashidate Kanko Kaikan near the cable car station. The food was great and plentiful and since it wasn't so crowded, I had an air-conditioned room all to myself.

My next goal was the Tango-hanto Peninsula. Judging from its jagged coastline on the map, I could expect a rocky shore with lots of ups and downs. I debated whether or not to leave my bike at Amanohashidate and take the one-day sightseeing bus around the peninsula to save time and sweat, but in the end I decided to do it the hard way.

The seaside Route 178 was very scenic and flat up to Ine, a small fishing village, where the houses are built on stilts over the water, providing park-ing space for small boats. After Ine, it was another story. The peninsula turned out to be a real test of stamina with endless killer slopes one after another. Although I had to walk my bike up the steeper hills, this was the most scenic segment of the entire trip and traffic was not too heavy. I rode to nearby Kameshima to see if there was a path going around the small cape. There was none, so I backtracked to Route 178. Shortly after Ine and

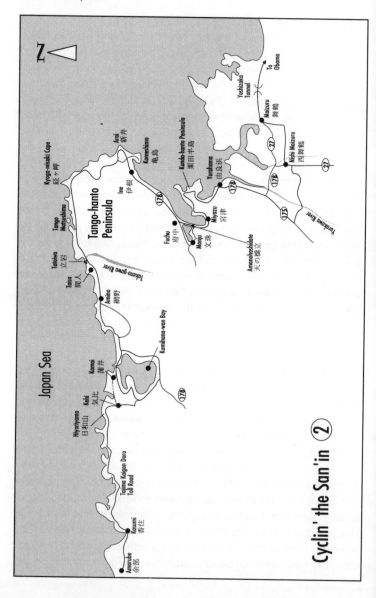

Cyclin' the San'in ②

N

To Obama

Yoshizaka Tunnel

Maizuru 舞鶴

Nishi Maizuru 西舞鶴

27

27

Arai 新井

Kameshima 亀島

Kando-hanto Peninsula 栗田半島

Kyoga-misaki Cape 経ヶ岬

Ine 伊根

178

Yurahama 由良浜

178

178

175

Yurakawa River

Miyazu 宮津

Fuchu 府中

Monju 文珠

Amanohashidate 天の橋立

Tango Matsushima

Tango-hanto Peninsula

Tateiwa 立岩

Taiza 間人

Tokeno-gawa River

Amino 網野

Kumihama-wan Bay

178

Japan Sea

Kamoi 蒲井

Kehi 気比

Hiyoriyama 日和山

Tajima Kaigan Doro Toll Road

Kasumi 香住

Amarube 余部

a long uphill climb, I took a grueling detour on a road leading to the seaside town of Arai and gladly went back to Route 178 at Honjo-hama where more killer slopes awaited.

I rested at Kyoga-misaki Cape, declining the thirty-minute hike to the lighthouse. Starting at Nakahama was a small seaside road which passed Tango Matsushima, a few small islands with pine trees. Cycling on I found Tate-iwa, an impressive wall of stone jutting up from the sea near the beach. At Taiza I stopped over at the almost empty Tango Hanto Youth Hostel fronting the ocean. My odometer read eighty kilometers.

On the fourth day, I rode from Taiza to Amarube, in Hyogo Prefecture—another day of endless ups and downs. Right before Amino I found a nice long beach path and then I went on the seaside road which eventually merged with Route 178. Thereafter, I tried to stay as close as possible to the coast. I rode along the northern shore of Kumihama-wan Bay to Kamai, a small village on the coast. From there, my map showed a dashed line over the mountain to Hyogo. I couldn't tell if it was a dirt road or what, but it looked like an irresistible shortcut. A farmer working his field told me that it was possible to cross over the mountain but I would have to carry my bike. I took my chances and ended up hiking up a steep and often narrow trail while pushing my bike. I was the only one on the mountain.

I finally hit the top and began going downhill much to my relief—it took about an hour and a half to clear the mountain. The long (but probably faster) way to Hyogo is to ride south of Kumihama-wan and cross Mihara-toge Pass. After lunch at Kehi-hama I rode to scenic Hiyoriyama-koen Park on Route 178.

The Tajima Marine Line toll road charged me ¥450 for the privilege of climbing up heartbreaking hills. A break came at Takeno-hama, then onward to Kasumi after more uphill climbing and thrilling downhill rides. In Kasumi you can stop off at Daijo-ji, a temple with a large collection of screens located about five minutes walk from Kasumi Station. After a few more slopes and a final steep 200m hill (the last straw!) I reached Amarube Youth Hostel, a run-down place with no air-conditioning.

The next morning I continued on Route 178, riding under the 41.5m high Amarube-hashi Bridge between Amarube and Yoroi stations on the San-in Honsen Main Line. The bridge achieved notoriety in 1986 when a train was blown off the top by strong winds, crashing into a crab cannery

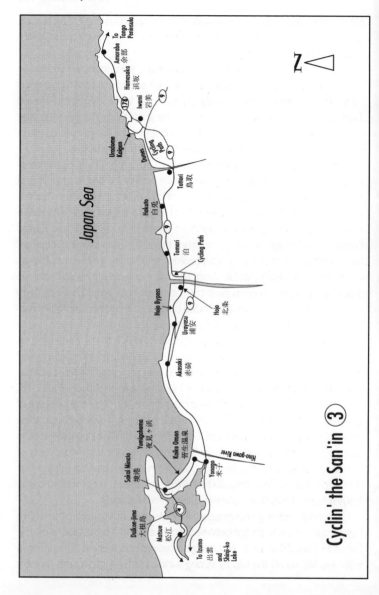

Japan Sea

To
Tongo
Peninsula

Amarube
余部

Hamasaka
浜坂

Iwami
岩美

178

Uradome
Kaigan

Dunes

Cycling
Path

9

Tottori
鳥取

Hakuto
白兎

9

Tomari
泊

Cycling Path

Hojo Bypass

9

Hojo
北条

Uroyasu
浦安

Akasaki
赤碕

Yumigahama
弓ヶ浜

Sakai Minato
境港

Kaike Onsen
皆生温泉

Hino-gawa River

Yonago
米子

Daikon-jima
大根島

Matsue
松江

To Izumo
出雲
and
Shinji-ko Lake

N

Cyclin' the San'in 3

directly below, killing a number of workers. Where the processing plant once stood is now a memorial Kannon statue .

Still on Route 178, there was a long uphill climb to a longer tunnel, after which came the immensely thrilling and longest downhill ride ever, toward Hamasaka. The coast is very beautiful in this area, but at the border with Tottori Prefecture, I had to walk my bicycle up the steep zig-zag slope into Iwami-cho. Shortly after the Uradome Kaigan route, a road with pleasant views but more exhausting than I had expected, I came to the Tottori sand dunes. I took the road running through the dunes until it ended at Route 9. and then dropped off my things at the nearby Tottori Cycling Terminal. This turned out to be the best lodging of the entire trip: the food was good and plentiful, the staff very friendly, and my room was air-conditioned. Tottori City has committed itself to being a cycling city: From the terminal there is a twenty-kilometer cycling course with good views of the sand dunes and the coast and there are also cycling paths along the Sendai-gawa River.

After a restful night at the cycling terminal and a big breakfast, I headed for Yonago and Kaike Onsen on a flat cycling path that ends at Hakuto-hama, the location of a legend about a deceitful rabbit that walked across the sea on the backs of sharks. I was glad that the killing grades which had plagued me so often up to Tottori were all but gone. After a few slopes between Aoya and Tomari on Route 9. I rode on a pleasant cycling path in Hawai-cho up to the Tenjin-gawa River. Instead of the busy, straight Hojo bypass, take a quiet farm road along the side. From Urayasu, there is a pleasant seaside road and path to Akasaki where it merges with Route 9. For the rest of the way to Yonago, I stayed on this relatively flat and easy going road.

Dinner in Yonago and then on to nearby Kaike Onsen where I spent the night, soaking up the much-welcomed hot spring waters. Kaike Onsen lies at the east end of a long sandy beach called Yumigahama. The next morning, I cycled this long and pretty shore (along busy Route 431) to Sakai-minato and then crossed to Daikon-jima. This quiet and scenic island offers pleasant cycling.

By lunchtime I was in Matsue, the "water capital" located on the shore of Shinji-ko Lake, and sliced into northern and southern sectors by the Ohashi-kawa River. A bicycle is the best way to see the main sights of Matsue, such as the castle, samurai houses, Yaegaki-jinja, and Kamosu-jinja, one of the oldest shrines in Japan. The next day I cycled south to the Fudoki-no-Oka Shiryokan, a museum housing ancient relics excavated in the vicinity.

From Matsue, it was onward to IzumoTaisha, my final destination. I rode on Route 431 to Hirata and then took a detour along the flat cycling path along the Hii-kawa River. Leaving the river near Takeshi Station, I rode westward until Taisha Station and IzumoTaisha-jinja. Since it was still light, I decided to cycle to Hino-misaki Cape, a short, exhausting trip, although the top of the lighthouse afforded a fine view of the surrounding coast.

I rode back to Izumo, where I found a *minshuku*. Later I discovered there is also a cycling terminal here with five courses in all, including a fifty-four-kilometer course around the Izumo Taisha area. The next day, after cycling to Tachikue Gorge, about sixteen kilometers away, I sent my bicycle back to Tokyo by *takkyubin*, and caught a flight home to Tokyo from Izumo.

About 720 kilometers in total, the cycling trip was a great success; no accidents, not even a flat tire, but I won't do it again in a hurry. If you plan on cycling the San'in and sampling the stunning ocean views, be mentally and physically prepared for endless hill-climbing from Amanohashidate to Tottori.   ✍ PO

❶ Field Information

For more information on the San'in, read *Along the San-in* by J.M. Daggett
Mihama-machi Tourist Information Center ☎ 0770 32-0222
Amanohashidate Tourist Information Center ☎ 0772 22-0670
Tango-machi Tourist Office ☎ 0772 75-0260 (ext. 36,35)
Tottori City Tourist Information Center ☎ 0857 22-3318
Hamamura Onsen Tourist Information ☎ 0857 82-0829
Matsue Tourist Information ☎ 0852 27-5843
Izumo Minshuku Association ☎ 0853 23-2873

⌂ Lodging Log

Mikata lakes area: Kokuminshukusha Baijo Lodge ☎ 0770 47-1234; Kogakujima-so (at foot of Baijo-dake between Suigetsu-ko and Kugushi-ko) ☎ 0770 45-0255
Amanohashidate: Amanohashidate Youth Hostel ☎ 07722 7-0121
Tango Peninsula: Tango-hanto Youth Hostel (on Route 178) ☎ 0772 75-1529
Kasumi: Hamakaze-so ☎ 07963 6-0773; Miuraya ☎ 07963 6-1091
Tottori: Tottori-shi Cycling Terminal (see page 265) ☎ 0857 29-0800
Hawai: Hawai Beach Minshuku ☎ 0858 35-4255; Drive in Tanaka ☎ 0858 35-2808
Matsue: Young Inn Matsue ☎ 0852 22-2000
Izumo Station area: Himebara-so ☎ 0853 23-2873; Inaba ☎ 0853 22-6178; Izumo Cycling Terminal (see page 265) ☎ 0853 23-1370

Shikoku: Japan's Fourth Largest Island

Shikoku still retains its out-of-the-way flavor despite the completion of the large Seto Ohashi Bridge connecting it with Honshu, and two more bridges planned for the near future. The rugged interior discourages the building of expressways and the presence of the cars that roam them. Most of the roads through Shikoku are still narrow, extremely winding, and idiosyncratic, thus depriving motor traffic of what it really wants most—speed.

The same goes for cycle tourists, albeit in a more nonlinear fashion. Should you want to cover a lot of terrain, and ride great distances, don't go to Shikoku. But, if you want to dawdle and don't mind retracing your route more than you would normally, then Shikoku is for you.

Shikoku is by no means remote or isolated—merely out of the way. Thus, one cycles in Shikoku to celebrate how little this island (apart from the main cities at least) has been affected by modernization, economic booms and busts, and so-called internationalization. Once away from the more populated areas, you will find yourself stopping several times an hour to check out something unusual; a small temple that seems to have been abandoned, a small rope bridge crossing a rushing creek, or a tiny roadside soba shop sporting a thatched roof of indeterminable age.

Since bicycles are prohibited on Seto Ohashi Bridge, the cyclist must arrive on public transport. Although each of Shikoku's four main cities (Kochi, Matsuyama, Takamatsu, and Tokushima) boasts an airport, and several trains cross the Seto Ohashi every hour, the most Shikoku-esque way to arrive is by boat. Not only does the slowness of ship travel decompress you for the dawdling cycling that lies ahead, but it also emphasizes the fact that you've arrived on an island. For Shikoku you will savor the effect.

By boat there are three main entry ports if coming from the direction of Tokyo: Tokushima, Kochi, and Imabari.

From Tokushima

Route: Scenic loop to Tokushima and back, taking in some of the best of Shikoku's coastal and highland routes via hot springs and a traditional vine bridge

Adrenalin-filled, we arrived at Ariake Ferry Terminal one December

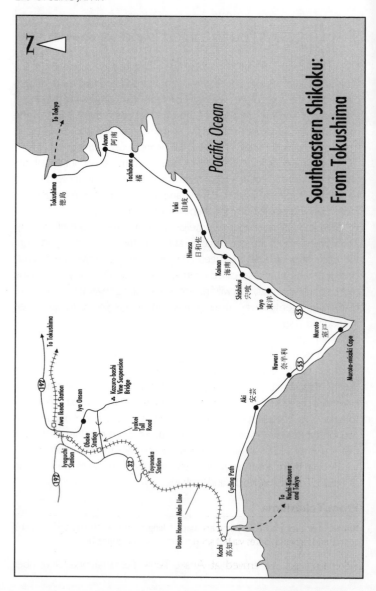

N

Pacific Ocean

To Tokyo

Tokushima 徳島
Anan 阿南
Tachibana 橘
Yuki 由岐
Hiwasa 日和佐
Kainan 海南
Shishikui 宍喰
Toyo 東洋
Muroto 室戸
Muroto-misaki Cape

55

55

Nawari 奈半利
Aki 安芸

To Nachi-Katsuura and Tokyo

Cycling Path

Kochi 高知

Dosan Honsen Main Line

Toyonaka Station
Iyeguchi Station
Oboke Station
Awa Ikeda Station
Iya Onsen
Kazura-bashi Vine Suspension Bridge
Iyakei Toll Road

To Tokushima

192

192

32

Southeastern Shikoku: From Tokushima

evening to catch the crowded 5:50 PM ferry to Tokushima. We hoped to get a glimpse of traditional Japan before the island's eventual "modernization" via the Seto Ohashi Bridge and also planned to explore some of the island's eighty-eight Buddhist temples, some dating back to about 800 A.D.

The ferry is slower than a plane or train, but cheaper and less hassle, allowing true relaxation. For simplicity, we rode our bikes on to the car deck, paying ¥2,200 extra. A bagged bike is only ¥300 extra. Basic second-class fare was ¥8,200 each way, with a ten percent discount on a round-trip ticket. The ferry leaves from Tokyo to Tokushima on even-numbered days, and from Tokushima to Tokyo on odd-numbered days. From Tokushima, the boat goes on to Kokura in northern Kyushu. Be warned that the ferry can be extremely crowded during the holiday season and the large lounge is often turned into a makeshift sleeping area. Landing in the early afternoon, we rode two kilometers to the clean, modern Tokushima Youth Hostel located on a small cove with a great private beach.

The next day we rode on Route 55 from Tokushima to Awatachibana, a distance of about twenty-eight kilometers with gentle hills and beautiful views. We took a narrow, curvy side road from Yuki to Hiwasa, which had some of the nicest cycling we've experienced anywhere in Japan. We rode along, sometimes through tunnels of trees, admiring the scenic, jagged coastline. Hiwasa is known for its protected sea coast and the Yakuo-ji Temple, the twenty-third stop on the temple pilgrimage. At the temple the custom is to drop a ¥1 coin on each step to protect oneself from all manner of calamities. Near the Yakuo-ji Temple is the Hiwasa Youth Hostel— a borderline dump, but sufficient for cleaning up and staying the night. From Hiwasa to Shishikuicho, Route 55 is a big, gentle roller coaster, making for fast descents and hammerable ascents. In Shishikuicho we stayed at Mitoko-so, a *kokuminshukusha* built on a scenic promontory.

The forty-seven kilometer stretch from Shishikuicho to Muroto proved to be one of most spectacular parts of the trip. Going south along Route 55, the rhythmic, azure ocean was on our left and towering, verdant mountains on our right. It was flat, and there was little traffic. With a strong tailwind, we flew along and were soon at Muroto-misaki Cape. The temperature plunged, rain or snow seemed imminent, and, as the last straw, we found the Higashi Youth Hostel was situated at the top of a very steep hill.

Part of a plaza of stout stone pagodas, ornate wooden structures, and golden Buddha figures, it is one of the most fascinating hostels I've ever visited. Also known as the Hotsumisaki Temple, it is the twenty-fourth stop on the temple circuit. Friends had recommended it after staying there during vacation time, along with thirty-five female motorcycle riders.

The next morning, the clouds parted and disappeared, and it was suddenly so warm that we wore only cycling shorts and T-shirts for the rest of the day, all the way to Kochi. The main road is fine, but from Aki, the birthplace of the founder of Mitsubishi, we found a bike path, almost all flat and lined with pine trees, that ran along the coast for at least twenty kilometers. It's always a little depressing to arrive in a big city after cycling out in the countryside, but Kochi isn't too bad. We stayed at the youth hostel near the station since it's centrally located.

The next day we decided to have a rest, and spent the morning exploring Kochi Castle, which is pretty well reconstructed, has a good view over the city, and houses an interesting museum. After lunch, we bagged our bikes and headed up to the center of Shikoku on a local train. The Jofuku-ji Temple, situated uphill from the town of Toyonaga, is also a youth hostel and a friendly place to stay. They are full of advice on hiking and cycling in the area, and have even made a list of challenges; people stay for weeks going on the various rides and hikes to qualify as "Smiling Buddha Federated National Citizens."

Two years ago, we took the train through the beautiful gorge that Route 32 follows, and thought that cycling there would be great. This time, we did just that, heading down the gorge for a while until we tired of the traffic. Just before Oboke, we turned right, and headed up a steep toll road (only ¥60 for bikes) to another tourist attraction, Kazura-bashi, one of the few remaining vine suspension bridges in Shikoku. It's worth a visit, especially since the cycling in this area is excellent. The hills are longer and steeper than those along the coast, but more rewarding. After lunch, we headed down through Iya, a dramatic valley with emerald water below and snow-capped hills above. We had to pull out our gloves for the first time, but it was quite beautiful and we mostly had the narrow road to ourselves. We eventually rejoined Route 32, and then met Route 192 near Ikeda. In the last few kilometers the traffic was terrible, and we were very glad to arrive in the shelter of Awa Ikeda Station at 3:00 P.M., just as it started to drizzle. Near the station, we found the Takaoka Ryokan, a friendly place to stay.

The morning greeted us with dark clouds, cold temperatures, and, luckily, strong tailwinds. We cycled off down the valley toward Tokushima, often on bicycle paths atop the dikes of the Yoshino-gawa River. It always seemed on the verge of pouring, but actually only drizzled on and off. With the favorable wind the seventy-kilometer ride took only three hours. A hundred meters from the station we found a business hotel, the Sakura, which, unusually, had friendly staff, large tatami rooms, and a real Japanese bath. After checking the tides, we took an hour-long bus trip to the Naruto Straits, famous for its fascinating tidal whirlpools. For a closer look take the thirty-minute boat trip.

Since it was the end of New Year, the return ferry was quite crowded but at least we weren't troubled with violent seas—friends had told us gruesome reports of vicious storms during their crossing which made the boat pitch so violently that an announcement was made warning people not to stand up.

All in all, this trip really exceeded our expectations. Maybe because this winter was warmer than usual, making it just fine for cycling. We brought the same clothes as we take on our summer tours, plus warm gloves. In nine days, we circled most of the eastern half of Shikoku, but never rode later than four o'clock, and had plenty of time off the bikes. We found Shikoku people friendly, and the slower pace a welcome change from Tokyo.   ✍NGH

ℹ Field Information

Kokura-bound ferry departs Tokyo 5:50 P.M., arriving Tokushima (Tsuda Futo, 20 min by bus from JR Tokushima Station) 12:50 P.M. the next day; for information and reservations, call Ocean Tokyu Ferry ☎ 03 3567-0971
Muroto-misaki Tourist Association ☎ 08872 2-0574

🛌 Lodging Log

Hiwasa: Hiwasa Youth Hostel ☎ 08847 7-0755
Shishikuicho: Kokuminshukusha Mitoko-so ☎ 08847 6-3150; Ebisu ☎ 08847 6-2769; Kuroko-so ☎ 08847 6-3438; Pacific ☎ 08847 6-3125
Kainan-machi area: Kaisan-so ☎ 08847 3-1326; Sushidake ☎ 0887 3-3252
Muroto-misaki area: Hotsumisaki Temple (Higashi Youth Hostel) ☎ 08872 2-0366; Ryokan Ota ☎ 08872 2-0004; Maruyama-so 08872 3-0279; Shimokawa ☎ 08872 2-1857; Yamashita ☎ 08872 2-1422; Muroto-so ☎ 08872 2-0409
Muroto City (4 km northwest of the cape): Drive-in Urashima-so ☎ 08872 2-2291

Kochi Eki-mae Youth Hostel ☎ 0888 83-50865
Toyonaga: Jofuku-ji Temple ☎ 0887-74-0301
Oboke area: Jisho-in Temple ☎ 0883 84-1934
Iya Onsen: Iya Onsen Hotel ☎ 0883 75-2311
Ikeda: Takaoka Ryokan ☎ 0883 72-1041, Hakuchi-so ☎ 0883 74-0487
Tokushima: Sakura ☎ 0886 52-9575; Tokushima Youth Hostel ☎ 0886 63-1505

From Kochi

Route: A loop from Kochi around the rugged southwestern peninsula to Ashizuri-misaki Cape, and Kashima-jima Island, famed for its monkey and deer

The crux of the entire trip was getting to Tokyo's Ariake Ferry Terminal on time. On the day of departure, heavy snow fell, much more than we could ride through, so we bagged our bikes and took the Yurakucho Line to Toyosu Station the closest to the terminal. The station has poor road access so it was hard to catch a taxi. Two of us finally got one though the other two of us spent another twenty minutes standing in the dark being spurned by all taxis. Luckily a kind workman picked us up and drove us to the terminal, and we arrived just minutes before the scheduled 6:10 P.M. departure—though the ferry was delayed ninety minutes waiting for passengers.

The ferry, run by the Blue Highway Line is more expensive but nicer than the Ocean Tokkyu Ferry (Tokyo to Tokushima to Kokura). The basic one-way fare is ¥13,910, with bikes ¥2,260 extra or, if bagged only ¥820 extra (or free if they forget to charge you). A two-person cabin with bunk beds (green *shindai* A class) costs an extra ¥3,600. In the economy class (*nito seki*) each person is assigned a space (about 2 x 6 ft) with pillow and blanket. No-smoking economy accommodation is not available.

After a comfortable cruise we arrived in Kochi a little before 5:00 P.M. As it stays a light a bit later there, we still had time before it got dark to assemble our bikes and ride the ten kilometers to Katsurahama to the *kokuminshukusha*. The ride was a little cold but the sunset was beautiful.

The next day we ambitiously rode over ninety kilometers to Kubokawa, avoiding the major Route 56 by riding along the coast. In Usa we opted for the longer toll road along the coast and were rewarded with fifteen kilometers of continuous steep climbs and spectacular ocean scenery. This was followed by short legs on Route 56, then onto one of

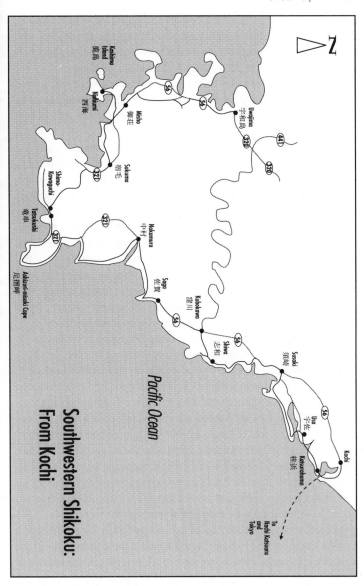

Southwestern Shikoku:
From Kochi

the smaller, deserted coast roads. When we headed inland to Kubokawa, it gradually started to snow in earnest. We cranked into the swirling wind and snow and finally made it to the Iwamoto-ji Youth Hostel by about 4:00 P.M., a clean and pleasant old temple with a *minshuku*-like dinner.

The next day, after a look round the temple at the hostel, we headed for Nakamura on Route 56, taking detours a couple of times. It was a shorter, warmer ride, and we arrived early and stayed right near the station at a *minshuku* that served a massive dinner.

New Year's Eve saw us heading off for Ashizuri-misaki Cape, the southern tip of Shikoku. In perfect weather we hugged the coast, avoiding the main road. For the first time we were down to shorts and T-shirts, although after lunch it became cloudy but not too cold. The final fourteen kilometers to the tip of the cape are highly recommended. After enjoying the scenery and the relatively quiet, narrow road, it was quite a shock to find lots of activity at Ashizuri. We checked into Kongofuku-ji Youth Hostel and went for a walk to the "best eroded granite sea-cave in Japan." Despite the crowds on the paved paths, the area is quite picturesque. After an unusually good dinner at the hostel, we tried to stay up until midnight but failed. At 11:40 P.M. the alarm went off, and we walked over to the temple with the other guests under a sky filled with brilliant stars.

The first day of the New Year we cycled off in a light-to-medium rain on an excellent road, but the rain intensified by the time we reached Tatsukushi at lunchtime. Turning right at Shimokawaguchi, we took a shortcut inland to Sukumo. The strong rain finally let up and the quiet little road ended at Route 321, where we turned right to reach Sukumo six kilometers later.

The following day we headed along the coast on a small road. We were enjoying the scenery so much that we ignored the warnings from two women about the road being impassable ahead. We found one part under construction, but went ahead in the dirt anyway. It wasn't until we'd rounded the point that the road suddenly ended. Retracing our steps, we faced a steep, 400m climb with a great descent bringing us back down to Route 56. After lunch we headed off toward Nishiumi on Route 34—a great road, curvy with quite hilly terrain but perfect grading. We took a ferry for the short hop to Kashima and stayed in the only building on the island, the *kokuminshukusha*, where we met a Tasmanian cyclist. It was windy but warm on the island, and although there's no place to cycle, we were entertained by semi-wild deer and monkeys and had an enjoyable ride in a glass-bottomed boat which circled a coral reef inhabited by colorful fish.

The next morning the wind had increased so much that the 9:00 A.M. boat was the last one for the day. Heading for Uwajima, we found an inland route that avoided the main road. The first pass took two hours to climb, but the road was so little used that it was covered with pine needles. We were climbing in shorts, which made for a chilly, long descent on the other side. Navigation was a bit tricky through here, but we finally managed to join back up with Route 56 only eight kilometers from Uwajima, where we had another little adventure. Two bearded foreigners dressed in lycra were probaby too much for the locals and we were refused accommodation at the first *minshuku* we tried. No matter, there were plenty of *minshuku* around and we ended up staying only a block away in a much friendlier place.

From Uwajima we returned to Kochi via Kubokawa by train. The weather was perfect and we were kicking ourselves for riding a train through such beautiful-looking cycling country, particularly the route from Uwajima to Kubokawa. Back in Kochi, the ferry departed on time at 6:20 P.M. but was more crowded than before. By 3:15 P.M. the next day we were cycling along Harumi-Dori and in an hour we were home.   ✍ NGH

❶ Field Information
Kochi-bound ferry leaves Tokyo on odd-numbered day at 6:20 P.M. stopping in Nachi-Katsuura (Kii-hanto) at 7:40 A.M., arriving at Kochi around 2:30 P.M.; return ferry leaves Kochi 5:50 P.M. arriving Nachi-Katsuura 1:10 A.M., and Tokyo 2:40 P.M.; for more information and reservations, call Blue Highway Line ☎ 03 3578-1127
Nakamura Tourist Office ☎ 0880 35-4171
Ashizuri Tourist Information ☎ 08808 8-0939

⚓ Lodging Log
Katsurahama: Katsurahama ☎ 0888 41-3898; Kokuminshukusha Katsurahama-so ☎ 0888 41-2201
Kubokawa: Iwamoto-ji Youth Hostel ☎ 08802 2-0376
Nakamura: Minshuku Sakura ☎ 0880 34-3062
Ashizuri: Kongofuku-ji Youth Hostel ☎ 08808 8-0038
Sukumo: Minshuku Ayu ☎ 0880 63-1870
Nishiumi: Ishigaki-so ☎ 0895 82-0421; Kokuminshukusha Nishiumi-so (Kashima Island) ☎ 0895 82-1121
Uwajima: Minshuku Katsuma ☎ 0895 23-1398

From Imabari   🚲

Route: A select menu of three routes all starting from Imabari, including hot springs and routes to lakes in the heart of Shikoku

One of the best places to arrive on Shikoku for a short, casual trip is Imabari, which is well served by hourly ferries from Mihara Port on Honshu near Mihara Shinkansen Station, only about two hours from Osaka. The fare is ¥1,310; call 0898 32-1500 for more information.

In addition, the Shikoku Orange Ferry from Osaka lands at Toyo, about ten kilometers south of Imabari. There are two sailings each day from Osaka: early afternoon arriving late evening, and late evening arriving the next morning. Take the overnighter to save lodging costs and allow for more daytime cycling. Fares start at ¥3,600. For details, call 06 612-0951

After arriving at Imabari Port, head inland toward the center of town. Turn left on Route 317 and go straight. Don't turn right on Route 317, but continue straight onto Route 196 through Toyo.

Those arriving from Osaka by Orange Ferry should ride from Toyo Port south and follow the signs to Matsuyama, which will put you onto Route 196 just before it finishes at the intersection of busy busy busy Route 11.

From this point you have a choice of three routes, all different in terms of riding, but all interesting nonetheless.

⇨ To Matsuyama

The most leisurely of these three Shikoku suggestions is the route to Matsuyama, a major ferry terminal. Matsuyama is also home to Dogo Onsen, one of the oldest and most interesting hot spring resorts in Japan. Best of all, Matsuyama is close, and in no time at all you can find yourself enjoying the luxury of a huge, hot mineral bath. So let's get going.

Turn right onto Route 11 for about four kilometers, then take the turnoff to the right for Tambara-cho. Go straight on this moderately traveled road, through the town of Tambara, until it deadends about eight kilometers later at a T-junction. Go left until the road forks at Sekiya; go right and head up and over a tough but short pass, followed by a long downhill into Shigenobu-cho. The road then crosses Route 11; go right for about three kilometers until you come to a smaller road that forks off to the right heading more directly toward Matsuyama. This road serves numerous hot-spring resorts, including

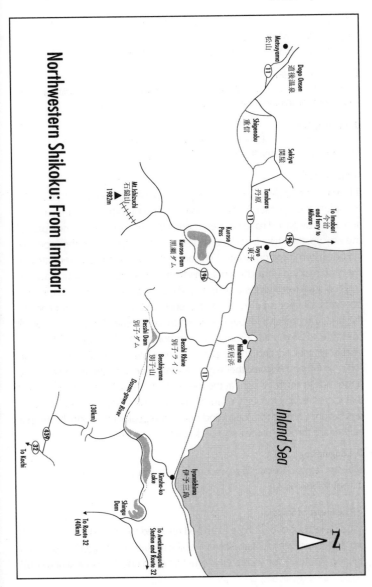

Northwestern Shikoku: From Imabari

Takanoko Onsen, Hoshigaoka Onsen, Higashi Dogo Onsen. and historic Dogo Onsen, where the main hot springs are open to the public, much like the public baths in most Japanese neighborhoods.

❶ Field Information

Ferries operate from Matsuyama to Hiroshima, Kobe, Iwakuni, Kure, Mihara, Yanai, and Onomichi on Honshu, and Beppu, Oita, and Kokura on Kyushu

♨ Lodging Log

Imabari: Komecho Ryokan (1 min from Imabari Port) ☎ 0898 32-0554
Matsuyama: Matsuyama ☎ 0899 24-8386; Miyoshi ☎ 0899 77-2581

⇨ Mt. Ishizuchi

If the weather is clear, you can't help but notice Mt. Ishizuchi (1,982m) to the south, the highest mountain in Western Japan. While the summit is not accessible by paved road or even mountain bike trail, you can ride part of the way up, then hike and climb your way to the top, or take the ropeway. To begin, turn right on Route 11, then right about two kilometers later on the road marked Ishizuchi-yama. This turns into a tough, winding road that goes up and over Kurose-toge Pass and down to a small lake. The climbing only gets rougher, so if you've had enough and decide to bail out back to flat land, turn left and follow the lakeshore to Kurose Dam, then downhill to Route 11. If you want more of the mountain, turn right and follow the lakeshore around and then up the Kamo-gawa River. When the road forks, go left and ride another eight kilometers or so to the ropeway. For a better ride, though, go right at the fork and ride a smaller, more scenic road that forges its way through a narrow river canyon for about fifteen kilometers before coming to a dead end below the peak of Ishizuchi. Note that neither are through routes, so a back-track is in order.

♨ Lodging Log

Ishizuchi: Tamaya Ryokan (in grounds of Ishizuchi-jinja, 20 mins. from top cable car station) ☎ 0897 59-0415

⇨ The Heart of Shikoku

If you bailed out over Kurose Dam and returned to flat land, but would still like some more mountain scenery—albeit over less-rugged land—turn right on Route 11 for about ten kilometers or so until Niihama, when you'll see signs beckoning you to turn right for Besshi. Do it and you'll be taken through an area called the Besshi Rhine, no matter how tenuous the scenic similarities with Germany. It is, however, an extremely beautiful area with a rushing river. On hot summer days, the water becomes awfully inviting . . .

The road continues uphill along the river, passes over a small dam, and continues more viciously uphill for another seven kilometers or so before going through a long tunnel (take a breather, this is the pass) and out into the village of Besshiyama, which spreads out over the hills surrounding a small lake formed by Besshi Dam. The road follows the Dozan-gawa River canyon through picture-book terrain and cozy settlements, rising and dropping, but mostly dropping.

At the next major intersection, about twenty kilometers from Besshi Dam, you can go straight and follow the river to the next lake, or go right and head further inland on an even smaller road that heads toward the other side of Shikoku, a wild mountain ride that ends up in Motoyama-cho about thirty kilometers later. Another thirty kilometers (via a stretch on Route 439) will take you to the middle of downtown Kochi.

If you go straight and follow the Dozan-gawa, you can continue through some spectacular mountain scenery while avoiding long, hard climbs. A few kilometers along there'll be a bridge on your left; turn onto it if you'd like to head back to civilization—you'll be treated to a long tunnel followed by a stupendous downhill that almost simulates an aircraft landing as you roll headlong into Iyomishima City.

If you continue along the shore, you'll be treated to views of Kinsha-ko Lake on your left until Yanagise Dam, where the road plunges to a smaller lake behind Shingu Dam, then to an intersection at Kumano-jinja Shrine. From here you can go left and follow the Iyogawa river to Route 32 (the main artery between Takamatsu and Kochi), or go right for nearly forty kilometers of wild mountain riding before you join up with Route 32 about thirty-seven kilometers north of Kochi.   ✍ BH

❶ Field Information
Ehime Tourist Information (Tokyo office) ☎ 03 3231-1804

♠ Lodging Log
Iyomishima: Grand Foret Ishimatsu (5 mins from Iyomishima Station) ☎ 0896 23-3355

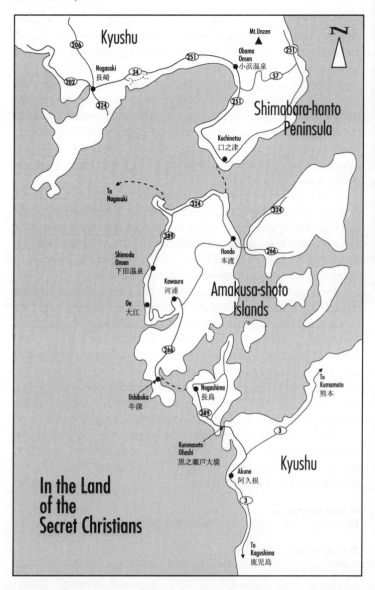

Kyushu

Mt.Unzen

Obama
Onsen
小浜温泉

Nagasaki
長崎

Shimabara-hanto
Peninsula

Kuchinotsu
口之津

To
Nagasaki

Shimoda
Onsen
下田温泉

Honda
本渡

Kawaura
河浦

Amakusa-shoto
Islands

Oe
大江

To
Kumamoto
熊本

Ushibuka
牛深

Nagashima
長島

Kuronaseto
Ohashi
黒之瀬戸大橋

To
Kagoshima
鹿児島

Akune
阿久根

Kyushu

In the Land
of the
Secret Christians

Kyushu 🚲🚲🚲🚲🚲🚲🚲🚲🚲🚲🚲🚲🚲🚲🚲🚲

In the Land of the Secret Christians 🚲

Route: Island-hopping off the coast of Nagasaki in the land of Japan's secret Christians
Start: Nagasaki (JR Nagasaki Line from Hakata; or JR Kagoshima Honsen Main Line from Kumamoto to Tosu Station and change to the JR Nagasaki Honsen Main Line)
Goal: Akune Station (JR Kagoshima Honsen Main Line)

The Amakusa area south of Nagasaki is considered among the most scenic in Japan. Noted for the seven bridges (actually there are more) linking a number of islands, the region is where Japan's early Christians holed up to avoid persecution. Don't be surprised to see the towering spire of an old Catholic church beyond the next hill or turn. This course can be done in two days, but three is best.

From Nagasaki, climb up Route 34 over the hill, then turn right on Route 251 heading east toward Unzen on the Shimabara-hanto Peninsula. I went in spring, and the wildflowers were tremendous on this stretch. Stay along the coast, passing Obama Onsen. At Kuchinotsu on the end of the peninsula, take the thirty-minute ferry ride (every forty-five minutes until 6:45 P.M.) over to Amakusa Island. At the other side, go toward the right (west) and follow the coast facing the sea on Route 324. There are only a few grades along here until you get to Shimoda Onsen, where there are several good places to spend the night along the river which runs through town. As I remember, the seafood was very good.

From here to Ushibuka is perhaps the best part of the journey. Route 324, now Route 389, narrows and climbs up the bluffs overlooking the sea, and then plunges down into Kawaura. You can't miss the church here, which looks like an odd European transplant. The uneven road then creeps along at ocean level through what might be called fjords—rugged rock cliffs framing peaceful inlets. Where Route 324 ends, turn right on Route 266 for Ushibuka. The road gets wider and better, but you leave the ocean scenery. At Ushibuka, board the small yet luxurious ferry (on the hour from 7:00 A.M. to 7:00 P.M.) over to Nagashima.

On the other side, take Route 389, passing over the beautifully painted Kurono Seto Ohashi Bridge to Akune on the Kyushu mainland. From here

o Kagoshima (which offers plenty of interesting sights) on
y or less, or board the Ariake Express on the Kagoshima
ne at Akune and get to Hakata in about three hours. (The
kkyu gets to Osaka by 9:30 the next morning.)　　✐ BH

ᴏ"ıg Log

Nagasaki Station area: Nagasaki Youth Hostel ☎ 0958 23-5032; Fumi Minshuku ☎ 0958 22-4962; Minshuku Senju-so ☎ 0958 23-1954; Ryokan Sansui-so ☎ 0958 24-0070

Nagasaki Peace Memorial Park area: Tanpopo ☎ 0958 61-6230

Amakusa: Kokuminshukusha Amakusa-so ☎ 0969 42-3131

Hondo: Amakusa Youth Hostel ☎ 0969 22-3085

Obama Onsen: Kokuminshukusha Seiunso ☎ 0957 73-3273

Shimoda Onsen area: Minshuku Sakamoto ☎ 0969 42-3563; Takahama-so ☎ 0969 42-0887; Yamada-so ☎ 0969 42-1136; Shirohama-so ☎ 0969 42-0690; Ueno ☎ 0969 42-1179

Oe (church with tatami floor built by French priest in 1933) Umekawa ☎ 0969 42-5302

Ushibuka area: Chinosaki-so ☎ 09697 3-4773; Satsuki-so ☎ 09697 2-3773; Haiya ☎ 09697 2-4605; Shirohama-so ☎ 09697 2-9130; Hatsumaru-so ☎ 09697 2-9427

Crossing Mt. Aso　　🚲

Route: Crossing Mt. Aso, an awesome crater at least twenty three kilometers in diameter, from the castle town of Kumamoto to the hot-spring town of Beppu via the scenic Yamanami Highway

Start: Kumamoto (JR Kagoshima Honsen Main Line from Hakata)

Goal: Beppu (JR Nippo Honsen Main Line from Kokura)

I took Route 57, cutting right through the center of Kumamoto City north-west toward Mt. Aso, Mt. Kuju, and the Pacific coast. It was noon Friday, and the traffic was light. On weekends, Route 57 becomes a slow-moving parking lot stretching all the way to Aso.

In Ozu, about twenty-five kilometers from Kumamoto, the road begins its climb into the Aso basin. Not too steep or too narrow, the road starts to flattens out after the junction with Route 325, and the air begins to feel crisper, and cleaner—the difference between above and below is too much to miss.

Route 57 then cuts around the north of Aso and heads to Ichinomiya. Aso Shrine, near JR Miyaji Station, is said to have been founded in 281 B.C. by Emperor Korei. I turned left in the middle of town, following the signs pointing to the Yamanami Highway.

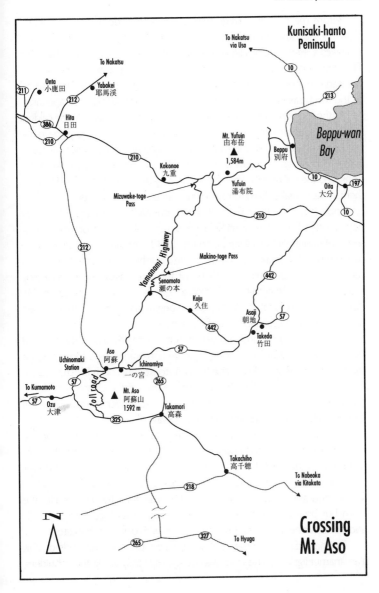

To Nakatsu

Onta
小鹿田

211

212

Yabakei
耶馬渓

386

Hita
日田

210

210

Kokonoe
九重

Mizuwake-toge
Pass

212

Yamanami Highway

To Nakatsu
via Usa

Kunisaki-hanto
Peninsula

10

213

Mt. Yufuin
由布岳

1,584m

Beppu
別府

Beppu-wan
Bay

10

Oita
大分

197

Yufuin
湯布院

210

10

Makino-toge Pass

Senomoto
瀬の本

Kuju
久住

442

442

57

Asaji
朝地

57

Takeda
竹田

Aso
阿蘇

Uchinomaki
Station

57

Ichinomiya
一の宮

265

57

Ozu
大津

Toll road

Mt. Aso
阿蘇山
1592 m

Takamori
高森

325

To Kumamoto

Takachiho
高千穂

To Nobeoka
via Kitakata

218

N

265

327

To Hyuga

Crossing
Mt. Aso

Before me rose the inside wall of the Aso caldera. The Yamanami Highway (also known as the Beppu-Aso Toll Road, or simply as Highway 11) takes a leg-pounding climb up switch-backs that is strenuous, but short. The views, however, are apt compensation. As you rise out of the caldera, you can see more of the basin and more of Aso, which becomes framed by the south caldera wall while the mountains of Takachiho soon appear.

At the top of this climb, the land and atmosphere change. On the caldera rim, at the southern edge of the Aso highlands, I could see Kuju-yama in the northeast. The highlands themselves are altogether different from the basin below. Pampas grass, yellow and dying in the fall, moved with the wind and blanketed the rolling hills. The hills are on a plateau, and as the road follows them, it has to make sharp turns and quick ascents and descents.

Soon, however, the rolling hills flatten out and the Yamanami Highway begins a steady climb toward Kuju. I could see what lay before me; a long series of switchbacks snaking up to the 1,330m Makinoto-toge Pass. The round trip to the peak is a pleasant three-hour hike, and once on top, you can take in the beautiful panorama of the Aso valley and surrounding mountain peaks. Worth the effort on a clear day. A ride to the top of Mt. Kuju (or Mt. Aso, for that matter) is best begun in the early morning when the weather is coolest and the traffic lightest.

Where the Yamanami Highway meets Route 442, I paid the toll, and since it's lowest by far for bicycles, I splurged on orange juice and coffee. At this junction of Route 442 is the Senomoto Kogen Youth Hostel. About four kilometers north of the Makinoto-toge there is the Cosmos-so Koku-minshukusha. Further accommodation is available over the pass in *onsen minshuku* about ten kilometers off the highway.

Climbing the pass gave me even more good views. Far, far off I could see Kumamoto, and was glad to be so far, far away. Over the pass into Oita Prefecture I paid another toll and rolled down onto the Kuju highlands, a popular resort area. The region has some very confusing place names. The characters for the mountain are pronounced Kuju; the same characters are used for the town but bizarrely the town is called Kokonoe. Don't confuse this with another town nearby called Kuju but written with different characters.

The next day found me continuing across the Kuju highlands on the Yamanami Highway. The road was frosty, especially along the shoulders, but cars were few so I didn't feel apprehensive. Instead of pampas grass, these highlands have dense pine forests and cedar groves. The rolling hills become bigger, yet the road continues its sharp curves and quick climbs and drops. At the junction of Route 210 and the Yamanami Highway, about six kilometers before Yufuin at Mizuwake-toge Pass, there is an *onsen* where, in June, the attraction is fireflies in the open-air baths.

I soon arrived in Yufuin, a small, beautiful village surrounded by hills and forests, and said to have the last free public baths in Japan. Mt. Yufu rises 1,584m to the northwest of the village, while the highway skirts around its southern edge. *Minshuku* are available in the ¥5,300 to ¥10,000 price range; most are in the center of the town and have open air baths. Leaving Yufuin, I followed the highway up and over a pass. At the summit is the start of a well-traveled trail to the top of Mt. Yufu, which only takes an hour or two. From the summit I could see Kuju and the rest of the Kyushu mountains to the west and south, and Shikoku off to the east.

Down the trail and back on my bike, I coasted almost all the way into Beppu. The road was long and steep, and I felt glad to be going down, not up. In Beppu, I searched in vain for the tourist office; one map showed it on Highway 10 near the Cosmopia shopping complex, while another put it near the station. On a subsequent trip I found it, brimming with useful information, southeast of the station.

I found the youth hostel in the Kankaiji Onsen area (near Suginoi Palace), dropped my bags there, got back on the bike, and rode to the Kannawa Spa area. Eventually I found my way down to the beach. The Pacific Ocean was my ultimate destination for reasons that were unclear at the time. Back at the youth hostel, I thought about how I got to Beppu and soon fell fast asleep.

The next day I took another soak in the baths and then headed off from the center of town on Route 10, which runs along the beach to Oita. It was Sunday morning, and the traffic was heavy. This stretch of road has a very narrow shoulder, so ride with caution. Less than a kilometer into Oita is a sign for the bypass to Route 210. I took it, turning right and heading southwest through empty streets. This bypass is well marked, and soon turns right onto Route 210. The road stays narrow, but at the intersection of Route 210 and Route 442, both roads become wider and easier to ride.

I went straight onto Route 442, which winds up and around rice paddies and terraced fields, passing through farming villages on its way southwest toward Route 57. The villages seem far apart and the road wound just enough to keep my concentration.

As the road goes deeper into the hills, the land becomes less and less populated. Pedaling far from a city, without too many distractions, I can almost lose myself and forget the world around me. The feeling is not forgetting about the land, but rather becoming so immersed in it that I do not think about it anymore. Almost a trance, but a trance very much aware of what's going on under my feet.

Continuing on Route 442, I finally reached the summit and descended. A little before Route 57, a turnoff on the left leads to the Fukouji Magaibutsu, one of the largest cliff-carved Buddhas in Japan, measuring 11.2m at its tallest point. Next to the stone Buddha, the monks have built a platform and temple into the cliff.

I returned to Route 442 and eventually turned right onto Route 57, back on track to Mt. Aso. For lunch, I stopped in the town of Takeda, which has a good market, many shrines, a waterfall (with no obvious point of origin, except maybe an electric pump), and the remains of Oka Castle. Although it was destroyed in the late nineteenth century, its stone walls and foundation still dominate a local hill.

Continuing west on Route 57 toward Aso, the road rises and falls. I thought I was in for another stretch of roller-coaster riding like on the Aso or Kuju highlands, but the road soon begins a steady and marked climb, just enough to fight against, but not enough to kill you. For almost thirty kilometers, the road climbs to the caldera rim. This stretch of Route 57 is wide and well-traveled, with an excellent shoulder. With Mt. Aso right before me, I kept track of my destination and spun on.

After a considerate truck driver descending slowly into the Aso basin passed me, I had the whole road to myself. With lots of speed, I coasted through Ichinomiya on Route 57 and pedaled my way to the Aso Toll Road, about one kilometer west of the intersection of Routes 57 and 212. Three kilometers up the toll road is the Aso Youth Hostel, where I stayed.

The fourth day started with rain, which stopped after breakfast. As I cycled up the toll road to the summit, the clouds began to clear. Circling the mountain, I could see Kumamoto and beyond, across the Ariake Sea into Nagasaki Prefecture. Then the southern caldera wall came into view, with the Takachiho mountains behind. The clouds started to clear and coming full circle near the top, I could see all the land I had just cycled over.

The Aso highlands and the Kuju mountains stretched and rose on the land. The summit of Mt. Kuju had snow, and soon passed behind a cloud. The highlands and mountains looked more massive than they really are. Maybe this was because my eyes deceived me; maybe because bicycling, as you go farther from home, makes the land smaller and more intimate. I would prefer to think the latter.

Descending Mt. Aso on the south side (Yoshida-sen), I turned right onto Route 325 and followed it back to Route 57, which I rode back to Kumamoto. Pedaling in familiar territory, I felt Kyushu was a little smaller and the Pacific Ocean a little closer, but my world larger for the experience.　　✍ AA

ॐ Route Extensions

⇨ The Old Railway Line

From Beppu, Route 213 around the Kunisaki-hanto Peninsula provides some interesting distractions from cycling, including Usa Jingu, said to date back more than a thousand years, and Fuki-ji, one of the oldest wooden temples in Japan. From Usa, Route 10 or the coastal road takes you into Nakatsu. Turning left onto Route 212 at Nakatsu, follow the Yamakuni-gawa river valley toward Hita. Watch for the bike path, beginning five kilometers from town, which follows the old local train route, tunnels and all, for about thirty-five kilometers. One is completely removed from the highway traffic and left to enjoy the scenery. About ten kilometers from town, to your left, are the Ao-no-Domon, a series of tunnels carved into the valley walls by a diligent monk. The nearby trout and carp farm is quite touristy but still a nice place to stop for a cold one.

Twenty-four kilometers from Nakatsu, you can turn left toward Yabakei Dam. Better than the scenery is the *onsen* about ten kilometers up the road. To connect with the Yamanami Highway, continue on this road and go right when it meets Route 387. Ride for a few kilometers, then turn left onto Route 210. About twenty kilometers down Route 210 is a turning on the right to the Yamanami Highway.

Coming down from Yabakei Dam, turn left onto Route 212 and head toward Hita, an old-fashioned provincial town with some well-preserved buildings. From Hita, the ancient pottery village of Onta located deep in the mountains is well worth a visit. Head out of town toward the west on Route 210, turning right just after Yoake Station onto Route 211. When the road forks after about eight kilometers, turn right onto a narrow, winding road that crawls up to Onta.

⇨ Takachiho Gorge

From Route 57 running through Aso-cho, go left onto the road that takes you to Mt. Aso. An early start up the mountain will reward you with dramatic views of the valley below and the mountain above. Upon reaching the crest in the road, you can appreciate the size of this enormous crater. An approach to the current area of activity crosses the ancient crater floor, now carpeted in grasses that feed the grazing cows and horses. There is also a small snow skiing area; no doubt the view is dramatic after a new snowfall: a pure whiteness with dark clouds of ash and steam billowing in the background.

Once you've inched your way up the grade to the Mt. Aso crater, there's a choice of ways to get to the top. You can walk, cycle up a short toll road, or ascend in the luxury of an aerial tram that any major ski resort would be proud to own. The top affords a view into the crater itself. Note that concrete bunkers have been provided for refuge, just in case.

Continue on the toll road to the end, then go left (east) on Route 325 for another free-falling descent into Takamori. From there, the ride to the scenic Takachiho Gorge is rolling and green, with a few long downhill stretches. Takachiho Gorge was formed by lava that has cooled into pillars of rock, some up to 80 meters high. The Gokase-gawa River winds through the gorge on its way to the sea. At the bottom of the gorge are a number of waterfalls and a small tourist center. Don't miss the famous Yokagura Dance that is performed every night from 8:00 at the Takachiho-jinja Shrine.

From here, Route 218 is the main road to Nobeoka on the coast, though if you're a bit of a masochist you may opt to go via Route 327, which can be picked up from the gorge bottom near the town, or again a ways down Route 218. Route 237 travels along the river, in a quiet world all its own. Though the pain inflicted in the initial climb to road level must be considered, I found it worth the effort. Either way, Route 327 is the road of choice. A pleasant ride to the sea and Nobeoka follows. ✍ KP

❶ Field Information
Yamanami Highway: 63 km from Ichinomiya to Yufuin area
Beppu Tourist Information ☎ 0977 23-1119
Kumamoto Minshuku Reservation Center ☎ 096 352-4543
Kokonoe Tourist Information ☎ 09737 6-3150
Yufuin Onsen Tourist Information Center ☎ 0977 84-2446

⌂ Lodging Log
Kumamoto Station area: Ryori-ya ☎ 096 324-3839; Komatsu-so ☎ 096 355-2634; Ryokan Hanasato ☎ 096 354-9445; Minshuku Kajita ☎ 096 353-1546
Aso Station area: Aso ☎ 0967 34-0194; Aso no Fumoto ☎ 0967 34-0624; Asosan ☎ 0967 34-0224; Aso Youth Hostel ☎ 0967 34-0804
Uchinomaki Station area: Asomoto ☎ 0967 32-2986; Aso no Yu ☎ 0967 32-1521
Junction of Route 442 and Yamanami Highway: Senomoto Kogen Youth Hostel ☎ 0967 44-0157
Makinoto-toge Pass area: Kokuminshukusha Cosmos-so ☎ 09737 9-2221
Mizuwake Toge area: Mizuwake ☎ 09737 7-7383
Yufuin Station area: Yufuin Sanso Kokuminshukusha (2 *rotenburo* in addition to large indoor bath) ☎ 0977 84-2105
Beppu: Beppu Minshuku (owner cooks organically grown food) ☎ 0977 23-2228; Kokage Minshuku ☎ 0977 23-1753; Beppu Youth Hostel ☎ 0977 23-4116
Hita: Yorozu-ya ☎ 0973 22-3138
Onta: Soba Chaya ☎ 0973 29-2228; Sakamoto ☎ 0973 29-2312
Takachiho: Folkcraft Ryokan Kaminoya ☎ 09827 2-2111; Ryokan and YH Yamatoya ☎ 09827 2-2243

In the Deep South   🚲

Route: Hugging the coast of southern Kyushu for much of the way, the route offers stunning views of the Nichinan Coast and then takes you inland for a final spin around Sakura-jima before meeting up with the ferry for Kagoshima
Start: Hyuga (ferry from Kawasaki or Kobe; JR Nippo Honsen Main Line)
Goal: Kagoshima (JR Kagoshima Honsen Main Line)

This is a nice stretch in a remote part of southern Japan that seems pretty much like summer most of the year round. Hyuga is a small town smack in the middle of the east coast of Kyushu, distinguished mostly as the destination of convenient ferries from Kanto (Kawasaki) and, even more conveniently, from Kansai (Kobe).

In the Deep South

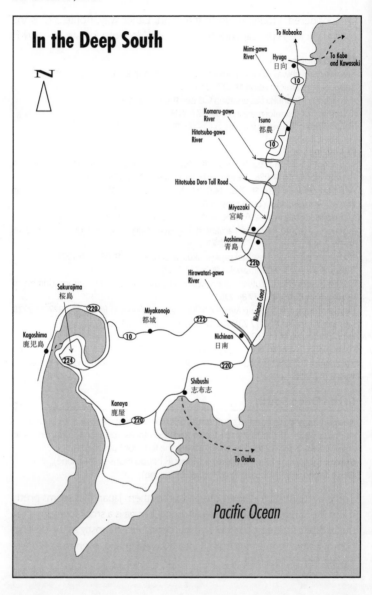

N

To Nobeoka

To Kobe and Kawasaki

Mimi-gawa River

Hyuga
日向
10

Komaru-gawa River

Tsuno
都農
10

Hitotsuba-gawa River

Hitotsuba Doro Toll Road

Miyazaki
宮崎

Aoshima
青島

220

Hirowatari-gawa River

Nichinan Coast

Sakurajima
桜島
220

Miyakonojo
都城

222

10

Nichinan
日南

Kagoshima
鹿児島

224

220

Shibushi
志布志

To Osaka

Kanoya
鹿屋
220

Pacific Ocean

From Kawasaki Port (the ferry to Chiba departs from here, too) the Marine Express Ferry leaves most nights at 7:00, arriving in Hyuga the next morning at 9:20; the return boat leaves Hyuga most evenings at 8:50, arriving in Higashi Kobe Port at 10:50 A.M. One-way fares start at ¥7,260.

Once in Hyuga, leave the ferry terminal and follow the coast road south. After you cross over Oguragahama Ohashi, a large bridge with a great ocean view on your side, the road connects with Route 10 heading for Miyazaki, with more stunning ocean views to your left. There are many good swimming beaches along this stretch, but they get better further down the coast.

About seven kilometers later, after crossing the Mimi-gawa River, Route 10 moves inland a little, although the JR Nippo Line stays close to the sea, sharing the coast with Kyushu's famous Linear Motor Car test track. About ten kilometers later, take the left turn for Tsuno Station to get off the highway and back along the coast.

A ways after Kawaminami Station you'll have to leave the coast again, but if you take the next main road to the left you can keep off Route 10 until you cross the Komaru-gawa River a few more kilometers along. After that you're pretty much stuck with Route 10 until you get past Sadowara Station and to the start of the Hitotsuba Doro, a toll road that hugs the coastline until Miyazaki.

Follow along until the road intersects with Route 220, then turn left and head south. For the next fifty kilometers or so, the towns are fewer and farther between, the road becomes steeper and more challenging, and the seascapes are often breathtaking. Sights along this stretch include the famous "Washboard Coast" at Aoshima where ridges of rock in the shallow ocean resemble a washboard, Udo-jinja Shrine built in a cave by the sea, and a cactus garden tourist attraction.

When you finally get to level ground and a straight road, the ride is over. After crossing the Hirowatari-gawa River, you've got the choice of staying on the more coastal Route 220 to get to Kagoshima, or of turning right and taking the more direct mountain route via Route 222 to Miyakonojo, then Route 10 to Kagoshima.

If you stay on Route 220, about thirty kilometers later you'll arrive in Shibushi, where you can take the Blue Highway Line ferry back to Osaka.

Boats depart almost nightly at 6:00, arriving in Osaka the next morning at 9:40. From Osaka the departure is 8:00 P.M., arriving in Shibushi at 11:30 A.M. One-way fares start at ¥9,270.

From Shibushi, if you continue on to Kagoshima you'll pass by the famous volcano on Sakura-jima. Instead of following the bayshore all the way around Kagoshima Bay, ride instead around Sakura-jima once (thirty-five kilometers), then backtrack to the other side and take the ferry over to Kagoshima. While the southern side is shorter (fourteen kilometers), the northern side (twenty-one kilometers) is narrower, less traveled, and more interesting. The ferry over to Kagoshima takes about fifteen minutes, costs ¥100 and runs several times an hour.   ✍ BH

❶ Field Information
Marine Express Ferry (Kawasaki to Hyuga): for further details and reservations, call 06 311-1533 in Kansai, or 0982 52-8111 in Kyushu
Blue Highway Line (Shibushi to Kobe): for more details call 06 203-4551 in Osaka, 0994 73-0661 in Shibushi, or 03 3578-1127 in Tokyo.
Hyuga Minshuku Association ☎ 0982 57-1550
Nichinan Tourist Information ☎ 0987 23-1111

⌂ Lodging Log
Aoshima: Aoshima Kokuminshukusha ☎ 0985 65-1533; Senriki ☎ 0985 65-0215; Suzuya ☎ 0985 65-0457; Akashiya ☎ 0985 65-0822; Aoshima ☎ 0985 65-1580; Oro ☎ 0985 65-0908
Miyakonojo: Minshuku Miyakonojo ☎ 0986 38-0022
Kushima (near Fukushima Takamatsu Station on the Nichinan Line): Yoshino-ya ☎ 0987 72-1095; Takamatsu-so ☎ 0987 72-0670; Ebisu-ya ☎ 0987 72-1097
Sakurajima: Yogan Lodge ☎ 0992 93-2111; Murayama ☎ 0992 93-2734; Miwa-so ☎ 0992 93-2615; Sakurajima ☎ 0992 21-2130
Kagoshima: Nakazono Ryokan ☎ 0992 26-5125

All Those Islands 🚲🚲🚲🚲🚲🚲🚲🚲🚲🚲🚲🚲🚲🚲

It seems strange to recommend cycling on islands in Japan. After all, Japan is made up of islands, right? However, the island of Honshu is so vast and in many places so densely populated that it doesn't fit anybody's idea of an island. The same goes for Kyushu and, at least in terms of vastness, Hokkaido.

The real islands for cycling in Japan are very small and, owing to their volcanic origins, usually have but one main road circling the perimeter. There are many islands that fit this description, and despite the varying degrees of difficulty getting you and your bike on them, there are several reasons why they are great for cycling. For one thing, it's hard to get lost amidst their limited geography, and for another, as people from Tokyo, Nagoya, and Osaka can't drive there on weekends, vehicle traffic is light.

There are two major strings of islands, the Izu Islands that run south from Tokyo and the Amami and Ryukyu islands that run from Kagoshima to Okinawa to the small island of Yonaguni, from where you can see Taiwan on a clear day. In addition, there are countless other coastal islands that make good overnight destinations—let a good map and a reliable ferry schedule be your guide. Although it's possible to fly to many islands, all are served by ferries.

Keep in mind that some islands are so small that there are very few roads to ride, particularly if you prefer pavement. Those on mountain bikes will always fare better in this regard.

Izu Islands 🚲

When the typhoon season is finally over, cruise out of Tokyo by boat and go cycling on one of the seven Izu islands. The best islands for cycling in the chain are Oshima, Miyake-jima, and Hachijo-jima, as the roads are good and cars are few and far between. The smaller Nii-jima also offers some pleasant cycling, but the other islands have too few roads for a good ride.

These three islands are always a few degrees warmer than Tokyo during the day, but winds in the evenings can cool everything down quite a bit. For cycling, a sweater/windbreaker combination is recommended, as are gloves in case it gets cold.

Ferries run by Tokai Kisen leave Takeshiba Sanbashi Pier, about seven minutes on foot from Hamamatsucho Station on the JR Yamanote Line. Turn right out the north exit of the station, go under the tracks, and head straight past the expressway to where you'll see the pier. To the right is the building where you buy the tickets. Get there about thirty minutes early so you'll have time to go through the line and fill out the little form to get your passage squared away.

Most ferries to the islands leave in the evening, arriving early the following morning; blankets can be rented on the ships for a few hundred yen, and passengers sprawl out on huge, tatami-like surfaces for the duration of the voyage. In summer the boats are crowded and noisy, and it's sometimes hard to sleep. In the winter the crowds are much thinner, people are quieter, and the Pacific Ocean is almost always as smooth as glass. If you pay about double the economy fare, you can move up to somewhat better accommodations away from the noisy lower decks. If you venture out onto the deck, be prepared for some pretty cold blasts of wind.

If you've bagged your bike, you can carry it on as luggage for a few hundred yen. Or, you can wheel it up the gangplank and put it on the boat as is, though you'll have to pay extra.

⇨ Oshima

Oshima, the closest and most easily accessible island from Tokyo, is a volcanic island with a big mountain in the center. A highway circles the perimeter with another road going over the top for those who like a bit of rugged climbing. It's best to circle the island counterclockwise because you'll finish the quick steep uphill at the south end of the island early on in your ride, followed by a long, gradual downhill as you ride north along the eastern side.

Oshima is close enough to visit in a single day—fast riders can circle the island before noon, have a leisurely lunch, and take the boat back to Tokyo at 2:50 P.M. However, it's better to make it an overnighter, and for those on a sightseeing pace over a hundred *minshuku*, two youth hostels, and five campsites are available. It's easiest to find a place to stay in or around Motomachi (pop. 12,000), though there are inns in the fishing villages of Okada and scenic Habu. Rental bicycles are available in Okada.

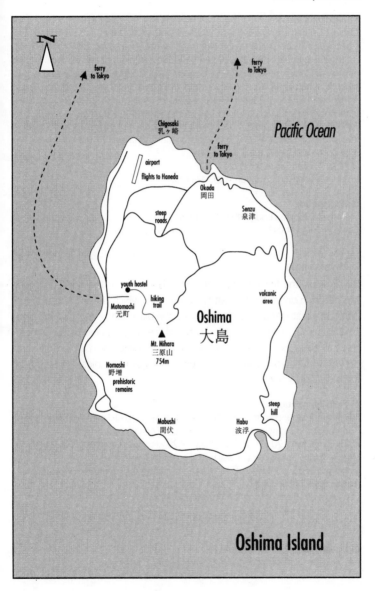

N

ferry
to Tokyo

ferry
to Tokyo

Chigasaki
乳ヶ崎

Pacific Ocean

airport

flights to Haneda

ferry
to Tokyo

Okada
岡田

Senzu
泉津

steep
roads

youth hostel

volcanic
area

Motomachi
元町

hiking
trail

Oshima
大島

Mt. Mihara
三原山
754m

Nomashi
野増

prehistoric
remains

steep
hill

Mabushi
間伏

Habu
波浮

Oshima Island

❶ Field Information

Oshima-bound ferry leaves Takeshiba Pier nightly at 10:00 P.M. arriving Motomachi (the main port) or Okada (depending on the weather) at about 5:30 A.M. the next morning.; return ferry leaves 2:50 P.M.; basic fare is ¥2,760, plus ¥750 to take your bike on as is. High-speed boats make several runs to Atami in the afternoons, but bikes must be bagged; from Atami, it's fifty-five minutes to Tokyo by shinkansen or an hour and a half by Odoriko Express. Boats also leave from Ito; for further information on boat schedules contact Tokai Kisen Ferries ☎ 03 3432-4551

Air Nippon makes three runs daily from Haneda.; the flight takes about forty minutes and costs about ¥7,000 one way; for more details and reservations call Air Nippon ☎ 03 3552-6311

Oshima Tourist Office ☎ 04992 2-2177

Izu Islands Tourist Association ☎ 03 3436-6955

⌂ Lodging Log

Izu Oshima People's Lodge ☎ 04992 2-1285

Habu: Habu-ya ☎ 04992 4-0675; Yoshimura ☎ 04992 4-0009

▷ Miyake-jima

Miyake-jima, the third largest of the Izu Islands, is a round island thirty-six kilometers in circumference with a live volcano, which last erupted in 1983. Attractive features of the island include the black sandy beaches and two small lakes surrounded by cliffs. Lush and scenic, the island has an almost tropical feeling. Riding on Miyake-jima is pretty rugged with a lot of ups and downs, though you won't encounter any long grades unless you stray off the road that circles the island.

❶ Field information

Miyake-jima–bound boat leaves Takeshiba Pier at 10:10 P.M. every evening except Tuesday and Sunday, arriving Miyake-jima at 5:00 A.M.; returning the boat leaves Miyake-jima at 12:20 P.M., arriving Tokyo 7:20 P.M.; basic fare is ¥4,160 with ¥750 extra for bike; for details call Tokai Kisen Ferries ☎ 03 3432-4551

Two flights a day from Haneda to Miyake-jima taking forty minutes; for more information call Air Nippon ☎ 03 3552-6311

Miyake-jima Tourist Association ☎ 04994 6-1144

Hydrangea Festival: Mid-June

Toka-jinja Festival: August 4–9

⌂ Lodging Log

Minshuku are available at Hirata, Ako, and Okubi

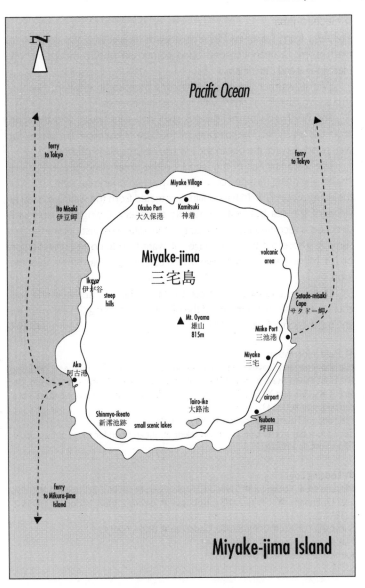

Pacific Ocean

ferry
to Tokyo

ferry
to Tokyo

Miyake Village

Ito Misaki
伊豆岬

Okubo Port
大久保港

Kamitsuki
神着

volcanic
area

Miyake-jima
三宅島

Ikaya
伊ヶ谷

steep
hills

Satado-misaki
Cape
サタドー岬

▲ Mt. Oyama
雄山
815m

Miike Port
三池港

Miyake
三宅

Ako
阿古港

airport

Tairo-ike
大路池

Shinmyo-ikeato
新澪池跡

small scenic lakes

Tsubota
坪田

ferry
to Mikura-jima
Island

Miyake-jima Island

⇨ Hachijo-jima

The ferry from Takeshiba Pier that stops at Miyake-jima also goes on to Hachijo-jima, a peanut-shaped island composed of two mountains, Mt. Hachijo-Fuji and Mt. Mihara.

With its warmer climate and distinctly subtropical atmosphere, Hachijo-jima is enjoyable for all riders, with two distinct courses.

The north side of the island is stark and windswept, and the road around is largely flat. The road around the base of Hachijo-Fuji is almost flat with good views of the ocean and Hachijo Ko-jima Island offshore.

The southern half of the island, on the other hand, presents more challenging riding (hills and curves) and more greenery and sights. Most of the riding around Mt. Mihara is fairly protected from the wind, with fewer views of the sea but quite picturesque scenery. Going in a clockwise direction is recommended, stopping at the vista point just before the first summit. Those out for a challenge will want to ride up to Loran Station on Mt. Mihara, about 700m high, which comes up toward the end of the loop.

There are a number of places to stay in the flats between the two courses, but the southern end of the island has hot springs, many *minshuku* and much more of the island flavor.   ✍ BH

❶ Field Information
Hachijo-jima ferry leaves Takeshiba Pier at 10:10 P.M. arriving 8:30 A.M.; returning the boat leaves Hachijojima at 9:40 A.M., steaming into Takeshiba at 7:20 P.M.; the fare is ¥5,180, and ¥1,050 for your bike as is; for more information contact Tokai Kisen Ferries ☎ 03 3432-4551
Hachijojima Tourist Association ☎ 04996 2-1377
Six flights a day from Haneda Airport taking about an hour; for more details call Air Nippon ☎ 03 3552-6311

⌂ Lodging Log
Mitsune area: Yanagi-ya ☎ 04996 2-0210; Asahi-so ☎ 04996 2-2171; Sasao ☎ 04996 2-0547; Funami ☎ 04996 2-0731; Rokusan ☎ 04996 2-1067; Midori ☎ 04996 2-2218
Sueyoshi: Yuki-so ☎ 04996 8-0358; Gaden-so ☎ 04996 7-0014
Nakanogo: Jiyugaoka ☎ 04996 7-0440
Kashidate: Yutori-so ☎ 04996 7-0528

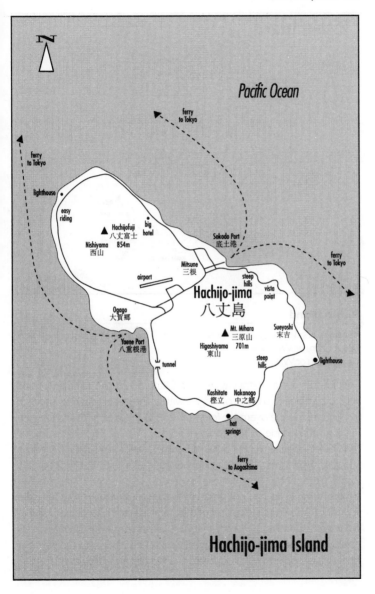

Pacific Ocean

ferry
to Tokyo

ferry
to Tokyo

lighthouse

easy
riding

▲ Hachijofuji
八丈富士
854m

Nishiyama
西山

big
hotel

Sokado Port
底土港

Mitsune
三根

ferry
to Tokyo

airport

**Hachijo-jima
八丈島**

steep
hills

vista
point

Ogago
大賀郷

▲ Mt. Mihara
三原山
701m

Sueyoshi
末吉

Yaene Port
八重根港

Higashiyama
東山

steep
hills

tunnel

lighthouse

Kashitate
樫立

Nakanogo
中之郷

hot
springs

ferry
to Aogashima

Hachijo-jima Island

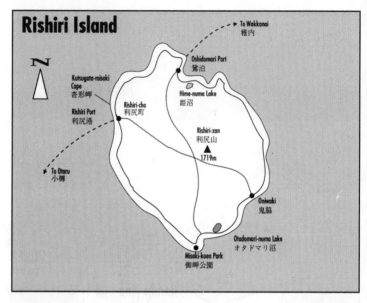

Rishiri Island

Route: A loop for the gourmet round the island of Rishiri off the coast of Hokkaido
Start: Otaru or Wakkanai
Goal: Otaru or Wakkanai

Should you have an extra day when in Otaru during the summer, a good way to combine two nights of lodging with an interesting day ride is to take a round trip on the overnight ferry to Rishiri Island, a remote and fascinating cone-shaped isle off the northern tip of Hokkaido. The boat is smaller than other large car ferries but is still quite comfortable. Rishiri is really a string of small fishing villages around its perimeter with the imposing Mt. Rishiri in the center. The main marine product is sea urchins (*uni*), and during the summer as you ride through the small villages you can hear the sounds of *uni* being shucked out of the urchin shells. This delicacy is somewhat less expensive on Rishiri, so if you have a taste for it, splurge on *uni donburi* (*uni* on rice) at one of the restaurants near the port. Also delicious on Rishiri is the fresh milk produced by a small ranch on the west side.

The main road around the island, a circuit of about forty kilometers, can be covered easily in a day, with a little time here and there for stops and plenty of time left over for a leisurely early supper. Late spring and summer, when the cherry trees and mountain flowers are in full bloom and when *uni* is in season, are the best times to visit, as Rishiri is cold, windy, and desolate during its long winter. ✍ BH

❶ Field Information

Ferry leaves Otaru at 9:00 P.M. arriving Rishiri-cho Port at 7:20 A.M. the next morning. The return boat leaves at 10:20 A.M. arriving in Otaru at 7:30 P.M. the same day; one-way fares start at ¥7,210; for more information contact Hokkai Shosen Ferry ☎ 0134 22-0830; hovercraft also leave from Wakkanai for Oshidomari Port
Rishiri Minshuku Information (May 15–October 15) ☎ 01638 2-1837
Thanksgiving Festivals held all over island last week of June; Hokkai Island Festival August 2–3; Floating Island Festival August 4–5

♠ Lodging Log

Rishiri-cho (western side of island about thirty minutes by bike from Oshidomari): Kutsugata-so ☎ 01638 4-2038; Nagori-so ☎ 01638 4-2233; Kokuminshukusha Rishiri ☎ 01638 54-2001
Rishiri Fuji-machi (about five to ten minutes walk from port): Umeya ☎ 01638 2-1016; Pension Herasan no Ie ☎ 01638 2-2361; Yamada ☎ 01638 2-1543; Wafu Pension Misaki ☎ 01638 2-1659

Awaji Island

Route: A relatively easy loop through picturesque fishing villages and dramatic cliff scenery on mostly flat coastal roads with a little climbing around the southeastern cape, where you'll be rewarded with spectacular views of the Inland Sea and the opportunity to see wild monkeys and wildflowers
Start: Tsuna (ferry from Kobe, Osaka, Nishinomiya, Misaki)
Goal: Awaji (ferry to Akashi)

Awaji-shima , the largest island in the Inland Sea is a popular destination for cyclists, particularly those training for Century Rides as it is slightly over 160 km in circumference. The island is a short, inexpensive ferry ride from the Osaka-Kobe metropolitan area, is less developed and has less traffic than the mainland, the roads are good, and besides, you might even spot a member of the top road teams that sometimes train here. However, with plenty of places to stay over or camp, the island is the perfect weekend

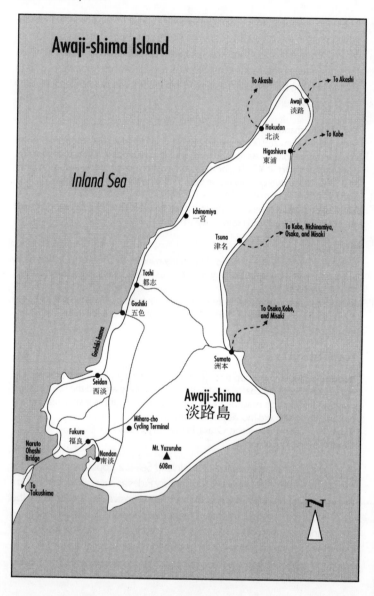

Awaji-shima Island

Inland Sea

To Akashi

To Akashi

Awaji
淡路

Hokudan
北淡

To Kobe

Higashiura
東浦

Ichinomiya
一宮

Tsuna
津名

To Kobe, Nishinomiya,
Osaka, and Misaki

Toshi
都志

Goshiki
五色

To Osaka, Kobe,
and Misaki

Goshiki-bama

Sumoto
洲本

Seidan
西淡

Awaji-shima
淡路島

Mihara-cho
Cycling Terminal

Fukura
福良

Naruto
Ohashi
Bridge

Nandan
南淡

Mt. Yuzuruha
608m

To
Takushima

N

getaway for cyclists in the Kansai region with a less hectic schedule. The best time to visit is from June to November, though the wildflowers are most spectacular in April and May, as are the rains. Watch out for typhoons in August and September, especially on the south coast.

To enjoy the coastal scenery and to take advantage of the prevailing winds, a clockwise route from Tsuna, halfway down the east coast, is recommended. Tsuna is the major ferry port on the island, one hour from Kobe and seventy-five minutes from Nishinomiya. Traffic on the east coast on Route 28 is always heavy but beyond the town of Sumoto the sandy beaches gradually become more inviting. The new Route 28 that will connect the Akashi Ohashi Bridge in the north and the Naruto Ohashi Bridge in the southwest will reduce coastal traffic but will also change the rural flavor of the island. Already tourist hotels, restaurants, and other eyesores are being built in anticipation of the new business the route will generate.

However, once past Sumoto Onsen, the tacky tourist attractions dwindle, traffic disappears, and the road starts climbing into the hills of the Yuzuruha Range , where the best riding of the trip starts. Numerous old logging roads and hiking paths abound, twisting their way into the mountains waiting for MTB riders to explore them. Here the going can get a bit tough, but a thrilling descent over the southeastern flanks of the range brings you down to the clean, clear Pacific Ocean past Ikui-saki Cape. Typhoons regularly pound this area and the road is rougher, often paved with concrete and the beach flanked with concrete tetrapods, the houses cowering behind protective walls. It's also possible to climb Mt. Yuzuruha —a muscleburner, but the views from the top just over a kilometer from the coast are breathtaking.

On the southwest coast, heading toward the Naruto Ohashi, the road moves inland. Explore the lanes in the small villages on the coast and inland and peel fifty or a hundred years off the clock. This area could well earn the title of Onion Capital of Japan, for in the summer every possible hut, house, and shed is dripping with onions hung out to dry so that they will last through the winter.

The Naruto Ohashi, closed to bicycles, is worth a look mostly for the views of the immense whirlpools caused by the over-one-meter difference in elevation between the waters of the Inland Sea and the Pacific Ocean.

The bridge observation area is a good place to grab some food, stretch the muscles, and fill your water bottles. Winds can be fierce here even in good weather—on one ride in May I was blown horizontally off my bike while heading down to the bridge.

From the bridge to Seidan, you can continue around the picturesque coast or head inland. The inland route is most direct but is hilly, offering some good views of Shikoku. In the Seidan area are some of the best swimming beaches on Awaji, including the famous Goshiki-hama (Five-Color Beach), so named because its stones change color as they become wet from the surf and then dry in the sun. Seaweed is cultivated on the west shore, and you'll see it laid out to dry on the sand, rocks, fences, and even well into the road at times. The area is also well known for the manufacture of ceramic roof tiles, evident in the seemingly infinite variety of colors and designs of the roofs in the villages. It's possible to have a look at the process of making the tiles in some of the small operations that abound in this area. *Minshuku* are available in Nandan, Seidan, and Goshiki-hama areas for those who prefer to take it leisurely. If time permits there's a good chance to see the famous Awaji puppets, said to be forerunners of the *bunraku* puppets. Performances are held every day at the Awaji Ningyo-za in Fukura, near Nandan.

Toward the north end of the island past Hokudan, the ocean pollution increases, which rather tends to spoil the view. Around Awaji there is a lot of activity due to the construction of the Akashi Ohashi, the longest suspension bridge in the world, so watch out for traffic. From Awaji you can take the ferry for the fifteen-minute ride to Akashi. If you're determined to complete the loop back to Tsuna, the often fierce tailwinds in this area will help you on to your destination twenty kilometers away.

On the final stretch you'll come across enormous covered conveyor belts snaking their way out from the hills, for this is where much of the soil for the new Kansai International Airport comes from. Up in the quarries, huge grinding machines endlessly gobble mountains and spit them onto the belts leading to barges lined up for the voyage to their final resting place twenty-five kilometers across the waters. One short trip into the mountains reveals all: dust covers everything, the waters are fouled—the hills have simply disappeared along with the birds and wildlife. A quick return to the coast restores flagging spirits as none of this is visible from the shore. Fortunately activity has declined somewhat with the completion of the first phase of the airport, but hills are still quietly disappearing to fill the offshore islands being built around the bay.

Just past Higashiura, you can't miss the 100-meter tall Kannon statue towering over the coast, and you may be tempted to pay for a ride to the top. The first time I saw it was from the ferry to Tsuna when I saw a shining white figure, hands clasped in prayer looming up out of the mist. I had to rub my eyes several times before I realized that I hadn't just seen a miracle.

Before jumping on the ferry, replenish your fluids and stretch. If you've done the whole island loop in one go, you will have just done a little over 160 kilometers. No matter how many days you take to do the loop, pace yourself, enjoy the views, explore when you can, drink and snack often, and above all have fun.   ✍ MS

❶ Field Information
Ferries: Tsuna to Kobe, Nishinomiya, Osaka, and Misaki (Kii-hanto Peninsula); Awaji (Iwaya) to Akashi; Hokudan to Akashi; Higashiura to Kobe; Sumoto to Osaka, Kobe, and Misaki
Nandan Tourist Information ☎ 0799 52-2336
Seidan Tourist Information ☎ 0799 36-3311
Keino Minshuku Association (Seidan area) ☎ 0799 36-2299
Goshiki-hama Tourist Information ☎ 0799 33-0160

⌂ Lodging Log
Seidan area: Kokuminshukusha Keinomatsubara ☎ 0799 36-3391
Nandan area: Minami Awaji Kokumin Kyukamura ☎ 0799 52-0291; Awaji Youth Hostel ☎ 0799 52-0460
Mihara-cho Cycling Terminal ☎ 0799 42-5310 (see page 265)

Out of the Saddle   🚲 🚲 🚲 🚲 🚲 🚲 🚲 🚲 🚲 🚲 🚲 🚲 🚲

For those days when you're aching to get out of the armchair and onto the saddle, *Oikaze* suggests some books to help you plan your next adventure:

Round the World on a Wheel by John Foster Fraser, 1899 (Reprint: Futura Publications, 1989)

A Pedaller to Peking by Christopher Hough. Methuen, 1986

Full Tilt: Ireland to India with a Bicycle by Dervla Murphy, 1965 (Reprint: Overlook Press, 1986)

Round Ireland in Low Gear by Eric Newby. Viking Penguin, 1989

Hey Mom, Can I Ride my Bike Across America? Five Kids Meet Their Country by John S. Boettner. SBF Productions, 1990

Cycling to Xian and other Excursions: Travels by Bicycle through China and Tibet by Michael Buckley. Gordon Soules, 1988

Bicycling Across America: A Journal on the Open Road by David H. Fenimore. Pinedrop Pr., 1989

Seeing Myself, Seeing the World: A Woman's Journey Around the World on a Bicycle by Martin Krieg and Sally Vantress. Cycle America, 1991

Chesapeake Reflections: A Journey on a Boat and a Bike by Ken Carter. Amantha Publications, 1991

Two Wheels Around New Zealand: A Bicycle Journey on Friendly Roads, by Scott Bischke. SBF Productions, 1990

Pedalling to the Ends of the World by David Duncan. S and S Trade, 1986

Ten Thousand Miles on a Bicycle by Karl Kron. E Rosenblatt, 1982

Miles from Nowhere: Round the World Bicycle Adventure by Barbara Savage. Mountaineers, 1985

Around the World on a Bicycle by Thomas Stevens. Seven Palms, 1984

Two Wheels and a Taxi: A Slightly Daft Adventure in the Andes by Virginia Urrutia. Mountaineers, 1987

The Great Bicycle Adventure by Nicholas Crane. Oxford Illustrated Press, 1987

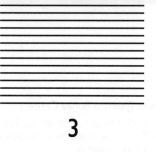

3

Nuts and Bolts

Bicycle Resources

Bicycle Culture Center (Jitensha Bunka Center)

Jitensha Kaikan Bldg. 3, 1-9-3 Akasaka, Minato-ku, Tokyo ☎ 03 3584-4530
• Open 10:00 A.M. to 4:00 P.M.; closed weekends and national holidays
• Toranomon Station (Ginza Line, exit 3)

The Bicycle Culture Center is a mine of information on anything concerning the bicycle. Located just opposite the American Embassy, the center has three whole floors devoted to the bicycle. On the first floor, new bicycles are displayed and films, lectures, and photo exhibitions are often held in the "communication space." If you've often wondered what the first bicycles looked like, or whether the Emperor can ride a bicycle, then take a look at the extensive overview of bicycle history on the second floor, which features everything from Penny Farthings to *Ukiyo-e* prints showing Meiji gentlemen trying out the latest fad.

Maps and cycling books are available at the souvenir shop on the second floor. On the third floor is a large library of books and magazines on cycling, including the latest foreign editions. On hand to answer your questions about cycling in Japan, or indeed anywhere in the world, is Suzuki Kunitomo, a veteran of cycle-touring around the world. The library is also well equipped with various kinds of video games and quizzes to test and top up your knowledge of bicycles.

From exit 3 at Toranomon Station, follow the road toward the NCR Building and turn immediately left after you pass it. Take the second street on the right and you'll find the center opposite the American Embassy.

Bicycle Information Center (Cycle Joho Center)

Osaka-kyujo Bunka Kaikan, 2-8-110 Namba-naka, Naniwa-ku, Osaka
☎ 06 643-5231
• Open 11:00 A.M. to 7:00 P.M.; closed Thursdays
• Namba Station, Midosuji Subway Line

Located in the former Osaka Baseball Stadium, a five-minute walk from Namba Station, the Bicycle Information Center is a useful resource for cyclists in the Kansai area, holding frequent exhibitions of bicycles and bicycle parts.

Oikaze (English-language Cycling Newsletter)

2-24-3 Tomigaya, Shibuya-ku, Tokyo ☎ 03 3485-0471

Although Japanese magazines such as *Cycle Sports* have comprehensive list-ings of the bike scene in Japan, *Oikaze*, a newsletter filled with fascinating articles and a useful ads section, has all the news and views—in the English language. The newsletter appears quarterly; a subscription is $15 for over-seas readers and ¥1,000 in stamps for readers in Japan.

For more information, call Bryan Harrell at the above number.

Cycling Clubs

Do any of the following statements describe you? You'd like to cycle in Japan, but you don't know where to ride, or who to ride with. You'd like to get to know some Japanese cyclists. You don't feel it's worth the trouble to organize rides for only a few riders. You lack a good source of information on Japanese cycling events.

If the answer is yes to any of these, then what has worked for me may work for you: join a cycling club. I've belonged to MCC (the Minato Cycling Club) for three years, and what makes it special is its wide range of activi-ties, its efficient organization, and, most of all, its members. MCC is orga-nized to involve all members in the planning of activities. Everyone gets to be a leader, and this has become a tradition of the club.

Activities include easy day rides for all members of the family, more serious riding, time trials, tours, and camping. Some rides feature a special theme, like big trees, or an activity, like rowing, that one would not normally associate with a cycling club. Activities run year round, weather permitting.

For more information about MCC, contact the Cyclo Salon (near Mita and Tamachi stations), 5-20-22 Shiba, Tokyo, ☎ 03 3452-6968.

For more information about cycling clubs and associations throughout the country, contact the Tokyo Cycling Association ☎ 03 3833-3969, or the Japan Cycling Association on the third floor of the Jitensha Bunka Kaikan, ☎ 03 3583-5628. For a fee of ¥4,000, you can become a member of the Japan Cycling Association and receive their newsletter four times a year.

Cycle Sports Centers

There are several centers throughout the country where bicycles can be rented to enjoy courses in the surrounding area. Ideal for family breaks, these centers offer other entertainment such as small amusement parks, swimming pools, go-carts, and dirt buggies. Accommodation is sometimes available. These centers also host professional and amateur cycling races, serving as useful sources of information on the racing world in Japan.

Cycle Sports Center

1826 Ono, Shuzenji-cho, Shizuoka
☎ 0558 79-0001, Tokyo office ☎ 03 3586-0625
• Closed Thursdays
• Take Tokai bus bound for Cycle Sports Center from Shuzenji Station

This cycle sports center offers 5km and 2km circuit courses, rental bikes, and other attractions such as a cycle monorail and indoor swimming pool. Accommodation is available at the Cycle Lodge ☎ 0558 79-0311

Kansai Cycle Sports Center

1304 Amano-cho, Kawachinagano-shi, Osaka ☎ 0721 54-3100
• Closed Tuesdays
• Take Nankai bus bound for Kansai Cycle Sports Center from Kintetsu or Nankai Kawachinagano Station

The Kansai Sports Center has a 3km course, a BMX and BRT dirt course, and rental bikes. Camping is available at the center.

Gunma Cycle Sports Center

Omineyama Aramaki, Niiharu-mura, Tone-gun, Gunma ☎ 0278 64-1811
• Closed Thursdays
• Take bus (Apr. to Oct.) or taxi for Gunma Cycle Sports Center from Jomokogen Station (Joetsu Shinkansen Line)

The Gunma Cycle Sports Center has a 6km course with stunning views, sports buggies, snowmobiles, a variety of rental bikes and many other attractions. A recent innovation is the rather bizarre Apollo Museum containing a collection of trick art—reproductions of masterpieces with unusual twists.

Cycling Terminals

HOKKAIDO

Shibetsu-shi Cycling Terminal
9-7 Higashi Shichijo-kita, Shibetsu-shi, Hokkaido

☎ 01652 2-3822

From Shibetsu Station take a northbound city loop bus, get off at Suigo-koen Mae; 18km park course, 30km course to Iwaonai-ko Lake

Abashiri-shi Cycling Terminal
4-7-2 Katsura-machi, Abashiri-shi, Hokkaido

☎ 0152 43-2078

From Abashiri Station take bus to Komaba Minami 1-chome, terminal is 6 mins. walk from bus stop; good views of Mt. Tento and other peaks and Sea of Okhotsk; interesting Iceberg Museum

Akan-machi Cycling Terminal
23-36 Akan-cho, Akan-gun, Hokkaido

☎ 0154 66-2331

From Kushiro or Otanoshike stations, take Akan bus bound for Akan-ko Lake, get off at Tancho no Sato; official BMX course, hot springs, sports facilities, close to Kushiro-Akan C.R. and crane migration ground

Higashi-Kagura-cho Cycling Terminal
25 Higashikagura-cho, Kamikawa-gun, Hokkaido

☎ 0166 83-3727

From Asahikawa Station 30 mins by taxi, from Asahikawa Airport 15 mins. by taxi; built in the shape of an alpine *Schloss*, 15km riverside cycling route

Otofuke-cho Cycling Terminal
14-4 Tokachigawa Onsen-kita, Oto-fuke-cho, Kato-gun, Hokkaido

☎ 0155 46-2114

From Obihiro Station take bus to Tokachi-gawa Onsen; cycling road from Tokachi-gawa River to Tokachigaoka with stunning views of Tokachi Plain

Takikawa-shi Cycling Terminal
3-119-6 Higashi Ninosaka-cho, Takikawa-shi, Hokkaido

☎ 0125 24-0055

From Takikawa Station take Chuo bus bound for Asahikawa and Amaryu, get off at Seinen Taiiku Center Mae; close to Ishikari-gawa C.R. and Suigo Takikawa Nature Park, sports facilities

Shimukappu-Mura Cycling Terminal
234-5 Ni-ni-u Shimukappu-mura, Yufutsu-gun, Hokkaido

☎ 0167 56-2014

Transport available from Shimukappu Station on request; birdwatching, hiking

Tomakomai-shi Cycling Terminal
19-1 Takaoka, Tomakomai-shi, Hokkaido

☎ 0144 35-1800

From Tomakomai Station take bus bound for Shikotsu-ko Lake, get off at Midorigaoka-koen Mae; 22km C.R. to Shikotsu-ko Lake, nearby Tarumae volcano affords spectacular views of the Pacific Ocean

Yubari-shi Cycling Terminal
1-8 Shako, Yubari-shi, Hokkaido

☎ 01235 2-3196
From Yubari Station 15 mins. walk,
from Sapporo Station take Yutetsu bus
or Chuo bus to Sekitan no Rekishi
Mura; 18km C.R. to Furano; tasting sessions at nearby melon brandy factory

TOHOKU AREA

Morioka-shi Tonan Cycling Terminal
1-1-41 Yuzawa, Morioka-shi, Iwate-ken
☎ 0196 37-0876
From Morioka Station take bus bound
for Yahaba Eigyo-sho or Tsudoi no Mori
(from April to Nov.), get off at Yuzawa
Ken'ei Jutaku; 37km lakeside cycling
path, 24km cycling path to Yahaba Hot
Springs

Ogawara-ko Cycling Terminal
100-8 Michinoshita Oura, Kamikita-
machi, Kamikita-gun, Aomori-ken
☎ 0176 56-2393
From Kamikita-machi Station 10 mins.
by taxi, from Misawa Airport 30 mins.
by taxi; close to Ogawara-ko Lake,
9km forest cycling path

Yuri-machi Cycling Terminal
Yurikogen, Nishizawa Yuri-machi, Yuri-
gun, Akita-ken
☎ 0184 53-3055
From Gohonjo Station take Yuri-kogen
Line to Maego Station, 25 mins. by taxi
from station; lakeside cycling path

Koromogawa-Mura Cycling Terminal
60-2 Hinata, Shimokoromogawa, Koromo-
gawa-mura, Isawa-gun, Iwate-ken
☎ 019752 3520
From Hiraizumi Station take bus bound
for Mizusawa and get off at Sehara;
10km to Chuson-ji Temple (national

treasure), many other historical sites
nearby

Yuwa-machi Cycling Terminal
193 Tsubakikawa, Yuwa-machi, Kawabe-
gun, Akita-ken
☎ 0188 86-3766
From Akita Airport 5 mins. by bus,
from Akita Station take bus bound for
Akita Airport and get off at Sportsu Zo'on
Iriguchi; near Akita Koen C.R. (27km)
and Nibetsu-Omonogawa C.R. (35km)

Natori-shi Cycling Terminal
2-1 Higashisuga, Yuriage, Natori-shi,
Miyagi-ken
☎ 02238 5-1000
From Natori Station or Sendai Station
take bus bound for Yuriage Shako, get
off at terminus; 4km cycling circuit, near
Sendai-wan Bay C.R. (44km)

Naraha-machi Cycling Terminal
27-29 Uenohara Kitada, Naraha-machi,
Futaba-gun, Fukushima-ken
☎ 0240 25-3113
From Tatsuta Station 20 mins. walk;
located in Tenjin Misaki Sports Park
near Iwasawa Beach

Izumizaki-mura Cycling Terminal
12 Sasatateyama Izumizaki, Izumizaki-
mura, Nishi Shirakawa-gun, Fukushima-
ken
☎ 0248 53-4211
From Izumisaki Station 20 mins. walk;
cycling circuit, sports facilities within
walking distance

KANTO AREA

Utsunomiya-shi Cycling Terminal
1074-1   Minowa,   Fukuoka-machi,

Utsunomiya-shi, Tochigi -ken
☎ 0286 52-4497
From Utsunomiya Station take Kanto Bus bound for Shin Kanuma or Kogashi Nagahata, 40 mins. walk from the Shinrin Koen Iriguchi bus stop (direct bus service is available from Apr. to Nov.); 1990 World Cycling Championship held here

Tatebayashi-shi Cycling Terminal
2916-3 Obukuro, Hanayama-cho, Tatebayashi-shi, Gunma-ken
☎ 0276 75-8484 (fom June 1993)
15 mins. from Tatabayashi Station on the Tobu Isesaki Line; (expected completion June 1993)

Oarai-machi Cycling Terminal
1212-57 Maehara, Onuki-cho, Oarai-machi, Higashi Ibaraki-gun, Ibaraki -ken
☎ 02926 7-5417
From Oarai Station 5 mins. by taxi; from Mito Station take Ibaragi Kotsu Bus bound for Oarai-Hokota, get off at Maehara; 23km Karenuma C.R., near Oarai Beach

Takamori-machi Cycling Terminal
850 Ushimaki, Takamori-cho, Shimoina-gun, Nagano-ken
☎ 0265 35-8260
From Ichida Station 10 mins. by car; in heart of scenic Japan Alps, camping; golf course

Nagano-shi Cycling Terminal
4268-151 Mamejima, Nagano-shi, Nagano-ken
☎ 0262 21-1731
From Nagano Station take Kawanakajima Bus bound for Daizujima Higashi Danchi, get off at Saikuringu Terminaru Mae;

19.2km C.R. along Chikuma-gawa River

Yamato-machi Cycling Terminal
70 Arakane, Yamato-machi, Minami Uonuma-gun, Niigata -ken
☎ 0257 79-3230
From Urasa Station take bus bound for Muika-machi via Aragane, get off at Aragane; camping area

Irihirose-Mura Cycling Terminal
886-514 Oshirokawa, Irihirose-mura, Kita Uonuma-gun, Niigata-ken
☎ 02579 6-2077
Transport available from Oshirokawa Station on request; located on shores of Hamagawa-ko Lake; 10km C.R. at lakeside

Itoigawa-shi Cycling Terminal
214-2 Ono, Itoigawa-shi, Niigata-ken
☎ 0255 52-6700
From Itoigawa Station take bus to Tamamizu, 20 mins. walk from Tamamizu bus stop; near Kubiki C.R.

CHUBU AREA

Oyabe-shi Cycling Terminal
119-9 Jodoji, Asaji, Oyabe-shi, Toyama -ken
☎ 0766 61-3596
From Isurugi Station take bus bound for Fukuno-Shogawa, get off at Yabunami; 40km C.R. to Toyama, near sports center

Togi-machi Cycling Terminal
Satohongo, Togi-machi, Hakui-gun, Ishikawa-ken
☎ 07674 2-2303
From Kanazawa Station take Hokuriku Tetsudo Bus bound for Togi-Monzen, 25 mins. walk from Togi Bus Terminal;

80km oceanside C.R. to Uchinada-cho with stunning views

Uchinada-machi Cycling Terminal

1-3 Miyasaka-ni, Uchinada-machi, Kahoku-gun, Ishikawa -ken

☎ 0762 86-3766

From Uchinada Station take bus bound for Unoki, get off at Miyasaka; 80km C.R. to Togi-machi, hot spring baths in terminal

Imajo-Cho Cycling Terminal

Imajo, Imajo-cho, Nanjo-gun, Fukui-ken

☎ 0778 45-0073

5 mins. walk from Imajo Station; 7 cycling paths including 25km Tannan C.R., 12km course to Yashaga-ike Lake

Horai-cho Cycling Terminal

31-54 Furikomatsu, Horai-cho, Minami Shitara-gun, Aichi-ken

☎ 05363 6-0211

From Hon Nagashino Station take bus bound for Horai-ji; get off at Saikuringu Terminaru-mae; located by Kansa-gawa River, 7 cycling paths

Hachiman-cho Cycling Terminal

945-1 Ichijima, Hachiman-cho, Gujo-gun, Gifu-ken

☎ 05756 2-2139

From Gujo-Hachiman Station take Gifu bus bound for Myogata, get off at Chuo-bashi; riverside cycling path to the old castle town of Gujo-Hachiman

Omiya-cho Cycling Terminal

Takihara, Omiya-cho, Watarai-gun, Mie-ken

☎ 05988 6-2501

15 mins walk from Takihara Station, or take Nanki Tokkyu Bus from Matsuza-ka Station, get off at Takiharagu-mae; 4 cycling paths including one to scenic waterfall

Nagahama-shi Cycling Terminal

1016-1 Nagoshi-cho, Nagahama-shi, Shiga-ken

☎ 07496 3-9285

From Nagahama or Maibara stations take bus to Nagoshi; near Biwa-ko Lake, cycling path at north end of lake

KANSAI AREA

Sonobe-cho Cycling Terminal

1-8 Hirotani, Okawachi, Sonobe-cho, Funai-gun, Kyoto-fu

☎ 07716 5-0800

From Sonobe Station take bus to Oku-ruri; 2km cycling path, many sports facilities

Joyo-shi Cycling Terminal

26-8 Terada Okawahara, Joyo-shi, Kyoto-fu

☎ 07745 5-7811

From Kintetsu Terada Station take bus bound for Uji Shako, get off at Kono-suyama Koen-mae; near Kyoto Yahata C.R., many historical sites nearby

Kashihara-shi Cycling Terminal

855-2 Kawanishi-cho, Kashihara-shi, Nara-ken

☎ 07442 7-3196

From Kashihara Jingu-mae Station on Kintetsu Minami Osaka Line take bus bound for Gosho, get off at Kawanishi-cho; 15km countryside path, 11km path around ancient tombs

Kawabe-cho Cycling Terminal

2095 Wasa, Kawabe-cho, Hidaka-gun, Wakayama-ken

☎ 0738 53-0234

15 mins. walk from Wasa Station; 5 cycling paths including one to Dojo-ji Temple

Haga-cho Cycling Terminal

Kotaki, Hara, Haga-cho, Shiso-gun, Hyogo-ken

☎ 07907 5-2355

From Himeji Station take bus bound for Hara/Tokura or Tottori, get off at Hara; 13km riverside C.R., hot spring bath in terminal

Mihara-cho Cycling Terminal

1040-3 Jindai Urakabe, Mihara-cho, Mihara-gun, Hyogo-ken

☎ 07994 2-5310

From Sumoto Port take bus bound for Fukura, one hour's walk from Ichi bus stop; 3 cycling paths

WESTERN JAPAN

Takahashi-shi Cycling Terminal

2281-3 Kobara, Matsubara-cho, Takahashi-shi, Okayama-ken

☎ 08662 2-0135

From Bichu Takahashi Station take bus to Wonda Landu; 3 cycling paths, near sports center and golf course

Yachiyo-cho Cycling Terminal

1194-1 Haji, Yachiyo-cho, Takada-gun, Hiroshima-ken

☎ 082652 2841

From Hiroshima Station take Hiroshima Dentetsu Bus bound for Oasa or Izuba, get off at Haji Kinen Koen-mae; 20km C.R. around Haji-ko Lake

Hofu-shi Cycling Terminal

2886 Higashi-sabarei, Hofu-shi, Yamaguchi-ken

☎ 0835 38-4488

From Hofu Station take bus bound for Hisakane, get off at Hitomaru; near many historical sites

Tottori-shi Cycling Terminal

1157-115, Hamasaka, Tottori-shi, Tottori-ken

☎ 0857 29-0800

From Tottori Station take bus bound for *sakkyu* (sand dunes), get off at Kodomo no Kuni; located at the start of Inaba C.R.

Izumo-shi Cycling Terminal

2-10 Enya Arihara-cho, Izumo-shi, Shimane-ken

☎ 0853 23-1370

10 mins. walk from Izumo-shi Station; 5 cycling paths including 17km path to Izumo Taisha Shrine

Nita-machi Cycling Terminal

558-2 Minari, Nita-machi, Nita-gun, Shimane-ken

☎ 0854 54-2100

In front of Izumo Minari Station on the Kisuki Line from Matsue; 4 cycling paths including 22km lakeside path (expected completion May 1993)

Uchinomi-cho Cycling Terminal

Sakate, Uchinomi-cho, Shozu-gun, Kagawa-ken

☎ 0879 82-1099

Located at Sakate-ko Port on the east side of Shodo-shima Island, take ferry from Kochi, Osaka, or Kobe; 5 cycling paths including 30km path around cape

SHIKOKU

Yasu-cho Cycling Terminal

1304 Teiyama, Yasu-cho, Kami-gun, Kochi-ken

☎ 08875 5-3196
From Tosa Dentetsu Bus Terminal take bus bound for Kannoura, Muroto, or Aki, get off at Teiyama Kanko Hoteru-mae; 4 cycling paths including 25km Kochi-Muroto-misaki Cape C.R.

Shido-cho Cycling Terminal
1-20 Kamosho Shido-cho, Okawa-gun, Kagawa-ken
☎ 0878 95-1000
Transport available from Shido Station on request;10km cycling path around cape, near local winery open to public, hot spring baths

KYUSHU

Kitakyushu-shi Cycling Terminal
828 Takenami, Wakamatsu-ku, Kitakyushu-shi, Fukuoka-ken
☎ 093 741-2527
From Orio or Tobata Station take bus to Saikuringu Terminaru-mae bus stop; located beside lake in Hibikinada Ryokuchi-koen Park

Yabakei-machi Cycling Terminal
Kakisaka, Yabakei-machi, Shimoge-gun, Oita-ken
☎ 09795 4-2655
From Hida, Toyogomori, or Nakatsu stations take bus to Kakisuka bus stop, or cycle on cycling path from Nakatsu Station; 36km Yabakei C.R. to Nakatsu

Kunisaki-machi Cycling Terminal
2662-1 Owara, Kunisaki-machi, Higashi Kunisaki-gun, Oita-ken
☎ 09787 2-3196
From Kinezuki Station take bus bound for Kunisaki; get off at Bokaien-mae; 4 cycling paths including 2km seaside course

Yamaga-shi Cycling Terminal
2085 Nabeta, Yamaga-shi, Kumamoto-ken
☎ 09684 3-1136
From Sekata Station take bus bound for Yamaga Onsen, get off at Shiritsu Hakubutsukan-mae; near Kumamoto-Yamaga C.R.

Aya-cho Cycling Terminal
3765 Kitamata, Aya-cho, Higashi Morokata-gun, Miyazaki-ken
☎ 0985 77 1227
From Miyako City at Miyazaki Station take bus to Aya bus stop; 3 cycling paths including 26km riverside path

(C.R. = Cycling Road)

Rental Bike Stores in the Kyoto Area

Yasumoto Rental bikes
☎ 075 751-0595
At Kawabata Sanjo, Sakyo-ku
Open 9:00 A.M. to 5:00 P.M.
1 day: ¥1,000; 1hr.: ¥200
Closed the first and third Sundays every month

Kyohan Rental Bikes
☎ 075 861-1656
In fronty of Arashiyama bus stop, Ukyo-ku
Open 9:00 A.M. to 5:00 P.M..
1 day: ¥800; 4hrs.: ¥600
Open all year round

Saga Rental Bikes
☎ 075 871-3717
West of Futagaoka Bridge, Maruta-machi, Ukyo-ku
Open 8:00 A.M. to 7:00 P.M.
1 day: ¥1,000; 2hrs.: ¥300
Open all year round

Arashiyama Cycles
☎ 075 882-1111
In front of Hankyu Arashiyama Station, Nishikyo-ku
Open 9:00 A.M. to 5:00 P.M.
1 day: ¥1,000; 2hrs.: ¥500
Open all year round

Rental bikes Kyoto
☎ 075 861-0117
Northeast corner of Togetsukyo-bashi Bridge, Arashiyama, Ukyo-ku
Open 9:00 A.M. to 5:00 P.M.
1 day: ¥800; 1hr.: ¥200
Open all year round

Daikaku-ji Cycles
☎ 075 872-9739
In front of Daikaku-ji Temple bus stop, Saga, Ukyo-ku
Open 10:00 A.M. to 5:00 P.M.
1 day: ¥800; 2hr.: ¥400
Closed Wednesdays

Saga Station Rental Bikes
☎ 075 881-4898
In front of JR Saga Station, Ukyo-ku
Open 9:00 A.M. to 5:00 P.M.
1 day: ¥1,000; 2hrs.: ¥500
Open all year round

Rentopia Service
☎ 0875 672-0662
In front of Hachijo Exit, Kyoto Station, Minami-ku
Open 8:00 A.M. to 8:00 P.M.
1 day: ¥1100; ¥900 from Dec. to Feb. and May to July
Open all year round

Higashiyama Youth Hostel Cycles
☎ 075 761-8135
Near Shirakawa-bashi Bridge, Sanjo, Higashiyama-ku
Open 8:00 A.M. to 6:00P.M.
1 day: ¥800
Open all year round

Keihan Uji Rental Bikes
☎ 0774 24-7775
In front of Keihan Uji Station, Uji-shi
Open 9:00 A.M. to 6:00 P.M.
8 hrs.: ¥800; 4hrs.: ¥600
Open all year round

Arashiyama Ladies' Hotel Cycles
☎ 075 882-0955
In front of Tenryu-ji Temple, Arashiyama, Ukyo-ku
Open 8:00 A.M. to dusk
1 day.: ¥1,000; 3hrs.: ¥600
Open all year round

Iwai Rental Bikes
☎ 075 341-2101
Near Kizuya-bashi Bridge, Omiya, Shimo-gyo-ku
Open 9:00 A.M. to 6:00 P.M.
1 day.: ¥800
Open all year round

Cycling Roads throughout Japan

HOKKAIDO

Kusshiro Akan Jitenshado
26.5 km
From: Yanagi-machi, Kushiro-shi
To: Akan-cho, Akan-gun
☎ 011 231 4111 ext. 2782

Shikotsuko Koen Jitenshado
22.9 km
From: Morappu, Chitose-shi
To: Shin-machi, Chitose-shi
☎ 011 2311 4111 ext. 2782

Tokachi Daiheigen Jitenshado
27.3 km
From: Tokachigawa Onsen
To: Ichikawanishi-machi, Obihiro-shi
☎ 01 231-4111 ext. 2782

Ishikarigawa Jitenshado
27.2 km
From: 4-jyo, Fukagawa-shi
To: Hokko, Sunagawa-shi
☎ 011 231 4111 ext. 2782

Toyohiragawa Jitenshado
37.7 km
From: Makomanai, Minami-ku, Sapporo-shi
To: Higashikariki, Higashi-Oku, Sapporo-shi
☎ 011 211-2617

AOMORI PREFECTURE

Aomori Tashiro Daira Kogen Course
21.7 km
From: Aomori-shi
To: Towadako-cho
☎ 0177 22-1111

IWATE PREFECTURE

Hanamaki Onsen Jitenshado
26 km
From: Kitakami-shi
To: Hanamaki-shi
☎ 0196 51-3111 ext. 3542

MIYAGI PREFECTURE

Sendai-wan Jitenshado
40.4 km
From: Sendai-shi, Iwakiri
To: Watari-cho, Watari-gun
☎ 022 211-3162

Oku Matsushima Jitenshado
40.8 km
From: Shinbashi, Ishinomaki-shi
To: Takagi, Matsushima-cho
☎ 022 211-3162

YAMAGATA PREFECTURE

Sakuranbo Cycling Road
37.8 km
From: Nishikawa-cho, Nishimurayama-gun
To: Yamadera, Yamagata-shi
☎ 0237 86-8111 ext. 424

AKITA PREFECTURE

Nibetsu Omonogawa Cycling Road
35.4 km
From: Yuwa-machi, Kawabe-gun
To: Akita-shi
☎ 0188 60-2485

Akita Chuo Koen Jitenshado
29.9 km

From: Akita-shi
To: Yuwa-machi, Kawabe-gun
☎ 018860-2485

FUKUSHIMA PREFECTURE
Fukushima Michinoku Jitenshado
29.9 km
From: Oaza Maeda, Sukagawa-shi
To: Hiwada-cho, Koriyama-shi
☎ 0245 21-1111 ext. 2144

Abukuma-gawa Cycling Road
21 km
From: Kamihama-cho, Fukushima-shi
To: Datebashi, Taishobashi
☎ 0245 33-2267-8

IBARAKI PREFECTURE
Karenuma Jitenshado
20 km
From: Ibaraki-cho, Higashi Ibaraki-gun
To: Ooarai-machi, Higashi Ibaraki-gun
☎ 0292 24-5845

TOCHIGI PREFECTURE
Kinu-gawa Jitenshado
24.4 km
From: Ninomiya-machi, Haga-gun
To: Utsunomiya-shi
☎ 0286 23-2426

Watarase-gawa Jitenshado
22.1 km
From: Kiryu-shi, Gunma-ken
To: Fujioka-machi, Shimotsuga-gun, Tochigi-ken
☎ 0286 23-2426

GUNMA PREFECTURE
Takasaki-Isesaki Jitenshado

42.3 km
From: Takasaki-shi
To: Isesaki-shi
☎ 0272 23-1111 ext. 3355

SAITAMA PREFECTURE
Ara-kawa Jitenshado
45.6 km
From: Tokiwa, Urawa-shi (Route 17)
To: Namekawa-cho (Shinrin-koen Park)
☎ 0488 24-2111 ext 3126

Iruma-gawa Jitenshado
22.6 km
From: Oaza Nakaoibukuro, Kawagoe-shi (Kawagoe Ageo Line)
To: Oaza Negishi, Sayama-shi (Route 407)
☎ 0488 24-2111 ext. 3126

CHIBA PREFECTURE
Taiheiyogan Jitenshado
22.6 km
From: Wada-machi, Awa-gun
To: Tateyama-shi, Numaaza Shimodai
☎ 0472 23-3195

Taiheiyo Jitenshadosen
29.1 km
From: Katagai, Kujukuri-machi, Sanbu-gun
To: Fukabori, Isumi-gun, Ohara-machi,
☎ 0472 23-3195

Edo-gawa Cycling Road
37.8 km
From: Matsudo-shi
To: Sekijuku-machi
☎ 0472 23 3195

TOKYO METROPOLITAN AREA

Edo-gawa Jitenshado
21.4 km
From: Minami Kasai 5-chome, Edogawa-ku,
To: Higashi Kanamachi 8-chome, Katsushika-ku,
☎ 03 3692-4651

YAMANASHI PREFECTURE

Fuefuki-gawa Cycling Road
26.1 km
From: Daimon-cho, Ichikawa
To: Manriki-koen Park, Yamanashi-shi
☎ 00552 37-1111 ext. 2722

NAGANO PREFECTURE

Chikuma-gawa Jitenshado
23.3 km
From: Ueda-shi
To: Nagano-shi
☎ 0262 32-0111

Chikuma-gawa Cycling Doro
21.5 km
From: Usuda-cho, Minami Saku-gun,
To: Komoro-shi
☎ 0267 82-3111

TOYAMA PREFECTURE

Daimon Sho-gawa Oyabe Jitenshado
39.2 km
From: Daimon-cho, Imizu-gun
To: Ishido, Oyabe-shi
☎ 0764 31-4111

Shinkiro Jitenshado
24.9 km
From: Kamojima, Toyama-shi
To: Kyoden, Uozu-shi
☎ 0764 31-4111

NIIGATA PREFECTURE

Kubiki Jitensha Hokoshado
28.2 km
From: Mushioiwato, Joetsu-shi
To: Oshiage, Itoigawa-shi
☎ 025 284-7293

ISHIKAWA PREFECTURE

Hakui Kenmin Jitenshado
32.8 km
From: Kawahara, Hakui-shi
To: Ushishita, Togi-machi
☎ 0762 61-1111

Kaga Kaihin Jitenshado
25.5 km
From: Fushoji, Kanazawa-shi
To: Yasumi, Komatsu-shi
☎ 0762 61-1111

Noto Kaihin Jitenshado
31.7 km
From: Mukoawazaki, Uchinada-cho
To: Yanagida, Hakui-cho
☎ 0762 61-1111

SHIZUOKA PREFECTURE

Shizuoka Shimizu Jitenshado
25.2 km
From: Nakajima, Shizuoka-shi
To: Osa, Shimizu-shi
☎ 0542 21-3029

Shizuoka Omaezaki Jitenshado
46.3
From: Nakajima, Shizuoka-shi
To: Shimomisaki, Omaezaki-cho
☎ 0542 21-3029

Hamamatsu Omaezaki Jitenshado
40.3 km
From: Nakatajima, Hamamatsu-shi
To: Shimomisaki, Omaezaki-cho
☎ 0542 31-3029

Hamana-ko Lake Shuyu Jitenshado
34.2 km
From: Mikkabi, Mikkabi-cho
To: Bentenjima, Maisaka-cho
☎ 0542 31-3029

AICHI PREFECTURE

Taiheiyogan Jitenshado
34.5 km
From: Oaza-Irako, Atsumi-cho
To: Higashi Hosoya-cho, Toyohashi-shi
☎ 052 961-2111 ext. 2707

Toyota-Anjo Jitenshado
25.9 km
From: Arai-cho, Toyota-shi
To: Hujii-cho, Anjo-shi
☎ 052 961-2111 ext. 2707

GIFU PREFECTURE

Nagara-gawa Jitenshado
30.1 km
From: Gifu-shi
To: Kaizu-cho
☎ 0582 72-1111 ext. 3035

HYOGO PREFECTURE

Harima Jitenshado
30.8 km
From: Haneda-cho, Himeji-shi
To: Nishi Shin-machi, Akashi-cho
☎ 0794 21-1101 ext. 271

Haga-cho Jitenshado
23 km
From: Hara, Haga-cho, Shisa-gun

To: Otomizu, Haga-cho
☎ 0790 75-2220 ext. 26

SHIGA PREFECTURE

Biwa-ko Yoshibue Road
23.2 km
From: Horigami-cho, Omihachiman-shio
To: Notogawa-cho, Kanzaki-gun
☎ 0775 24-1121

KYOTO PREFECTURE

Kyoto Yahata Jitenshado
27 km
From: Yawata Ikenobukubi, Yawata-shi
To: Kizugumo-mura, Kizu-cho
☎ 075 432-2074

TOTTORI PREFECTURE

Inaba Jitenshado
20.3 km
From: Tottori-shi
To: Kawahara-cho, Yazu-gun
☎ 0857 26-7630

SHIMANE PREFECTURE

Izumo-ji Jitenshado
26.6 km
From: Rokuonji-machi, Hirata-shi
To: Kizuki Kita, Taisha-cho
☎ 0852 22-5194

OKAYAMA PREFECTURE

Kibi-ji Jitenshado
20.6 km
From: Ijima-cho, Okayama-shi
To: Mitsuwa, Shoji-shi
☎ 086224-2111 ext. 2565

Kibi Kogen Jitenshado
21.8 km

From: Shinjoshita, Okayama-shi
To: Yoshikawa, Kayo-sho, Kazusa-gun
☎ 086224-2111 ext. 2565

YAMAGUCHI PREFECTURE

Yamaguchi Ariyoshi Jitenshado
30.8 km
From: Miyajima-cho, Yamaguchi-shi
To: Akiyoshi, Shuho-cho, Mine-gun
☎ 0839 22-3111 ext. 3354

TOKUSHIMA PREFECTURE

Naruto-Tokushima Jitenshado
32.8 km
From: Muya-cho, Naruto-shi
To: Kawachi-cho, Tokushima-shi
☎ 0886 21-2549

KAGAWA PREFECTURE

Kotogawa Jitenshado
21 km
From: Shionoe-cho, Kagawa-gun
To: Takamatsu-shi
☎ 0878 31-1111 ext. 2747

KOCHI PREFECTURE

Aki Yoshikawa Jitenshado
24.3 km
From: Yoshiwara, Yoshikawa-mura, Kami-gun
To: Tsukumo-cho, Aki-shi
☎ 0888 23-1111 ext. 2842

FUKUOKA PREFECTURE

Chikugo-gawa Jitenshado
27.2 km
From: Yoshi-cho, Ukiha-gun
To: Higashikushihara-cho, Kurume-shi
☎ 0942 44-5222

Masubuchi Kawachi Jitenshado
24 km
From: Kokura Minami-ku
To: Yahata Higashi-ku
☎ 093 582-2279

SAGA PREFECTURE

Saga Jitenshado
24.6 km
From: Oaza Hagino, Kase-cho, Saga-shi
To: Oaza Hagino, Kase-cho, Saga-shi
☎ 0952 24-2111 2852

KUMAMOTO PREFECTURE

Kuramoto Yuraga Jitenshado
30.5 km
From: Shimazaki, Kumamoto-shi
To: Nabeta-cho, Yamaga-shi
☎ 096 383-1111 ext. 6117

OITA PREFECTURE

Yabakei Jitenshado
23.5 km
From: Nakatsu-shi
To: Yasukuni-cho, Shimoge-gun
☎ 0975 36-1111 ext. 3565

KAGOSHIMA PREFECTURE

Kimotsuki-gawa Kahan Jitenshado
20.8 km
From: Higashikushira-cho, Kimotsuki-gun
To: Aira-cho, Kmotsuki-gun
☎ 0992 26-8111 ext. 3054

(Jitenshado = Cycling path)

Cyclists' Phraselist 🚲🚲🚲🚲🚲🚲🚲🚲🚲🚲🚲

BASICS

Good morning: *ohayo gozaimasu*

Goodbye: *sayonara*

Good evening: *konban wa*

Good afternoon/hello: *konnichi wa*

My name is___: *watashi no namae wa___desu*

What's your name?: *onamae wa nan desu ka?*

Please (do me a favor): *onegai shimasu*

Yes/no: *hai/iie*

Please (take this, do this): *dozo*

Thanks (very much): *(domo) arigato (gozaimasu)*

No thank you: *kekko desu*

You're welcome: *do itashimashite*

Wait a minute: *chotto matte kudasai*

Hello (on the phone): *moshi moshi*

Can you say that again, please: *moichi-do onegai shimasu*

Do you understand English?: *ei-go ga wakarimasu ka?*

Excuse me: *sumimasen*

I'm sorry: *gomen nasai/sumimasen*

Is there somebody around who speaks English?: *dareka ei-go o hanasu hito ga imasu ka?*

I don't understand: *wakarimasen*

I don't mind: *kamaimasen*

What does this/that mean?: *kore/ sore wa doiu imi desu ka?*

How do you say___in Japanese?: *nihon-go de___o do iimasu ka?*

May I take a picture?: *shashin o totte mo iidesu ka?*

I have to go now: *mo ikanakere-ba narimasen*

USING PUBLIC TRANSPORTATION

Excuse me, but___?: *chotto sumi-masen ga___?*

Where is the bank/post office/station?: *ginko/yubin-kyoku/eki wa doko desu ka?*

• subway: *chikatetsu*

• bus stop: *basutei*

• police box: *koban*

• ferry terminal: *feri noriba*

• port: *minato* • airport: *kuko*

• ticket window: *kippu uriba*

• lockers: *koin-rokka*

• bike shop: *jitensha-ya*

• tourist information: *kanko annai*

How do I get to___?: *___niwa do iki-masu ka?*

How far is it to___?: *___wa dono-gurai toi desu ka?*

When is the next train/bus/ferry to ___?: *tsugi no___e iku ressha/basu/feri wa nan-ji desu ka?*

What number bus/platform is to ___?: *___e iku no wa nan-ban no basu/homu desu ka?*

Do I have to change?: *norikae ga hitsuyo desu ka?*

Can you tell me where to get off for___?: *___ewa doko de orire-ba ii ka oshiete kuremasu ka?*

Could you write it down on a piece of paper for me?: *kami ni kaite kudasai masu ka?*

What time does it open/close?: *nan-ji ni aki/shimari masu ka?*

How long does it take?: *dono-gurai (jikan ga) kakari masu ka?*

Is this reserved/unrestricted seating?: *kore wa shitei-/jiyu-seki desu ka?*